The Spicer & Oppenheim Guide to Securities Markets Around the World

WILEY

JOHN WILEY & SONS

New York • Chichester • Brisbane • Toronto • Singapore

ISBN: 0-471-61289-8
ISBN 0-471-61162-X (pbk.)

Printed in the United States of America

10 9 8 7 6 5 4 3 2 1

CONTENTS

CONTENTS

iv

Introduction

When of *Securities Markets around the World* was first published in 1986, the booklet filled a previously unsatisfied need among those doing business in—and with—the ever-changing securities industry.

This second, larger version features updated information and focuses on 26 of the most important securities markets in the world, double the number in the earlier compilation.

The globalization of the world's securities markets continues to accelerate, and both traders and investors are striving to come to terms with the opportunities and challenges presented by this environment.

The growth in foreign gross activity in U.S. equities from $159 billion in 1985 to $481 billion by the end of 1987 is just one illustration of the growth in international equities trading. Globalization is equally apparent in the dramatically increasing trading volumes of all financial instruments.

This globalization of financial markets is not simply about the increasingly large cross-border flow of capital and the related increase in corporate finance. More important, it is a process by which the world's financial markets are beginning to act as a single integrated marketplace in which the price of financial instruments in one market is significantly affected by supply and demand for funds in other markets.

Such pricing linkages are most visible in currency markets through covered interest arbitrages, but there are similar linkages in bond markets. Issuers in the primary markets take advantage of pricing discrepancies across markets, while in the secondary markets, arbitraging between bonds and currency swaps is becoming common practice. Although linkages in the equities markets are less well-developed, we have witnessed remarkably similar rises and falls in most of the world's equity markets in the second half of 1987.

INTRODUCTION

Traders and investors in the major financial centers are paying unprecedented attention to events in markets other than their own. And for good reason. During the second half of October 1987, for example, the best indicator of movements in the *London Financial Times Index* was the previous evening's changes in the *Nikkei* and *Dow Jones Indices*. Inevitably, world indices have been developed; these include the *World Stock Capital Interest Index* and the *Financial Times-Actuaries World Indices,* covering 2425 securities in 24 countries.

As institutional investors become a more important channel for the flow of financial assets in many nations, they are increasingly taking advantage of the investment opportunities presented by differences between national financial markets and overseas markets which allow greater returns relative to the risks taken. This is particularly true in countries such as Germany, Switzerland, and Japan where domestic investment options are limited and where there are enormous surpluses to invest.

Many financial intermediaries and investors are still uncertain of their position in the new international marketplace and have yet to answer satisfactorily such questions as whether they should trade securities from several centers around the world, or from one center, 24 hours a day. They also ponder the true nature of the risks of trading or investing in an increasing range of instruments internationally, as well as the regulatory and tax implications of doing so. Such unanswered questions, however, have not precluded banks and securities houses from investing significant sums in the technology and infrastructure needed to support global operations.

The Spicer & Oppenheim Guide to Securities Markets around the World is intended to assist in grappling with these issues by providing information that will help in the assessment of the relative advantages and disadvantages of trading or investing in different countries.

This book highlights the ramifications of the continued trend towards the deregulation of the securities markets. It is written specifically for those working within the securities industry, as distinct from those who seek to raise capital through that industry. Our purpose is to provide a convenient, easy-to-read reference for those who have developed an international dimension to their businesses or who may seek to do so in the future. While it is not exhaustive, it provides an outline of the most relevant facts for each market.

Despite the rapid pace of change in the international securities markets, we have attempted to ensure that the information contained in this book is as up-to-date as possible. Unless stated otherwise, the information is current as of March 1988.

Each chapter has been compiled by a Spicer & Oppenheim International office located in the respective country. If you seek more detailed

INTRODUCTION

information or wish to check the continuing validity of the information contained in this book, please contact either Peter Oliver in London or Joel Press in New York, the editors of the book, or the partner whose name and telephone number appear at the head of the relevant chapter.

Spicer & Oppenheim International is an international accounting, tax, and consulting organization comprising independent national accounting firms, with 250 offices in more than 50 countries, employing over 9000 individuals. Each member firm provides clients with a comprehensive range of services on both a national and international basis. Worldwide we are well-known for our expertise and experience in serving the international financial services community. Our international capabilities are available to all clients of our member firms, whether they are seeking advice, specific services, or even a base from which to explore local opportunities.

ACKNOWLEDGMENTS

The scope of experience reflected in this book is the result of the time, effort and cooperation from many professionals of Spicer & Oppenheim International. As accountants, auditors, consultants and tax advisors, Spicer & Oppenheim International advises a wide variety of large, medium, and small businesses on issues of finance, management and taxation. In particular, the Spicer & Oppenheim Financial Services Group has developed a worldwide reputation in providing services to financial service firms.

Spicer & Oppenheim Financial Service professionals throughout the world have spent hundreds of hours working on this book. Besides the partners identified in each chapter, others who deserve special thanks for their contribution in preparation, research and coordination of the book are Simon Haslam and Glen Sanford in London and Julio Herrera, Thomas Phillips, and Joel Wolf in New York.

AUSTRALIA

Duesburys

Contact: Warwick Higgs, Tel: (02) 250 9555

Australia's six Stock Exchanges (ASX) are located in Sydney, Melbourne, Brisbane, Adelaide, Perth, and Hobart. All Stock Exchanges are subsidiaries of the Australian Stock Exchange Ltd. which was formed by the unification of the Stock Exchanges on April 1, 1987. The Sydney and Melbourne Stock Exchanges are linked in operation and account for approximately 90% of total Australian trading volume.

Size

There were 48 member firms on the Sydney Stock Exchange and 31 on the Melbourne Stock Exchange as of December 31, 1987.

There is a significant amount of off-shore trading, with major business occurring on the Stock Exchanges of London and New York. Outside the formal markets, fixed interest bond trading is of major importance. An estimated 80% of trading in fixed interest securities is transacted off the Stock Exchange floor.

There is no over-the-counter market, but a market for smaller companies is provided by the Second Board Market. This market has companies listed on all of the regional exchanges, but the greatest number of listings and the greatest turnover is in Perth.

Major companies from all industry sectors are listed on both the Sydney and Melbourne Stock Exchanges.

The index of the Exchange is the "all ordinaries" share index, and past performance is as follows:

1

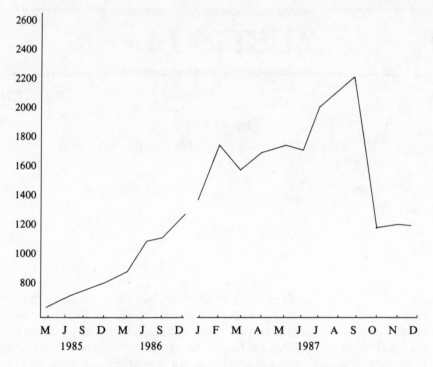

M J S D M J S D J F M A M J J A S O N D
1985   1986   1987

Market activity for the year ending December 31, 1987 was as follows:

	Equities	Fixed Interest
Turnover (A$ million)	77,684	52,819
Number of trades/bargains ('000)	100,669	N/A
Market capitalization		
(A$ million)	369,883	N/A
Number of securities	1,626	N/A

The Sydney Futures Exchange (SFE) is now linked with London International Financial Futures Exchange (LIFFE) and New York Commodity Exchange Inc. (COMEX).

OVERVIEW OF THE BOND AND EQUITY MARKETS

Structure

The hours of trading on the floor are Monday to Friday, 10:00 to 12:15 and 14:00 to 15:15. Apart from odd-lot specialists, there are no specialists or jobbers on the Australian Stock Exchanges.

Execution

The procedures for execution and settlement are identical for all Exchanges. Orders are placed through brokers who act as agents for their clients and do not deal for their own account without advising their clients first. Brokers deal directly with one another at trading posts on the Stock Exchange floor, where specific posts are designated for transacting specific types of securities. Each transaction must be reported before the opening of trading on the following day. There are no limits on the daily permissible price movements in stocks and there is no obligation to make continuous markets. Shares are generally traded in lots as follows:

Market Price of Share (A$)		Lot Size
1c–	25c	2,000
26c–	50c	1,000
51c–	$1.00	500
$1.01c–	$10.00	100
Over $10.00		50

The Stock Exchange Automated Trading System (SEATS), which permits screen-based trading from both the Exchange and brokers' offices, was implemented in October 1987. Initially only 20 stocks were traded on the system, but there are now 200 stocks traded in this manner.

Settlement and Clearing

For customers, settlement is within ten business days from the issue of the contract note. For settlement within the market, it is mandatory for all brokers to subscribe to the Broker/Broker Settlement System. The system provides an automated settlement operation for all transactions reported to the Exchange.

Market Characteristics

Commission Rates. Commission rates are negotiable, ranging between 0.25% and 5% of the value of the transaction. The only other cost incurred by the client in dealing is a stamp duty of 30c per A$100 contract value.

Margin Trading. Margin trading is not permitted on the Australian Stock Exchanges, although short selling is permitted in certain securities.

Investor Protection. Companies which are listed on the Stock Exchange are required to comply with Official Listing Requirements. Stockbrokers are required to comply with the rules and regulations of the Stock Exchange.

Specific measures to ensure investor protection are as follows:

- A broker must maintain an indemnity cover of at least A$500,000 against fraud; protection against fraud is also covered by the ASX indemnity fund.
- A national guarantee fund for the benefit of customers was established on April 1, 1987 through the Australian Stock Exchange and National Guarantee Fund Act 1987.
- A broker acting as principal must advise the client of that fact.
- There is no obligation upon a broker to trade or make prices.
- Annual audited financial statements must be filed with the ASX and the National Companies and Securities Commission (NCSC).
- Prices and transactions are monitored by the NCSC and the "Companies Department" of each Stock Exchange.
- Each Stock Exchange also conducts spot investigations of brokers.

New Issues

Although the underwriting of new issues is handled by brokers and merchant banks, each new listing must have a sponsoring broker who is a member of the ASX. The underwriting rate is generally 5%; however, once again these rates are subject to negotiation. Commissions are considered a private agreement between the parties concerned.

The number of new issues in 1987 were as follows

- Main Board : 266 companies
- Second Board : 168 companies

A register of all new issues is maintained with the Corporate Affairs Commission.

FUTURES AND OPTIONS TRADING

Futures

The Sydney Futures Exchange (SFE) provides trading, settlement, and technical facilities for the operation of the futures markets. It is a membership organization owned by its floor members who elect five of the ten directors on the Board.

The range of financial futures available is as follows:

- 90-day Bank Accepted Bills can be traded up to two years ahead and the settlement day is the second Friday of the delivery month.

4

- Ten-year Commonwealth Treasury bonds can be traded up to 12 months ahead and all positions held at the close of trading in the contract month are settled by the Clearing House at the cash settlement price.

- Three-month Eurodollar Interest rate contracts can be traded up to 12 months ahead; all positions are settled by the Clearing House at the cash settlement price. This contract is identical with that traded on the London International Financial Futures Exchange.

- U.S. Treasury Bond contracts can be traded up to 12 months ahead on an identical basis to the contracts traded in the United States and London.

- Share price index futures can be traded up to 18 months ahead; all positions at the close of trading in the contract month are settled by the Clearing House at the index value for cash settlement.

- U.S. Dollars can be traded up to 6 months ahead; all positions held at the close of trading in the contract month are settled by the Clearing House at the cash settlement rate of exchange. Contract unit: A$100,000.

Commodity futures are also traded in live cattle contracts, wool contracts, and gold futures.

Membership of the Futures Exchange is divided into four categories, the main three being floor members, local members, and full associate members. Floor members may deal on the Futures Exchange trading floor either for themselves or for their clients. Local members may deal on the Futures Exchange floor for their own account or for floor members, but not on behalf of clients. Full associate members may trade either on their own behalf or on behalf of clients, but are not permitted to operate on the trading floor. Full associate members must deal through a floor member but they may be members of the Clearing House in their own right. In addition to these categories, those who wish to maintain an association with the Futures Exchange may become market associate members, which allows them to be kept informed of new developments at the Futures Exchange. Market Associate Members are not allowed to trade on behalf of clients, but are eligible to join the Exchange's Clearing House and to clear in their own name.

The fourth category, Introducing Broker Associate Membership, is a new class of Associate Membership introduced in 1986. They may deal on their own behalf or introduce clients to members authorized to deal on behalf of the public. They can advise clients, but may not hold funds on the clients' behalf.

Nonresidents of Australia may become associate members or local members of the Futures Exchange, but firms or corporations which are not registered and conduct business in Australia may not become floor members.

The analysis of members of the SFE as of December 15, 1987 was as follows:

Total Numbers

Floor Members	29	
Full Associates	144	
Market Associates	130	
Local Members	71	(18 leased to 3rd parties)
Nonresidents	40	
Permit Holders	15	
Introducing Brokers	6	

There is no restriction on trading by nonresidents, except where transactions originate from a country designated by the Australian Government as a tax haven, in which case a Tax Clearance Certificate is necessary.

Users of the futures market enter into contracts to buy or sell through their brokers who transmit their clients' orders to the trading floor. Brokers' representatives then execute the orders through a system of competitive bids and offers by open outcry on the trading floor. Traders in the market and their customers are required to put up an initial margin, usually 5 to 10% of the value underlying the contract. Under the Futures Exchange's rules, additional margins must be paid when the unrealized loss on the position exceeds 50% of the original initial margin.

All contracts must be traded on the floor of the Futures Exchange and are registered and cleared by the International Commodities Clearing House, which also guarantees performances of all contracts to its members.

In late 1986, SFE joined trading links with LIFFE in London and COMEX in New York. The essence of the link is that contracts traded in Sydney and the Home Exchange are interchangeable, so a bought position in Sydney can be matched with a position sold in London or New York and immediate settlement obtained.

Options

Since 1985, the Futures Exchange has been phasing in options on bank accepted bills, Ten-year Treasury Bonds and share index futures. These are currently the only Exchange Traded Options available, but options on other instruments may be introduced later. The Sydney Futures

Exchange will be one of the first futures markets to offer margined premiums on options contracts. If the full option premium is greater than the current deposit on a particular option, it will only be necessary, in most cases, to pay an option deposit rather than the full premium when the option is traded.

In May 1984, the Sydney Stock Exchange entered into an association with the European Options Exchange in Amsterdam and the Montreal and Vancouver Exchanges to promote trading in options in gold, silver, and currencies guaranteed by the International Options Clearing Corporation.

Exchange Traded Options for securities are dealt on the Australian Options Market which is located on the floor of the Sydney Stock Exchange. The underlying equities must be listed on the ASX and be subject to the Stock Exchanges' listing requirements. Such option contracts are standardized at 1,000 shares of the underlying stock, but this is subject to variation at the discretion of the Stock Exchange. Clients dealing in options place orders with their stockbrokers or with clearing members to the Options Market in the same way that they deal in listed

The maturity dates for Exchange Traded Options are fixed at the end of the expiry month, and options are limited to a maximum of nine months' duration. Commissions on options, like those on futures contracts, are negotiable between brokers and their clients and payable as a flat fee per option bought and sold. Clearing House and Stock Exchange fees together amount to A$5.50 a round turn (one option bought and sold), and there is an additional fee of A$2.75 payable if the option is exercised.

The Australian Options Market has adopted the concept of competing market makers, known as Registered Traders. This approach is a major difference between trading in Exchange Traded Options and in the underlying securities.

Registered Traders trade on their own account, at their own risk and in competition with one another. In doing so they assume an obligation to make a market in an option when asked to do so and to trade in at least one contract, whether put or call.

REGULATIONS AFFECTING NEW ENTRANTS TO THE MARKETS

Australia's regulatory authorities are the State Corporate Affairs Commission (CAC) and the ASX. Currently the Attorney General has proposed a new independent commission, the Australian Securities

Commission, to take over the functions of the CAC. The statutory regulations which govern the securities industry are defined in the Securities Industry Act.

ASX Membership Requirements

All firms trading on the floor of the Exchange must be members of the Stock Exchange.

Corporate

Companies are admitted as member corporations of the Stock Exchange provided a majority of the directors of the applicant are Australian residents and:

1. If four or fewer directors, two directors are personal members.

2. In any other case, at least a quarter of the directors are personal members.

Where the applicant meets these requirements, it may be admitted as a member corporation if the joint Sydney/Melbourne listing sub-committee:

- is satisfied that each nonmember or substantial shareholder is of good name and character and high business integrity and has contracted to be bound by the rules of the Exchange
- is satisfied that the applicant has the required financial resources to meet its obligation as a member of the Stock Exchange
- has no reason to believe that, having regard to the number of members and member organizations of the Stock Exchange and the nature and capacity of the facilities of the Stock Market conducted by the Stock Exchange, it would be impractical to accommodate the applicant as a member of the Stock Exchange

Gaining membership does not require the purchase of a seat, but membership fees are:

1. For a natural person: $25,000

2. For a membership corporation: by tender with a minimum of $250,000

For natural persons, the following membership criteria applies:

- age not less than 21 years
- experience of not less than two years

- of reputable character
- of acceptable academic training

Liquidity Requirements

Regulatory requirements are:

- Unincorporated member organizations shall ensure that at all times the Adjusted Liquid Capital (as defined) in their business is not less than A$50,000 or 5% of their aggregate indebtedness, whichever is the greater.
- Member organizations which are corporations carrying on business on their own account or in partnership with other member corporations shall ensure at all times that the Adjusted Liquid Capital in their business is not less than A$250,000 or 5% of the aggregate indebtedness, whichever is greater.

All nonmember representative offices can trade on the market only through a member as agent.

OUTLINE OF CORPORATE AND INDIVIDUAL TAX CONSIDERATIONS

The Australian Taxation System has included a tax on capital gains since September 1985 and full imputation of company tax on dividends from July 1987.

Government Bonds—Current Income

Securities Issued before December 17, 1984. The interest on Treasury Bonds is assessable in the year of receipt and the discount of Treasury Notes is assessable in the year the notes mature. Securities traders have the option of valuing Treasury Bonds at cost price or market value at year-end and accordingly may deduct unrealized losses. The present rate of company tax is 49%, while for individuals rates range between nil and 49%.

Non-residents are subject to withholding tax of 10% in respect of interest and payments which are in the nature of interest.

Securities Issued After December 16, 1984. An accruals basis of taxation applies to discounted and other deferred interest securities which fall within the definition of qualifying securities. To be a qualifying security, the security must be issued after December 16, 1984, its expected term

9

must exceed 12 months and the sum of all payments (other than periodic payments of interest) under the security must exceed its issue price. Qualifying securities held by securities traders as trading stock and nonqualifying securities are excluded from the accruals basis of taxation.

Government Bonds—Capital Gains

Gains and losses made on sale of government bonds are assessable or deductible in the hands of a securities trader. However, in the case of an investor, a gain made on the sale of such a security acquired after September 19, 1985 will be taxable. Losses on the sale of such securities may be offset against capital gains of current and future years but not against noncapital gain income.

The withholding tax of 10% applies to discounts and other pecuniary benefits derived by nonresidents in relation to financing by way of discounted bonds and bills and by way of capital indexed and deferred interest securities. Generally the withholding tax provisions apply to the difference between the consideration received upon redemption or sale of the security, and the issue or purchase price, as the case may be.

Traded Options—Current Income

There are few legislative rules applicable to traded options. As a general rule, however, traders and speculators will be assessed or allowed a deduction for a profit or loss arising from a transaction when the option contract is closed out.

Traded Options—Capital Gains

In circumstances where an investor who does not usually trade in securities writes or takes an option for the purpose of hedging his investment in related securities, the premium received or paid would be subject to the capital gains rules. Where the option is exercised these rules operate to treat the option transaction, and the transaction entered into upon exercise, as a single transaction. Accordingly, any gain or loss made on the option contract will be taken into account in determining the taxable capital gain or loss arising upon sale of the security acquired upon exercise. Where the option is closed out or expires, the grantor of the option will be assessed on the premium received at the time of granting the option and allowed a capital loss upon closing out the position. The grantee of the option will be assessed on, or allowed an offsetting deduction for, the gain or loss arising on closing out the position.

AUSTRALIA

Financial Futures

There is no specific legislation applicable to these futures but it is generally accepted that a profit or loss resulting from the closure of open positions will give rise to either an assessable profit or deductible loss. However, the Taxation Office is likely to disallow losses incurred where profits have been deferred using straddle arrangements.

Nonresidents are subject to the same tax as residents although persons who trade in securities and are resident of a country with which Australia has a double tax treaty will generally be exempt if they do not have a permanent establishment in Australia.

Equities—Current Income

A system of imputation of company tax on dividends has been introduced in respect of dividends paid after June 30, 1987. The dividend imputation system will operate to impute the tax paid by the company as a credit attaching to "franked dividends" paid to resident individual taxpayers. ("Franked dividends" are generally dividends paid from profits derived by a resident company after July 1, 1986.) Both the dividend received and the imputation credit will be included in the assessable income of the shareholder who will then be entitled to a tax rebate equal to the amount of the imputation credit. Dividends, whether franked or unfranked or received by resident companies from other resident companies, will continue to be effectively a tax-free receipt because of the intercorporate dividend tax rebate.

The dividend imputation system credits will not apply to dividends received by nonresidents. However, nonresidents will not be subject to withholding tax in respect of franked dividends.

The rate of withholding tax on unfranked dividends is 30% or 15% if the nonresident is from a country with which Australia has concluded a double tax treaty.

Equities—Capital Gains

Equities Acquired before September 20, 1985. An investor who sells equities purchased prior to September 20, 1985 will not be assessed or allowed a deduction for the profit or loss he makes on the sale of the equities. Generally, a nonresident investor will not be subject to Australian tax on gains made on the sale of equities acquired before September 20, 1985 unless the place of the sales contract was in Australia and the equities were purchased and sold within 12 months.

11

Equities Acquired after September 19, 1985. For an investor, the gain or loss arising upon the sale of equities purchased after September 19, 1985 and held for longer than 12 months, will be subject to income tax under the capital gains provisions of the legislation. Upon sale, the capital profit to be assessed will be adjusted for an inflation factor in that the original cost will be inflated by an index applicable to the period of holding. Capital losses, however, will only be allowed as a deduction against capital profits in the same year of income. Any excess losses not deducted may be carried forward to be offset against future capital gains. There is no inflation adjustment allowed to increase the loss. Gains made on the sale of equities within 12 months of acquisition will be assessable without an inflation adjustment. For a trader, profits and losses will be assessed or allowed as a deduction as normal business income or outgoings. Equities on hand at the year end may be valued at either cost or market selling value at the option of the taxpayer. This option is available each year and may be exercised in respect of each separate holding.

In addition to the above, a nonresident will be assessed on, or allowed an offsetting capital deduction for, gains or losses made on the sale of taxable Australian assets acquired after September 19, 1985. Taxable Australian assets include a share in an Australian resident private company, and a share in an Australian public company where, at any time in five years before the sale, the investor held 10% or more of the public company's issued capital.

Stamp Duty

No stamp duty is levied on the purchase or sale of government bonds and on financial futures contracts. Transfers of equities transacted by a broker attract *ad valorem* duty of 30 cents per A$100 of consideration payable by both the vendor and purchaser. With regard to traded options both the vendor and purchaser pay an *ad valorem* duty on 30 cents per A$100 of the premium.

PROSPECTIVE DEVELOPMENTS

1. A new independent statutory commission, called the Australian Securities Commission, is being considered to take over the functions now performed by the state CAC, under proposals put forward by the Federal Attorney General.

2. The SFE is offering attractive financial incentives to traders from other Exchanges who would like to try their hand in the Sydney pits.

AUSTRALIA

The plan recently approved by the Exchange is known as the Locals Permit Plan and is aimed at further developing the SFE's pit population. Those who take it up will be known as permit holders. Permit holders, who may be either overseas or Australian traders, will be required to trade an average of at least 200 contracts (buys or sells) each month, of which 20 must be in one of four categories nominated by the trader, the four being those where SFE is keen to see further development such as agricultural contracts or the US Dollar contract.

Permits will be available for a minimum of three months and a maximum of six months, with extensions of a further six months being permitted to those who achieve the required level of trading. The permit fee will be A$200 a month.

There will be several incentives for permit holders with respect to:

1. A rebate of 50c per contract (up to $75) for every contract traded over 20 in one day.

2. A rebate of 50% of Exchange fees (75c a trade), if more than 40 contracts a day are traded on a monthly basis.

3. Permit holders who trade minimum volumes over a six-month period will be entitled to take up full permanent Local Membership of the SFE at the going secondary market price.

To streamline entry into Australia and access to the SFE pits for non-residents, the SFE has obtained official approval from the Australian Immigration Department to bring in 60 overseas traders in any one year (up to 20 at any time) to Australia to trade under the sponsorship of a SFE Floor Member.

Overseas or Australian traders who wish to take up permits under the plan must:

- Have a relationship with a floor member of the Exchange willing to take responsibility for the Local's trading and to clear on the Local's behalf.
- Demonstrate to a sponsoring SFE floor member an appropriate level of expertise and financial strength.
- Pass an oral examination on trading rules and procedures on the SFE trading floor.
- Agree to abide by the rules and regulations of the SFE, which among other things prohibit Locals from dealing on behalf of clients.

BRAZIL

Campiglia & Cia. S/C Auditores Independentes
Contact: A.O. Campiglia, Tel: (011) 288 0822

There are nine Stock Exchanges (Bolsas de Valores) in Brazil. The Stock Exchanges of São Paulo and Rio de Janeiro are the largest, handling between them approximately 90% of all Stock Exchange transactions. The operation of all Brazilian Exchanges, including Rio de Janeiro, must comply with the general rules issued by the Banco Central do Brazil as well as with the specific rules issued by the Council of Stock Exchanges.

This review is primarily concerned with the São Paulo Stock Exchange (BOVESPA) unless otherwise indicated.

Size

On June 30, 1987, BOVESPA had 85 member firms and 23 nonmembers authorized to trade.

The market figures for the São Paulo Stock Exchange for the six months to June 1987 were as follows:

	Equities
Turnover (US$ million)	2,865
Number of trades/bargains ('000)	806
Market capitalization as at 30 June 1987 (US$ billion)	21

The BOVESPA index is the indicator that provides the most widely recognized measure of the overall market price movement in Brazil. The index is calculated based on a basket of shares which represent over 80% of the trading volume.

14

BOVESPA Share Index

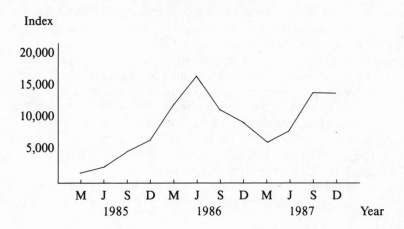

Index

OVERVIEW OF THE BOND AND EQUITY MARKETS

Structure

Floor trading hours in São Paulo and Rio de Janeiro are 10:00 to 13:30.

Trading is carried out at trading posts around the floor, with bid and offer prices being announced both by open outcry and via the Exchange computer. Off-floor block transactions are also displayed but these can be challenged and cancelled at the end of the trading period in favor of more competitive prices.

Most trades are carried out for cash settlement, representing approximately 67% of total trades, and a further 14% of total trades are for forward settlement. The remaining trades are in futures and options as described below.

Listed stocks may be traded only on the Stock Exchanges. There is a growing over-the-counter market for unlisted stocks which is supported by securities dealers who do not have a seat on a Stock Exchange.

Brokers may act as principals as well as agents.

Execution

Executed trades are confirmed by the buying and selling brokers and immediately entered into the Stock Exchange computer. Details of trades are then displayed immediately on the trading floor and at brokerage houses.

Settlement and Clearing

Clearing and custody functions are fully computerized. Shares are normally registered in the name of the individual investor, although bearer shares and book-entry transfer systems are both in use.

In the cash market, physical settlement occurs on the third business day after the trade and financial settlement occurs on the fifth business day. Since 1986 it has also been permitted to carry out day-trade operations (purchase and sale in the same trading session of the same stock for the same investor) with settlement of the financial difference only.

In the forward market, trades can be made for settlement up to 30, 60, 90, 120, 150, and 180 days ahead. These trades are settled on the contract expiry date, or earlier if the purchaser so wishes.

Registration and settlement are regulated both by law and by BOVESPA, and are on the same general principles as in other countries.

Market Characteristics

Commission Rates. Commission rates are fixed depending on the value of the transaction. Rates start at 2%, and fall to 0.5% for transactions valued at US$2,650 or more, with a minimum commission of US$1.50.

There are also registration fees based on the contract value for futures contracts and 0.2% of the premium for options contracts.

Margin Trading. The provision of a margin is mandatory for forward and futures operations. As a guarantee both brokerage houses involved in the trade must deposit an initial margin either in cash or in securities. Additional margin may be called up in accordance with the present value of the position.

Margin deposits are placed with Calispa (Caixa de Liquidadao da Bolsa de São Paulo) which is legally set up for that purpose and for the settlement of all Exchange forward and futures operations.

Securities provided as margin guarantee shall not be the ones traded in the contract, and the depositor must prove he is the legal owner. In the event that the securities belong to a third party, the owner must give a declaration that he knows the regulations concerning forward or futures operations and that he agrees to the use of his securities as a guarantee margin.

The amount of cash initial margin cannot be less than 20% of contract value. Securities deposited as guarantee margin are valued at 80% of their quotation on the previous day. The administrative council of the Stock Exchange is empowered to alter the margin percentage and other applicable regulations.

Investor Protection

The Brazilian Stock Exchanges each maintain a guarantee fund covering securities and funds delivered by a client to a broker for trading or safe custody purposes. The investor is protected against wrongdoing or defective title, and also against failure of the broker's business. A maximum amount applies in the case of reimbursement of securities of approximately US$80,000 per client.

Insider trading is prohibited.

New Issues

When a company wishes its shares to be traded publicly it must be registered with the securities commission (Cum-comissao de Valores Mobiliarios—CVM) as a publicly held company. Every new share issue, as well as bond issues, after they have been approved by a general stockholders meeting must be registered with the CVM with the assistance of an official broking house before public trading can commence.

1986 data on total capital raisings, in Brazil including public and private held companies, and trade turnover for São Paulo and Rio de Janeiro Exchanges is as follows:

a) Total capital issues in Brazil for 1986

	US$ '000
i) New companies	472,373
ii) New issues of existing companies	6,773,906
Total	7,246,279

b) Registration of new issues by São Paulo Exchange in 1986

Shares	1,106,565
Bonds	132,011
Total	1,238,576

FUTURES AND OPTIONS TRADING

In the futures market, standard stock lots of 100,000 shares are purchased and sold, with settlement on dates previously established by BOVESPA. Losses must be settled daily. Gains may be either withdrawn or accumulated until settlement day. There is no trading in options on securities.

REGULATIONS AFFECTING NEW ENTRANTS TO THE MARKETS

The Securities Commission (Commissao de Valores Mobiliaros, or CVM) is responsible for regulating the market. The Central Bank of Brazil also controls the constitution, organization and operation of the stock Exchanges and of the brokerage houses.

BOVESPA guarantees the settlement of intermember payables and receivables, but brokerage houses are themselves guarantors of their clients' debts.

Regulations for the Brazilian securities market are entrusted to the National Monetary Council in order to monitor the capital market. Only brokerage companies which are:

- Properly constituted as limited liability companies
- Authorized by the Central Bank of Brazil
- Registered with the Security Commission (C.V.M.)

can be members of the Stock Exchanges. Each member company must acquire a membership share in the market to be a member of the Exchange. This membership is transferrable at its market value.

The number of members is established in by-laws of each Exchange and is limited dependent on the characteristics and requirements of the region where the Exchange is located. The São Paulo Exchange allows 85 members only—at present no vacancies exist. In addition 23 nonmember companies are authorized to trade on the Exchange. Overseas companies and individuals can own a broker only through a subsidiary company legally established in Brazil, as several foreign banks already do.

A membership share grants the privilege of guaranteeing, by means of a security interest enforceable against third parties, any indebtedness of a brokerage company with the Stock Exchange, and the proper settlement of the transactions effected thereon.

The required minimum capital value of a brokerage company located in São Paulo or Rio de Janeiro varies from US$486,000 up to US$3,239,000 (at December 1987 rates of exchange) in accordance with scale and diversity of its operations.

Directors of brokerage companies must be individuals resident in Brazil who meet the conditions set out in the current laws and regulations. The election of directors to the board of a brokerage house must be submitted for the approval of the Central Bank of Brazil and the Security Commission. In general the requirements concern the proven identity and technical qualifications of the member elected. Any brokerage company can nominate floor brokers, even foreign nationals, provided they are permanent residents in Brazil who meet the conditions established in current laws and regulations.

The Stock Exchanges also maintain a guarantee fund, for the purpose of guaranteeing the clients of a brokerage company up to a specified limit. The fund is made up from 25% of the members' subscription fees to the Exchange in addition to other periodic contributions by the members.

OUTLINE OF CORPORATE AND INDIVIDUAL TAX CONSIDERATIONS

Residents—Current Income

Interest and dividends paid or credited are subject to income tax.

Capital Gains

Individuals are not subject to capital gains tax on disposal of securities, unless there is a simultaneous purchase and forward sale when a rate of 40% may apply (depending on the period of the funding and the return relative to bank bills).

Nonresidents—Current Income

Remittances to foreign investors are generally subject to 15% tax at source. Dividends paid to foreign shareholders are subject to withholding tax of 25% (or a lower treaty rate if applicable).

If profits are distributed in excess of approximately 12% on registered foreign capital, then a supplementary tax starting at 40% and rising to 60% (for a 25% return or higher) is payable.

Capital Gains

As for residents. No capital gains tax is payable on repatriation of funds.

Financial Operations Tax

This tax is payable on purchase transactions only. For forward and futures transactions it is 1% of the purchase price; for options it is 0.5% of the premium.

PROSPECTIVE DEVELOPMENTS

The level of Brazil's national debt (approximately US$110 billion) has led to a tendency for foreign creditors to be allowed to convert their assets into securities issued by Brazilian companies or joint ventures. This is seen as a way to promote greater liquidity in the market and to encourage economic development.

Other recent initiatives to attract foreign investment in Brazil are "Foreign Capital Investment Companies," "Foreign Capital Investment Funds" and "Securities Portfolios." Foreign Capital Investment Companies are incorporated and managed in Brazil, with the proceeds of the sale of their shares abroad being invested in a diversified portfolio. Foreign Capital Investment Funds sell their "quotas" abroad to overseas persons, funds or collective investment schemes. The quotas are freely saleable after 90 days. The funds are managed in Brazil and again are invested in a diversified portfolio. Finally, Securities Portfolios allow foreigners to register resources with the Brazilian Central Bank for management by a Brazilian institution.

Until 1975 foreign portfolio investment was not allowed in Brazil. Subsequent measures to attract foreign investment were not very successful because of the poor performance of the market and severe restrictions on the funds. Indications are that the recent innovations are having more success.

CANADA

Mintz & Partners
Contact: Robert Landori-Hoffman, Tel: (416) 391 2900

There are five Stock Exchanges in Canada, located in Toronto, Montreal, Vancouver, Winnipeg, and Calgary. They are not linked in operation and compete for listings.

Based on the turnover of shares, Toronto is the largest Exchange, followed by Vancouver (where the shares listed are most commonly low value shares issued by mineral exploration companies), although on the basis of value of business, Toronto (with around 75%) is followed by Montreal with around 20%.

Since the Toronto Stock Exchange (TSE) accounted for the majority of the total value of trading on all five of Canada's Stock Exchanges in 1987, this review is primarily concerned with the procedures of that Exchange.

Volumes of trading on the TSE for 1987 were as follows:

	Equities
Toronto (C$billion)	103.0
Number of shares traded (billion)	7.6
Market capitalization at 12/31/87 (C$billion)	737.7
Companies listed (at 12/31/87)	1208
Issues listed (at 12/31/87)	1695

The Toronto Stock Exchange has established two-way electronic trading links with the American Stock Exchange and the Midwest Stock Exchange, while the Montreal Stock Exchange has developed links with the Boston Stock Exchange.

21

The TSE presently has around 75 member firms, which are now permitted to be publicly and foreign-owned, although member firms themselves have to be Canadian residents.

In addition to the five main Stock Exchanges, there is an over-the-counter market, which accounts for about 5% of the trade in securities each year. Since early last year, the Canadian over-the-counter automated trading system (COATS) has been giving stock dealers and investors more accurate information on the market. The new system shows a stock's high, low, and closing price for the day, together with the volume.

About 35 brokerage houses are now willing to become market dealers for OTC stocks. The Toronto Stock Exchange is responsible for the software for COATS while the Ontario Securities Commission (OSC) monitors trading to ensure that it conforms with securities legislation. Most securities traded over the counter are speculative, and there is a considerable amount of reverse takeover activity; however, not all the listings are of "second-tier" companies. Large offshore companies are represented, as are some preference shares.

Although there is no self-regulatory organization governing the OTC market, the fact that the OSC monitors trading, and the TSE is responsible for the software, has had the following effects:

- Better transaction visibility, improved stock pricing, and better market regulation.
- More dealers in OTC stocks giving junior companies better access to equity capital.
- Issues can now place stock without moving out of the province or paying high fees to the TSE.

Significant increases in the size of the OTC market have therefore resulted. In the first half of 1987, 277.4 million shares worth C$1.2 billion had been traded on COATS. More significant are increases in the number of stocks and marketmakers. By the end of June 1987, the number of stocks quoted had risen to 334, compared with 263 a year earlier, while the number of marketmakers increased to 40 from 27.

The main market index is the TSE 300 Composite Index system, introduced in January 1977. Using this index the performance of 300 listed stocks divided into 14 major groups is carefully tracked. The base year is 1975, with base value 1,000.

The last 3 years' movements of the Index are as follows:

**Toronto Stock Exchange Composite
Share Price Index**

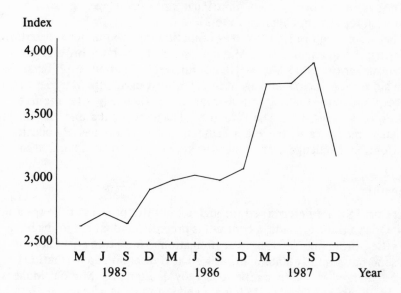

Index

OVERVIEW OF THE BOND AND EQUITY MARKETS

Structure

Trading on the TSE is conducted from 9:30 to 16:00, Monday to Friday, and these times are closely tied to New York's trading hours.

Orders are handled either by a floor trader at the TSE or by a computer system operated by the TSE. Trade orders are dealt with on an open-outcry system, at designated trading posts, all deals then being passed onto the TSE computer.

Stock dealt with solely by computer is dealt on either the MOST or LOTS trading system.

The MOST system routes small market orders directly from the brokerage firm to the trading post where the stock is traded. Trades are then carried out by the system, backed up by a guarantee from a floor trader who is responsible for the stock. Since 1986, that guarantee has been 1099 shares. Any market order less than 1099 shares is completed through the MOST system.

The LOTS trading system files the limit orders which come to the floor until market prices move to the specified price so that the order can be filled. LOTS ensures that floor traders have more time to trade larger and more complex orders.

The system has been leased to the Paris Stock Exchange, and trading in France on the system began in June 1986.

There is no required separation of function between underwriting and brokerage by member firms. Major firms perform both brokerage and marketmaker functions but conflict of interest regulations prohibit firms from acting as principal and agent in the same transaction. Member firms are responsible for making orderly markets, particularly after the underwriting of a new issue. The Canadian chartered banks and the Stock Exchange members all trade Government of Canada issues. By contrast, the Montreal Exchange uses a specialist system akin to New York.

Execution

Prices on TSE are determined through a bid-offer process at the trading post. Once a trade is made, a contract is prepared and issued to the buyer and seller. Brokerage firms have an obligation to maintain client accounts and send out monthly statements as well as transaction confirmations.

The market is made continuously by Designated Market Makers (DMM). Every stock on the TSE is assigned to a DMM who will maintain a market.

Of the approximately 500 traders working for member brokerage firms on the trading floor, 180 have been registered with the Exchange as DMMs. Approximately 32 TSE member firms have committed sizable amounts of capital to enable their DMMs to fulfill their marketmaking function. Trading privileges are not granted to the other traders working on the floor, who may only buy or sell stock through a registered representative with an approved member firm.

Although shares are normally traded in board lots (which are 100 shares for securities selling at C$1.00 and over and 500 shares for securities selling at C$0.10 to C$0.99), DMMs will buy or sell all odd lots, without charging any premium.

Publicly available information exists on an immediate basis for all listed stocks on the TSE, and details such as selling broker, buying broker, number of shares, time and price of trade can be obtained instantaneously through the use of the TSE instant access system.

There are no formal limits on daily permissible price movements in stocks. However, if an unusual price change does occur, the TSE's Markets Operation Division may investigate and intervene to stop trading in that stock until the circumstances underlying the price movement have been determined.

Settlement and Clearing

Normal settlement of transactions is within five business days. The Canadian Depository for Securities is available for both the Toronto and Montreal Exchange to provide automated facilities for the clearing and custody of securities. A system of continuous net settlement was introduced in late 1983.

Market Characteristics

Commission Rates. Commissions for executing trades are negotiable in Toronto and Montreal and have been so for a period of four years. Normal rates for small transactions (less than C$20,000) are 3% of contract value. One major bank and a number of brokerage houses have commenced operations as discount brokers executing trades at lower rates. Like U.S. discount brokers, they generally do not provide research or investment advice for their clients and therefore are able to charge lower commission rates.

Margin Trading. Margin trading is permitted by the TSE; the actual margin required depends on the security being traded. Margin trading includes transactions entered into as short (bear) sales. The rules applying to margin accounts require immediate settlement of margin deficiencies caused by a change in the loan value of securities in an account compared to the account balance. Most securities firms finance their margin lending through bank borrowing. Foreign investors are not precluded from margin trading.

Brokerage houses wishing to borrow stock to cover their needs are able to do so from the Central Depository for Securities or from another broker, but they normally pay a fee for this service.

Investor Protection. Investor protection is provided by capitalization requirements, the mailing of monthly client statements, net free capital calculations and filings, priority given to client orders and the existence of a National Contingency Fund. This Fund is sponsored by the Calgary, Montreal, Toronto and Vancouver Stock Exchanges and the Investment Dealers' Association of Canada. The Fund protects clients of a member firm from financial loss resulting from the insolvency or bankruptcy of the firm.

The Fund is responsible for the maintenance of accepted, financially related standards which must be observed by investment dealers and Stock Exchange members across Canada. The sponsoring organizations' member firms file monthly capital and quarterly operational and financial reports with the Fund's national examiner.

New Issues

The 1987 figures for new issues were as follows:

Number of new issues listed	190
Type of financing (C$'000)	
Fixed price offer	22,547
Public offer	10,091,832
Private placement	2,394,977
Rights	196,743
Total	12,706,099

The minimum listing requirements for the TSE are:

- The company must have at least 200 public shareholders, each holding one board lot or more.
- The market value of publicly held shares must be at least C$350,000.

The management and sponsorship of the company are also significant factors in determining the suitability of a company for listing.

FUTURES AND OPTIONS TRADING

In 1976, the TSE introduced an exchange-traded option market, which has since grown dramatically. By the end of 1981, both put and call options were available on all of the underlying securities listed for option trading.

Individuals or partnerships can trade for their own account in the options markets, and in 1985 the first independent traders Competitive Options Traders (COTS), started trading in all of the Exchange options products. In 1986 the TSE introduced a new Specialist Trading System for the options area. The specialist system ensures the following: guaranteed minimum board lots and posted bids and offers, a potential Automated Fill System for client market orders, and equality between COTS and other professional traders. The Specialist is responsible for full management control of the market environment and for maintaining an efficient and liquid trading environment.

Futures trading began on the TSE in September 1980 when interest rate futures such as contracts on Treasury Bills and Government of Canada Bonds were introduced.

The Toronto Futures Exchange was incorporated in October 1983 and opened officially in January 1984. At this time, the TSE 300 Composite Index Futures Contract began trading, followed six months later by the

U.S. Dollar Futures Contract. There are detailed TSE regulations concerning trading, settlement, and margin rules for both options and futures.

REGULATIONS AFFECTING NEW ENTRANTS TO THE MARKETS

Membership Requirements

A brokerage firm must be a member of the Stock Exchange to use its facilities.

Not all securities firms are Exchange members. Should a nonmember securities firm wish to buy and sell listed securities without formally joining an Exchange, it can do so by applying for authorized (or designated) nonmember status on the TSE, Calgary and Vancouver Stock Exchanges, or associated membership on the Montreal Stock Exchange.

In the case of authorized nonmember status, each applicant signs an agreement undertaking to abide by certain Exchange by-laws.

A member of a recognized Canadian Exchange is automatically treated as an authorized nonmember on all other Canadian Exchanges which grant nonmember status. Equivalent nonmember status is extended by those Canadian Exchanges to most members of recognized Stock Exchanges throughout the world without formal application. However, the Exchanges reserve the right to withdraw nonmember authorization or designation at any time, thereby terminating the entitlement to split commission. Thus, while carrying out Exchange transactions through a member firm, nonmember brokers retain their separate identities.

Member firms may be either incorporated or partnerships and may be publicly owned provided that no nonindustry person owns more than a 10% interest.

A firm must have ownership of at least one TSE seat and must be a resident of Canada to be entitled to use TSE facilities and conduct the business of buying and selling securities. The Montreal Exchange, however, allows foreign seat holders. A candidate must be the owner of a seat, have adequate and acceptable experience in the securities industry and have passed the necessary qualifying examinations. A firm must be approved by the Stock Exchange and comply with TSE rules that govern trading procedures and client accounts.

Equity ownership by nonresidents in TSE firms is limited to 10% for each individual nonresident with an aggregate limit of 25% for nonresident equity holdings. This limitation applies in aggregate to all classes of a member firm's equity.

Changes within member firms such as retirement of a director or partner, the naming of new directors and officers or a change in the firm's name require the Stock Exchange's approval prior to the change taking effect. For both corporate and partnership member firms, Stock Exchange requirements state that more than 40% of the directors or partners in the firm should be securities experts.

Capital, Liquidity, and Audit Requirements

The Stock Exchange monitors the financial status of each member firm. The amount of capital that member firms must maintain at any time depends upon such factors as the volume of the firm's business, the nature of its business and internal administrative efficiency.

The Stock Exchange's regulations state that a firm's available capital must at all times exceed the minimum requirements, and any capital deficiency must be notified to the Stock Exchange immediately. The minimum capital requirement is C$75,000.

The Stock Exchange defines available capital as working capital less funds required to margin fully the firm's inventory positions, unsettled cash transactions outstanding in excess of a stipulated time period, and margin account deficiencies. Required capital is calculated as a percentage of adjusted liabilities. There are further rules regarding subordinated loans when determining available capital. In addition, while the capital requirement is calculated on a percentage basis of adjusted liabilities, there are other factors which also enter into the calculation of minimum capital, for example, the deductible amount of the broker's blanket bond insurance policy.

Each Stock Exchange, as well as the Investment Dealers' Association of Canada, employs examiners who regularly review financial and other operating information submitted by members. In addition, the examiners visit each member at least once a year to conduct their own audits. They concentrate on assessing a firm's administrative procedures for ensuring compliance with regulations. If a member raises concerns about submissions, these would also be reviewed by examiners.

OUTLINE OF CORPORATE AND INDIVIDUAL TAX CONSIDERATIONS

With respect to corporations and individuals engaging in the business of securities, all securities transactions are treated as part of business operations and not as transactions giving rise to capital gains.

Such business profits would be subject to Federal Income Tax at 36%. Personal tax rates range from 6% to 34%; 34% applies to taxable income over C$63,347.

Residents

Government Bonds—Current Income. Interest income is fully taxable as part of total income. For individuals it is reported on a cash received basis or on the accrual basis if the interest is payable less frequently than once every three years. For corporations it is reported annually on the accrual basis.

Government Bonds—Capital Gains. Capital gains or losses are recognized in the year of disposal. The gain or loss is deemed to be the difference between the purchased and the selling price of the principal proportion of the bond only. Accrued interest purchased and sold is not part of the capital gain/loss determination.

Equities—Current Income. Dividend income is fully taxable on a cash received basis. For 1988 and subsequent years, the amount included in income is 125% of the actual dividend but a tax credit is granted equal to 16.67% of the actual amount of the dividend. Dividends received by corporations are generally liable to 25% tax, refundable when the dividends are redistributed to the companies' shareholders.

Equities—Capital Gains. For 1988 and 1989, two thirds of capital gains/ losses will be included in determining income. Commencing in 1990, the rate increases to three quarters.

For 1985 and subsequent years, individuals other than trusts who are resident in Canada throughout a taxation year, are eligible for a lifetime exemption of capital gains up to a limit of $500,000. Tax reform proposes to limit the lifetime exemption of $100,000 for all property except for shares of certain Canadian-controlled private companies.

Traded Options—Current Income. Profits or losses are on income account if realized by a trader in options and securities or by a nontrader in covered options who treats profits and losses on the underlying securities on income account. A nontrader, however, can make an irrevocable choice for an income account or capital account treatment of the profits or losses incurred.

Traded Options—Capital Gains. This only applies to a nontrader who chooses to report his options profits or losses under capital account treatment. In this case, all results will be reported in the year the contract is sold, closed, or otherwise disposed of.

Financial Futures—Current Income. Profits and losses are on income account if realized by a trader in futures or by a nontrader who voluntarily and irrevocably chooses the income account treatment. However, some exceptions are available for nontraders.

Financial Futures—Capital Gains. This only applies to a nontrader choosing a capital account treatment (see above).

Nonresidents

Government Bonds—Current Income. Interest on government bonds is exempt from income tax provided that it is not connected with a business in Canada. No withholding tax is levied.

Government Bonds—Capital Gains. Provided the bonds are not the property of a business carried on in Canada by a resident or by a permanent Canadian establishment of a nonresident, the capital gain realized on bonds sold is tax-exempt.

Equities—Current Income. Dividends paid abroad by a Canadian company are liable to 25% withholding tax or to a lower rate applicable to residents of treaty countries.

Equities—Capital Gains. Different treatment applies to shares of public and private companies. Half of the net gains of private company shares are taxable at the same rates applicable to residents. The same treatment applies to large shareholdings (more than 25%) of public companies. Gains from smaller shareholdings of nonpublic companies are tax exempt.

Traded Options—Current Income. The same rules apply as to residents if the activity is part of a business establishment in Canada.

Traded Options—Capital Gains. The same rules apply as for equities because an option on a share is deemed to be the same as the share itself.

Financial Futures—Current Income. The same rules apply as to residents if the activity is part of a business carried on in Canada or a business attributable to a permanent establishment in Canada.

Financial Futures—Capital Gains. This only applies to a nontrader as set above for residents. In that event any gain or loss is tax-exempt.

Stamp Duty. Canada does not levy any stamp duty or similar tax on securities, options, and futures transactions.

PROSPECTIVE DEVELOPMENTS

The Ontario cabinet has given final approval to the new regulations of the Ontario Securities Act that will open up the securities industry in the province. The regulations went into effect on June 30, 1987.

The new rules cover ownership and entry into the industry by foreign dealers, Canadian financial institutions and others. So far, 12 foreign dealers have applied for entry, and 7 of the applications have been approved.

Restrictions on foreign ownership of securities firms were eased in June 1987 to allow a 50% foreign stake, and all barriers are to go in 1988.

DENMARK

Scan-Revision International A/S
Contact: Søren Jensen, Tel: (01) 14 35 80

The only Stock Exchange in Denmark is in Copenhagen (The Koben-havns Fondsbors). Only a small percentage of total securities trading takes place on the Copenhagen Exchange, with most transactions being through banks, brokers, or privately.
The 1987 figures for the Copenhagen Stock Exchange were:

DKK 1,000,000	Equities (including unit trusts)	Fixed Interest (including floating rate bonds and index bonds)
Turnover – value	13,651	93,346
Number of trades/bargains	N/A	N/A
Market capitalization as of 12/31/87	124,015	943,942
Number of securities as of 12/31/87	433	2,215

The 1987 turnover for bonds on the Copenhagen Stock Exchange at nominal value of DKK 102,338 million represents only 3% of the total turnover on the Danish bonds market, which in total averages DKK 1 million turnover per capita, considerably more than any other country in the world.
The Stock Exchange in Denmark is currently undergoing major restructuring. Until the end of 1986, only 28 broking firms were members

of the Stock Exchange. 46 broking companies are now operational, of which 27 are the successors to the former broking firms, 13 have been established by clearing banks, and 6 are newly floated companies.

Indices

The Copenhagen Stock Exchange Index. All listed companies are included in the Copenhagen Stock Exchange Index (Kobenhavns Fondsbors Aktieindeks).

Copenhagen Stock Exchange Index

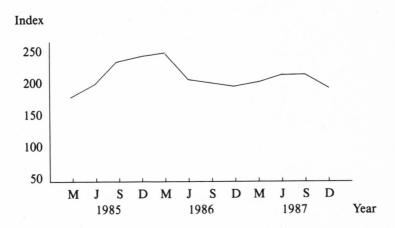

OVERVIEW OF THE BOND AND EQUITY MARKETS

Structure

Both the equities market and the bonds market on the Copenhagen Stock Exchange are divided into three sections. For shares these are broadly:

- *Section I.* Large companies with the most frequently traded shares and a paid-up capital of at least DKK 15 million.
- *Section II.* Companies with less frequently traded shares but still with paid-up capital of at least DKK 15 million.
- *Section III.* Small and medium-sized companies with a paid-up capital between DKK 2 million and DKK 15 million, for which the demands for Stock Exchange quotations are less strict than for Sections I and II. When the capital requirement is DKK 2 million a minimum of DKK 1 million must be offered for sale.

For bonds the sections are:

- *Section I.* All major and leading issues, including government bonds, unified mortgage credit bonds, indexed bonds, and bonds issued by special institutions.

- *Sections II.* Mortgage credit bonds, issued before the second mortgage credit reform in October 1980, separated into ordinary and special institutions.

- *Section III.* Bonds transferred from Sections I and II which have been closed for issue for at least 2 years and for which the amount in circulation is less than DKK 100 million, and bonds issued by organizations which ceased activity following mortgage credit reforms in 1970.

Only a small proportion of turnover (estimated at 10%) in bonds and equities takes place during the "official quotation." Over the last few years the percentage of bond trading during the official quotation has decreased but it is expected that the percentage of the official equity trading during the official quotation will increase when shares are transferred to central registration with the Danish Securities Center.

There is a large turnover in bonds due mainly to the active portfolio management policy of traders facilitated by the central computerized registration system. Traders finance their activities though the spread between bid and offer prices and are able to rearrange their bond holdings very quickly. Before the change from paper bonds to EDP-bonds registered centrally, turnover was hindered by the transport of papers, delivery dates and financing.

An unofficial over-the-counter (OTC) market has been established, mainly for shares in investment trusts. Price quotations are published daily in a number of newspapers, but market liquidity is relatively limited. There is no particular public control and the OTC is of insignificant size.

Trade at the Copenhagen Stock Exchange officially starts at 10:30 and ends when the last securities on the list have been quoted, normally at around 16:00. Trade outside the Exchange usually starts "at home" at approximately 8:15 and ends at around 17:00.

Stockbrokers must be organized in such a way that they are able to operate actively in all quoted securities and serve any potential customer.

Only stockbrokers (authorized by the Government Bank Inspectorate) and the Danish National Bank have access to the official quotation trading system of the Copenhagen Stock Exchange. However, certain other banks have the right to deal in securities outside the official quotation system.

DENMARK

Execution

Fundamental changes in the operation of the Danish securities market are in progress. A computerized system comprising trade, settlement, and information procedures was introduced in autumn 1987 and is expected to be fully implemented by the middle of 1989.

Until this new system is fully implemented, securities will continue to be traded through a call-over system at certain times of the day. All securities are only quoted officially once a day. The new system will change this practice completely and current quotations will be available throughout the day.

All bargains in securities quoted at the Copenhagen Stock Exchange with the assistance of a stockbroker or with one party associated with the Danish Securities Center must be reported to the Copenhagen Stock Exchange. However, there are no limits on the daily permissible price movements in bonds or equities.

Every day, the Copenhagen Stock Exchange issues an official quotation list containing a great deal of information in addition to quotations and size of turnovers for the day in question. The list of quotations is shown in full or partly in a number of daily newspapers the following day.

The New System

It will be the task of the Copenhagen Stock Exchange to implement and control the three new trading systems which will result from the restructuring of the markets. A brief description of the proposed three-stage system is given next:

The Pre-Opening System. This is based on the CATS system in Toronto. The purpose is to set the market going during a 15-minute period before the ordinary trade starts at 9:00. The system runs automatically and the broker needs only to make an offer. Offers are matched collectively and all deals are closed at a common rate.

Automatic Matching System. This is an automatic trading system with computerized quotations. All offers and bids input are ranked by price and by time of input. Trading takes place automatically whenever the prices of offers and bids match or overlap each other. Contrary to the pre-opening system which matches all offers collectively, this system will match whenever an offer is made which is better than or corresponds with one or more bids. The time of input determines which offer is matched with which bid in the case of identical offers.

35

The Accepting System. This is a trade-support system informing a central computer of offer and bid prices. The broker company can see all not-yet traded bids and offers on its computer monitor. A deal is entered through the pointing out of an offer and acceptance on the monitor. This accounts for the name "acceptance system."

Settlement and Clearing

Trades in shares and bonds are due for settlement on the third business day after the transaction (the value day) when the invoice amount is settled and papers exchanged, except for trading in Section III bonds where the transaction is settled on the fourth day. Shares are transferred by "physical delivery" but bonds are transferred from the seller's to the buyer's account in the Danish Securities Center. The buyer must arrange the physical collection of shares from the seller, unless other arrangements have been made. If the seller is unable to hand over the securities, the time of delivery can be postponed subject to the buyer's consent and the issue of an IOU.

Clearing between stockbrokers takes place by transfer between the brokers' accounts in the Danish National Bank.

Market Characteristics

Commission Rates. Commission rates, which were fixed until recently, are now negotiable and usually fall within the following ranges:

- Bonds 0.025% to 0.15%
- Shares 0.25% to 1.0%

Other than on trading between banks and stockbrokers there is also a 1% fee on the sale of shares payable by the seller to the State.

Margin Trading. Margin trading is permissible and as from September 1, 1987 there have been statutory rules governing this practice. If the customer purchases securities with borrowed funds, the broker must ensure that the loan is exceeded by the market value of the securities held by him, after applying a specified range of discounts to the market value.

Foreign investors may participate in margin trading and are governed by the same rules as Danish investors. Firms usually finance their margin lending by repurchase agreements and bank borrowing. Loans of share and bond portfolios may be made to bank/brokers/Stock Exchange when the owner has granted written permission and if the size of the loan is reported to the Stock Exchange.

DENMARK

Investor Protection

The main regulation for the securities industry is the Copenhagen Stock Exchange Act. One of the purposes of the legislation is to protect investors. However, brokers may act as both principal and agent in the same transaction.

Section 39 of the Copenhagen Stock Exchange Act contains the most recent provision restricting insider dealing, expanding on Section 53 of the Danish Companies Act. Section 39 says "The purchase or sale of a listed security may not be effected by anybody knowing of information not yet published concerning the particular issuer if any such information may be assumed to be significant to the security pricing."

New Issues

The 1986 figures for new issues are as follows:

	Equities	Bonds
Number	199	Not applicable*
Value	8,941	101.665
(DKK million)		

*Danish issues are usually issues of existing securities.

New issues of equity normally come to the market with the assistance of a bank or broker in the preparation of the prospectus and in planning the issue. Direct placement by banks or an offer for sale through newspapers are the usual means of issue. The bank would often also guarantee and administer the issue of the shares. Due to the fact that most bonds are supplied by the State and the mortgage credit institutes, they are often issued without help from brokers/banks.

Underwriting rates are negotiable, the banks handling the issue normally charge around 1.5% of the quoted value to cover both the initial planning and the issue itself. New issues of shares and bonds must be registered with the Copenhagen Stock Exchange and the Danish Securities Center and in addition shares only must be notified to the Registrar of Companies.

FUTURES AND OPTIONS TRADING

An organized option market is expected to commence during the spring of 1988. Initially only bond option contracts (call options of the European type) will be introduced based on a standard mortgage credit bond. It is the intention to introduce a wider spectrum of contracts as the market matures.

An organized financial futures market will be established in the same underlying instrument as the options market.

The Danish futures and option markets are established in connection with the Guarantee Fund for Danish Options and Futures, founded by the Danish Banking Association, the Danish Savings Bank Association, the Brokers Association, and the Danish National Bank. The purposes of the Fund are to:

- Stand as one of the parties in option and future contracts listed on the Copenhagen Stock Exchange
- Set up the administrative rules for issue, trade, and closing of futures and options contracts between users of the fund and their customers
- Clear and close contracts
- Issue information regarding the special character and risk connected with contracts

The potential users (members) of the Fund are the Danish National Bank, Danish banks, brokers, and credit institutes with special permits. The users must be registered as stockbrokers with the Danish Securities Center and have a clearing account with the Danish National Bank.

Transactions between members are reported to the Guarantee Fund by the issuing party to the contract. An initial margin is required and a daily margin is computed and settled.

Options and futures contracts for the time being are not negotiable. A contract can be closed by entering a "reverse contract." Contracts are closed only through cash payment as physical delivery cannot be demanded. In-the-money options are automatically exercised on the expiry date.

In the initial phase, there is no established link to foreign options or futures markets. Foreign investors may, however, deal freely in the market through established users of the Guarantee Fund.

REGULATIONS AFFECTING NEW ENTRANTS TO THE MARKETS

Stockbrokers must be approved by the Government Bank Inspectorate to participate through the trading systems of the Copenhagen Stock Exchange. An application must contain a statement of the type of business planned and the organization of the company. The Government Bank

Inspectorate carries out direct inspection of the brokers to ensure effective observance of the regulations.

The main statutory regulation is contained in the Copenhagen Stock Exchange Act (316 of June 4, 1986) which places the control of the Exchange in the hands of the Stock Exchange's board and management.

Stockbroking firms may only carry out normal Stock Exchange transactions. They must carry out the business entrusted to them with precision, accuracy, the speed dictated by the nature of the assignment, and in accordance with good business principles.

A stockbroking firm may not have subsidiaries and must use the word "stockbroking firm/company" as a part of its company name. The equity of a stockbroking company must amount to at least 8% of its total assets. However, it should be noted that in calculating total assets, various categories of assets are given different proportionate values. Monthly statements of equity are required as well as quarterly and annual accounts.

Foreign brokers cannot trade directly on the Copenhagen Stock Exchange although they may establish a Danish stockbroking company in order to gain entry. If an investment is made in accordance with the Exchange control rules governing direct investments, there are no restrictions on interest and dividends flowing therefrom nor on the payment of royalties or license fees.

Membership of the Exchange

Stockbrokers and the Danish National Bank have the sole right to trade on the Copenhagen Stock Exchange. A stockbroking firm is required to show that:

1. It is a limited company listed in the Register of Companies.

2. Its share capital is no less than DKK 5 million.

3. The company shares are registered in the holder's name.

4. It is linked to the clearing system of the Danish National Bank, and registered with the Danish Securities Center as a stockbroker.

5. The company's Memorandum and Articles are approved by the Government Bank Inspectorate.

If a firm meets all of the requirements, it can automatically obtain membership.

Brokers who at the time when the Stock Exchange reform came into force were licensed as members of the Copenhagen Stock Exchange, have been given the possibility of continuing their banking activities in the form of a registered company as credit institutions (credit banks)/banking firms. The share capital must—within 3 years from receipt of permission to run the credit institution—be raised to at least DKK 3 million; within 5 years to DKK 5 million; and within 10 years from the receipt of permission to DKK 10 million.

If 50% or more of the shares are no longer owned by a broker who (at the time of the Stock Exchange reform coming into force) was licensed as a member of the Copenhagen Stock Exchange, the share capital must then be at least that of the minimum capital requirement of a bank, i.e., DKK 25 million.

Brokers who were licensed as members at January 1, 1987 have also been given interim arrangements with regard to the share capital of stockbroker companies. They can start off with a share capital of DKK 5 million which is the minimum for others wishing to establish stockbroker companies.

OUTLINE OF CORPORATE AND INDIVIDUAL TAX CONSIDERATIONS

Corporate Taxes

Resident companies are liable to corporation tax on worldwide income including taxable capital gains. Nonresident companies are liable to corporation tax on business income earned through a permanent establishment in Denmark, on income derived from real estate situated in Denmark and on dividends from Danish companies. Capital gains are taxable only if related to a permanent establishment, or to real estate, situated in Denmark.

Personal Income Tax

Resident individuals are taxed on their worldwide income. Nonresident individuals are taxed on income arising from services performed in Denmark, from a permanent business establishment or from real estate in Denmark, and on dividends from Danish companies.

Capital Gains Tax

Capital gains on shares and bonds obtained by securities houses are usually treated as business income and are as such subject to corporate tax or personal income tax.

Stamp Duties

When shares are sold, a 1% stamp duty is paid on the quoted value. In the following cases no stamp duty is paid:

- On the issue of shares (but capital duty is payable, see below).
- When a stockbroker company enters into an agreement with a foreign broker or a foreign bank in relation to the purchase or exchange of listed shares.
- When the seller is a broker, i.e., no stamp duty is paid when shares are bought from the National Bank of Denmark, stockbroker companies, banks, and credit banks.

Capital Duty

Capital duty is payable by companies on formation or expansion of share capital as well as by a company moving to Denmark from a country which is not a member of the EEC. The duty is levied at a rate of 1%.

PROSPECTIVE DEVELOPMENTS

The Stock Exchange reforms—including the introduction of the electronic Stock Exchange—means that the Copenhagen Stock Exchange will become more efficient. It is expected that a considerably larger part of total trade will pass through the Stock Exchange making it easier for foreign securities houses to operate on the Danish securities market. But the intensified competition and increased demands on the market may result in some of the smaller participants finding it difficult to survive.

All Danish shares will, as from Easter 1988, be registered centrally at the Danish Securities Center (Vaerdipapircentralen) as bonds have been since 1983. From then on, no Danish shares or bonds will be on paper. The Stock Exchange expects that when all shares are computerized, about 20,000 deals will be settled daily.

In Denmark shares are currently quoted as a percentage of their nominal value. In order to make it easier for nonresidents investing in Danish shares and to enhance the international role of the Copenhagen Stock Exchange, the Danish system will be changed so that from Easter 1988 shares will be quoted in DKK per share. However, the new system will also contain an element for checking whether the nominal value of the shares is 20, 50, or 100 DKK.

FRANCE

Société Française d'Audit et d'Expertise
Contact: Patrice de Maistre, Tel: (1) 47 66 28 05

There are seven Stock Exchanges (Bourses) in France. The Paris Bourse is the largest, handling approximately 96% of all Stock Exchange transactions. The remaining 4% of activity occurs on the regional Exchanges located in Bordeaux, Lille, Lyon, Marseille, Nancy, and Nantes.

This review is primarily concerned with the procedures of the Paris Bourse.

Size

The market figures for the Paris Bourse for 1987 were as follows:

	Equities	Bonds	Others
Turnover (FFr billions)	522.1	2426.5	63.0
Number of trades/bargains (millions)	581.5	2430.0	N/A
Market capitalization as of 12/31/87 (FFr billions)	929.2	N/A	N/A

There are 61 member firms, including 45 on the Paris Bourse, which have a legal monopoly on trading.

All transactions in securities must be passed through member firms which are known as Agents de Change.

There is significant trading of French equities outside France, particularly in London where the main equities traded include Lafarge Coppee, L'Air Liquide, BSN, and Total.

42

Trading of overseas equities on the Bourse represents only a small proportion of total activity.

The index used to indicate overall market price movement is the Index Compagnie des Agents de Change (Index CAC), which is based on the market capitalization of 249 representative French equities quoted in Paris. Movements in the Index CAC since 1985 are:

Index CAC

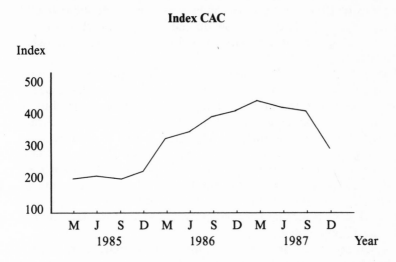

Another index is planned for introduction in September 1988 which is based on 40 securities traded on the monthly settlement market and weighted by market capitalization. It represents more than 40% of the total market capitalization of securities traded on the official list and more than 50% of the total turnover.

OVERVIEW OF THE BOND AND EQUITY MARKETS

Structure

The securities market can be divided into three categories: the Cote Officielle or official list, the Second Marché or second market, and the Marché Hors Cote or OTC market.

The official list is divided into two sections, the cash market and the monthly settlement market. For a quotation on the official list, at least 25% of the equity or 500,000 shares of a company must be available for distribution to the public.

FRANCE

The monthly settlement market is the more active market where the 250 or so most heavily traded French and foreign securities are traded. The cash market is the focus of trading for small volumes of smaller companies' shares. Any quantity can be traded for immediate settlement and delivery.

The second market was opened in 1983 to cater for smaller companies seeking a cheaper listing than that provided by the official list, where a minimum of 10% of shares are made available for public distribution. Approximately 258 firms are now quoted in this market, mostly in the high technology sector. Securities listed on this market are traded for cash settlement.

The OTC market deals in the shares of smaller companies. Transactions are carried out for cash. Turnover is small and is likely to decrease further as small companies now prefer to enter the second market. Trading on the OTC market is conducted solely by broker members of the Stock Exchange. The level of bond trading on the OTC market is minimal.

Trading on the Stock Exchange floor is conducted in the following way. The securities of the largest companies are dealt between 9:30 and 11:00. Dealings in most public bonds and all private debentures are conducted between the hours of 11:30 and 12:30. For dealings in shares and convertible bonds and securities on the second market, the trading hours are 12:30 to 14:30.

Foreign securities are traded on the forward market from 12:30 to 14:30. These are quoted again during a later one hour session which coincides with the first hour of trading on the NYSE, thus enabling these securities to be more widely traded. This is known as the "petit bourse" and its time varies according to the time difference between Paris and New York.

Off-floor trading takes place between 10:00 and 17:00.

No statistics are available for the proportion of on-floor trading. The "continuous market" which is the computerized off-floor market was created in 1986 and is growing significantly. It has been possible to deal in more than 100 securities since the end of 1987.

Agents de Change can deal for clients in any stock, but for stock listed on the cash market only one Agent de Change is designated as market maker.

All trading of bonds and shares is granted by law exclusively to the 61 member firms (Agents de Change) of the seven French Stock Exchanges. They are appointed by the Minister of the Economy after passing professional examinations. They may only deal in securities assigned to their own Stock Exchange. There is no separation of function between member firms in trading. Until 1987, foreigners were excluded by statute from becoming Agents de Change, but reform of this situation is now taking place.

Banks (including foreign banks) and other financial institutions are allowed to relay prices from the Stock Exchange floor, but all their trading activity must be conducted through Agents de Change.

PROCEDURES

Execution

There are two methods of on-floor trading, one for the cash market and one for the monthly settlement market. A system of "casiers" or pigeonholes is used for the cash market. There is one casier for each security and fixed blocks of casiers are assigned to different Agents de Change. Each firm is responsible for collecting all orders which belong to its block and delivering them to a clerk who determines the price which gives him the fairest balance between the total number of shares offered and bid for.

An auction system à la criée is used for the monthly settlement market. Agents de Change transact business by collecting all buy and sell orders and bringing them onto the floor to trade. Securities are assigned to six auction groups and officials of the Chambre Syndicale act as auctioneers—one for each group. The auctioneer opens the auction in each security at the previous day's closing price. Bids and offers are then called out. The auctioneer raises or lowers the price until he reaches the balancing price.

Off the floor, the quotation is obtained by matching the best bid and offer prices.

Generally, Agents de Change may not act as market makers but are allowed to deal directly with clients as principal in accordance with the following rules:

- They may only deal with clients when the floor is closed.
- These dealings must be on the basis of the latest price quoted at the previous trading session.
- They must resell any securities they have bought or buy any they have sold on the market as soon as possible since they are not allowed to own securities personally.

For official list stocks there are no obligations on member firms to make continuous markets in any one stock. However, companies listed on the second market can enter into an agreement with a sponsor (an Agent de Change and/or a bank) who is thereafter authorized to act as market-maker for the specific purpose of maintaining a fair and orderly market in the stock.

A deed assignment is prepared for each transaction. The Société Inter-professionnelle pour la Compensation des Valeurs Mobilières (SICOVAM) operates the clearing system for almost all the stocks and bonds.

At the end of each working day the Chambre Syndicale also publishes the *Bulletin de la Cote Officielle* (Daily Official List). This shows the opening price as well as the highest, lowest, and closing prices for each security. At the beginning of each month, the buy/sell information for each transaction is published for the previous month.

As part of its supervisory function, the Chambre Syndicale endorses all prices quoted on the Stock Exchange and enforces limitations on daily price variations.

On the cash market, the Chambre Syndicale does not allow the opening prices for French bonds to differ by more than 3% from the closing prices of the previous day. Similarly, the opening prices for French equities are not allowed to differ by more than 5% from the close of the previous day. If the disparity between supply and demand is such that the opening prices will exceed this limit, the Chambre Syndicale sets a fixed price for that day with a spread of about 2% for bonds and 5% for equities. Supply and demand are then balanced by reducing buying or selling orders (depending on which side is in excess) at the price set. If fewer than 20% to 25% of orders can be carried out at the prices set, trading is suspended for the day and the price is marked "off" (offer in excess) or "dem" (demand in excess) in the daily official list.

On the monthly settlement market, if the opening price of a security differs by more than 8% from its closing price of the previous day, trading is stopped so that operators may have time to confirm or cancel their orders. Trading is later resumed in the same session.

On the continuous market there is no limit on daily permissible price movements, but a special Commission is permitted to stop the quotation after a 7% movement in the price. Prices of foreign securities are, however, free to move in accordance with the prices of their home market.

There is no obligation to trade in round lots on the cash market, but on the monthly settlement market shares are normally traded in round lots of 5, 10, 25, 50, or 100 shares and the Chambre Syndicale fixes the size of the lot for each security.

Odd-lot orders, which are orders for lower quantities than are permitted for trading, are handled on the market subject to a specific commission. Such orders are always settled immediately.

46

Clients must deposit a cover (margin) which is a percentage of the amount of the bargain and which can be adjusted if there is any variation.

Settlement and Clearing. Settlement and delivery are immediate for transactions carried out on the cash market. Transactions conducted on the monthly settlement market require settlement and delivery at the end of each month, although bargains can be deferred until the following settlement date by the Contango System (marché des reports). This market operates once a month on the day after settlement. A central depository system for bearer stocks is operated by SICOVAM. The preparation and delivery of certificates is computerized.

Market Characteristics

Commission Rates. Since July 1, 1985, clients have been able to negotiate the commission they pay for transactions above a level of FFr 2 million for equities and FFr 10 million for bonds. Below this level, fixed commissions are payable. For equities the negotiated commissions range between 0.65% and 0.215% of the amount of the consideration and for bonds between 0.45% and 0.01%, depending on the amount of the consideration and the term to maturity of the bond.

When an order is passed through a bank, the bank has a reduced charge commission from the Agent de Change but the bank adds its own negotiable commission.

The other dealing costs are: a Stock Exchange tax at the rate of 0.3% of the consideration up to FFr 1 million, and 0.15% thereafter; and VAT of 18.6% payable on the commission.

Margin Trading. The coverage required to trade on margin is 20% in cash on Treasury bonds, 25% on French bonds or on gold and 40% on shares. Foreign investors can deal on margin.

Stock borrowing is prohibited in France except through the Contango System (see *Settlement and Clearing* above).

Investor Protection. The Stock Exchanges are under the supervision of the Minister of the Economy, but investor protection is ensured by the Commission des Operations de Bourse (COB) which acts in a supervisory capacity similar to the U.S. Securities and Exchange Commission. Established in 1967, the COB's main responsibilities are to ensure that listed companies report all legally required information in time to prevent corporate insiders from using confidential information for their own purposes, and to register any complaints. The COB can suggest modifications to the rules governing Stock Exchange organization and procedures.

It also decides on the admission of securities to the Official list on the advice of the Chambre Syndicale. The COB makes regular investigations into abnormal price movements.

All firms trading in securities must be members of the Stock Exchange and must also belong to the Compagnie des Agents de Change (National Broker Association). Its executive body, the Chambre Syndicale, ensures the orderly operation of the market, enforces regulations governing the activity of members and manages the brokers' guarantee fund. This fund protects clients of a member firm from financial loss resulting from insolvency or bankruptcy of the firm.

Until recently, foreign firms or individuals were not permitted to join the Stock Exchange but they could have representative offices. This has not markedly changed except to the extent that foreign firms can have an interest in an existing member but not be a member of the Exchange in their own right. Refer to *Prospective Developments* for the planned changes to the current situation. Foreign firms' dealings must be conducted through an Agent de Change on the Stock Exchange.

New Issues

During 1987 the following new issues of equities were made:

French equities on the official list	7
Foreign equities on the official list	8
Equities on the second market	87
	102

Representatives from the French Treasury, the Caisse des Dépots et Consignations (CDC), the Caisse Nationale de Crédit Agricole and the four major French banks constitute the New Issues Committee which is responsible for controlling the primary market in bonds.

For each new bond issue one or more lead managing banks, an underwriting group and a selling group are involved. The underwriting group guarantees that the borrower will receive payment 10 days after the official opening of the issue of state bonds, 15 days after the opening for state guaranteed bonds, and one month after the opening for private sector bonds. The terms and conditions of each issue, including the coupon rate and issue price, are set by agreement among the issuer, lead manager and the French Treasury, generally a few days prior to the issue's official opening. Placement occurs at this fixed price and settlement is made the day before payment to the issuer (usually between two to four weeks after the official opening of the issue). Actual delivery occurs about six months after the official opening.

Once the official opening has taken place, the underwriting group forms a supervisory group which monitors the market to ensure price stabilization.

For equities, one Agent de Change is responsible for the issue. The price is calculated by the Agent de Change and agreed upon by the COB. Placement is carried out by the Agent de Change and the banks. The new issues are registered with SICOVAM.

FUTURES AND OPTIONS TRADING

On the monthly settlement market, it is possible to buy and sell options, but the option itself is not negotiable. An official market for traded options in six securities started in September 1987. These options are available for up to ten months forward.

The Marché Á Terme des Instruments Financiers (MATIF) or financial futures market is controlled by the Conseil du Marché a Terme (CMT), and is organized through the Chambre de Compensation des Instruments Financiers (CCIFP).

On the MATIF, the two instruments presently traded relate to interest rates. They are a long term gilt at 10% and a treasury bond. A currency future based on the ECU should start early in 1988. An option on the long term gilt has been traded on the MATIF since January 1988.

The margin is calculated every day, and payment is made accordingly. At the maturity date, settlement is on a cash basis.

The Agents de Change lost their legal monopoly on trading for the MATIF in September 1986. Since then, both domestic and foreign banks and trading houses have been able to become members of the market.

There is no formal link with any overseas options or futures markets.

REGULATIONS AFFECTING NEW ENTRANTS TO THE MARKETS

Membership Requirements

In order to be proposed by the Chambre Syndicale, four conditions must be fulfilled. An individual must be a French citizen, over 25 years old, have worked for at least four years in a stockbroker's office and be listed as capable of carrying out the business of stockbroking.

The minimum capital requirement for a member firm is FFr 152,000. However, in reality, net equity capital varies from FFr 4 million to FFr 40 million, depending upon the size of the firm.

OUTLINE OF CORPORATE AND INDIVIDUAL TAX CONSIDERATIONS

Residents

Government Bonds—Current Income. Interest income derived from government bonds is fully taxable at normal rates. Individual taxpayers can, however, make an option for a withholding tax of 26% which covers the whole tax liability.

Government Bonds—Capital Gains.

Individuals. Capital gains arising on the sale of securities are taxable at 16% if they are related to bonds or shares quoted on the Stock Exchange and the annual amount of the sales is over FFr 281,000. If any of these conditions is not met, capital gains are tax-exempt.

Corporations. For a company trading in securities, capital gains on securities sold are considered as a normal profit and will be taxed at 42%. For a company which does not trade in securities, capital gains will be taxable at 15% if the securities have been held over two years; otherwise the normal corporation tax rate of 42% is applicable.

Equities—Current Income.

Individuals. Dividends paid to resident companies or to individuals domiciled in France carry a tax credit (avoir fiscal) equal to 50% of the dividend. The tax credit may be offset against the income or corporate tax ultimately payable.

Corporations. Special provisions apply to French companies liable to corporate tax and which hold at least 10% of the shares of the company which pays a dividend. In this case only 5% of the dividends will be taxable.

Equities—Capital Gains.

Individuals. Capital gains on quoted or unquoted shares realized by individuals who have possessed over 25% of the company shares at any time in the five years preceding the sale are taxable at 16%. In addition, for quoted shares, the same rules apply as for capital gains on government bonds.

Corporations. The same rules apply as for capital gains on government bonds.

Traded Options and Financial Futures. These transactions, when carried out by firms, are taxed annually on a mark-to-market basis and the profits are considered as normal income subject either to corporate income tax (companies) at a 42% rate or to personal income tax (partnerships and individual firms) at the normal progressive rate (from 5% to 56.8% depending on the taxpayer's level of income).

The taxation of individuals depends on whether transactions refer to an underlying security (quoted bonds and shares) or not.

When transactions refer to such a security, the same rules apply as for capital gains on bonds and shares.

Profits realized on other transactions are taxed at a flat rate (33%).

However, individuals who usually trade in options and futures are subject to normal income tax. This is a question of fact which especially depends on the frequency of the transactions and the amounts involved.

Nonresidents

Government Bonds—Current Income. If the bonds were issued before October 1, 1984 a withholding tax of 25% will be levied on interest payments to nonresidents. For bonds issued since October 1, 1984 no withholding tax has to be paid.

Government Bonds—Capital Gains. Capital gains realized on government bonds by nonresidents are tax-exempt.

Equities—Current Income. Dividends payable by a French company to a nonresident are subject to a withholding tax of 25% or a lower rate applicable to residents of treaty countries. Some ʿreaties permit the refund to minority shareholders of the "avoir fiscal" attaching to French dividends.

Equities—Capital Gains. Capital gains arising in the hands of a nonresident will be taxable at 16% if the conditions for a qualified shareholding as defined above for residents are met.

Traded Options and Financial Futures. Profits realized by nonresident firms on traded options and financial futures are not subject to any French tax unless they are carried out through a permanent place of business located in France.

As a principle, the gains realized by nonresident individuals are exempt from French tax unless they are considered as carrying on a professional activity in France or they usually trade in such transactions in France.

Stamp Duty

There is no stamp duty as such on purchases and sales of bonds and equities. However, transfer taxes apply.

Transactions on shares which are quoted on the Paris Stock Exchange are subject to a transfer tax at a 0.3% rate up to FFr 1 million and 0.15% above. Quoted bonds are exempt from this tax.

The transactions which are realized on the Second Market, on the over-the-counter market, and on the regional Stock Exchanges are exempt from this transfer tax.

Wealth Tax

There is no longer any wealth tax in France.

PROSPECTIVE DEVELOPMENTS

A reform of the member firms is due to take place. The monopoly of the Agents de Change will be suppressed, and it will be possible for the share capital of the firms to be sold off as follows:

Up to   30% in 1988
Up to   49% in 1989
Up to 100% in 1990

This reform will allow the firms to increase their share capital; therefore they could do this by an association with a bank or by a listing on the second market.

The Agents de Change will also be allowed to act as marketmakers. There will be one Agent de Change for each security. This new function is important for the regulation of the market.

It is also proposed to change the name Agent de Change to Société de Bourse by January 1992.

The reform will also allow foreign securities houses to hold shares in the French Sociétés de Bourse. During the latter part of 1987, a significant number of Agents de Change have reached agreement with French and foreign banks and securities to sell some or all of their shares in accordance with the above timetable.

WEST GERMANY

BTR Beratung und Treuhand Ring GmbH
Wirtschaftsprüfungsgesellschaft
Contact: Jürgen Ott, Tel: (069) 77 20 06

There are eight Stock Exchanges in West Germany, located in Frankfurt, Düsseldorf, Münich, Stuttgart, Hamburg, West Berlin, Hanover, and Bremen. Together they generated a total turnover of approximately DM 2035 billion in 1987.

Frankfurt and Düsseldorf are the principal Stock Exchanges accounting for approximately 52% and 25% of turnover respectively. Hamburg and Münich each account for approximately 7%. The Exchanges are generally independent but are partially linked in databases and stock deposits, and are developing increasingly close relationships.

Size

The 1987 market figures are as follows:

	Domestic Equities	Foreign Equities	Options	Bond
Turnover (DM billion)	671.2	57.8	119.9	1185.8

There are 500 foreign equity stocks and 300 bond stocks listed on the German Stock Exchanges. There are 20 German equity stocks listed on overseas Stock Exchanges. The level of the Index der Aktienkurse over the past 3 years is as follows:

Data for West Germany

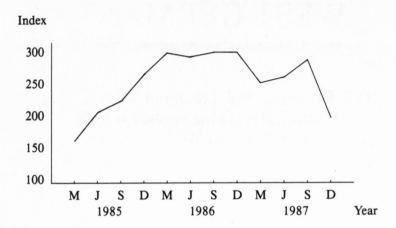

Index

OVERVIEW OF THE BOND AND EQUITY MARKETS

Structure

There are four markets on the German Stock Exchanges. The official market (Amtliche Notierung) is regulated by the Stock Exchanges in accordance with law. Most quoted companies, government and public authority bonds, financial and foreign bonds are traded in this market by the Official Exchange Brokers, the Kursmakler.

The second market (Geregelter Markt) was opened in May 1987 to cater to smaller companies seeking a cheaper listing than that provided by the official list.

On the second market, or Geregelter Freiverkehr, securities are traded on the floor of the Stock Exchanges by the Freimakler, who are independent dealers. Admission requirements for this market are less stringent.

The Telefonverkehr, or over-the-counter market (OTC), is a regulated market for securities which are not listed on the Stock Exchanges although officially listed stock may also be traded. Indeed, because it provides an "after hours" dealing facility, the turnover of listed securities can be higher in the OTC market than in the official market. Securities on this market are dealt with between the German banks and other financial institutions.

There is also an unregulated and unofficial market (the Ungeregelter Freiverkehr) which is of particular relevance to the smallest companies which cannot be traded on the three official markets. Securities can be traded both on the floor and by telephone.

All trading on the official market is determined by the Official Exchange Brokers, who participate in the determination of prices of individual securities according to the balance of supply and demand. All trading on the floor of the Stock Exchange is handled by the Exchange Brokers at their trading posts.

The Freimakler, the independent dealers, have a particular responsibility in determining the prices of nonofficial stock although they may also deal in the official market. The regulations of the Stock Exchange and the general regulations of the German Commercial Code (Handelsgesetzbuch) govern the operation of the Freimakler which are appointed by the Managing Committee of the Stock Exchange.

Trading on the floor takes place from 11:30 to 13:30, Monday to Friday, while trading off the floor takes place from 9:00 to 11:00 and 14:30 to 16:30. In general, off-the-floor trading is interbank trade in any security, but these deals are not publicly reported. Off floor trading can effectively take place at any time.

Execution

Dealing in the official market occurs using a trading post system, that is, each security is allocated a physical location on the exchange floor. The Official Exchange Brokers participate in the determination of the price of the orders in hand, by setting a price that enables the greatest match between open buy and sell orders. The fixed price so determined is that which will apply for all contracts in that security in that session. Variable prices are determined generally for larger listed companies by means of a continuous quotations process, with the Exchange Broker ensuring the price is adjusted to reflect the open orders. Prices are made available to the public at the end of each day via a daily list (Börsenblatt); however, continuous prices are available during the course of the trading hours.

A similar basis of price determination is used on the semi-official market, where the Freimakler takes the place of the Exchange Broker.

In general, there are no limits on daily permissible price movements. However, if the price of an equity or bond decreases or increases by more than 5% or 1.5% respectively, after the last fixed price, trading in the particular security concerned is stopped and the Official Exchange Broker has to inform a member of the Managing Committee of the Stock Exchange before trading is allowed to recommence.

Settlement and Clearing

Generally, dealing is on a cash basis with settlement for bonds and equities taking place two days after dealing. German shares are nearly always issued in bearer form, with settlement taking place by physical delivery. However, most German bonds and equities are now cleared through special financial institutions operating collective securities, deposits and giro transfer systems on a book-entry basis. Access to these institutions is only possible through the German banks.

Settlement is carried out by regional clearing agencies for domestic securities known as Wertpapiersammelbank AG and, for foreign securities, the central agency called Auslandskassenverein AG which is located in Frankfurt.

New Issues

The 1986 figures for new issues of equities and bonds are as follows:

Number 21
Value DM 102.7 billion

New equity and bond issues are managed by the banks which are also responsible for setting up underwriting groups. Since 1985, foreign banks with local branches have been allowed to operate as managing underwriters for the issue of foreign institutions' DM denominated bonds. Once an underwriting group has been established, the banks then partly sell the securities before their first quotation. Mortgage banks may issue their own bonds and these banks and the government manage the issues through the Bundesbank (German National Bank). The listing must meet the requirements of the Börsengesetz.

The price for equities is determined by negotiation between the company and the bank, and therefore generally determined by the market. Equities cannot be issued at less than nominal value.

There are no fixed rates for underwriting fees but they are at least 1% for government and domestic bonds, and at least 4% for equities.

The Listings Committee (Zulassungsstelle) is responsible for licensing securities prior to their being admitted to official listing. It examines the issue documents and ensures that all the requirements for listing have been met and all required information has been made publicly available.

Market Characteristics

Commission Rates. There are two types of commission rates, which are both negotiable, payable on both the purchase and sale of securities.

There is a commission to the Exchange Broker (the brokerage rate), as well as a commission payable to the bank, although the former is only charged where the trade is executed on the Exchange floor. The rates are summarized as follows:

- For bonds the brokerage rate paid to the Exchange Broker ranges from 0.075% to 0.0075% and for shares and share rights it is 0.1%.
- The commission to the bank ranges from 0.25% to 0.50% for bonds and 1% for shares and share rights with a minimum of DM10.

These rates apply to all authorized security dealers. The buyer as well as the seller must pay the brokerage rate and the bank commission on any transaction. Sellers and buyers are also subject to a turnover tax of 0.25% on all transactions, reduced by one half in certain cases.

Margin Trading. Margin trading is not permitted, although in exceptional circumstances, the banks will grant their customers credit to purchase shares.

Investor Protection. There are no regulations or procedures in existence, other than the disclosure by listed companies described above, specifically to ensure investor protection. Banks can act both as principal and agent in the same transaction. Banks which promote the issue of shares at the Stock Exchange must provide the public with the prospectus and they are liable for all statements contained in it. However, the government supervises the conduct of the Stock Exchanges and in turn the boards of the Stock Exchanges supervise the stockbrokers.

FUTURES AND OPTIONS TRADING

At present there is no financial futures market, although there is a forward market which deals only in currencies and takes place outside the Stock Exchange.

Options trading takes place according to the rules of the Stock Exchange Act (Börsengesetz) and the Besondere Bedingungen für Optionsgeschäfte an den deutschen Wertpapierbörsen.

Traded equity options must be listed on the Stock Exchange. In addition, before a particular security is eligible for options trading, certain general conditions and terms must be met. The nominal value of the traded equity options must be at least DM 10 million which will be traded on a continuous quotation on the Stock Exchanges. The company is obliged to publish an interim financial report. At present, option trading exists for 68 equity and 14 bond stocks.

The trading procedures for options require that both put and call options are for 50 shares or a multiple thereof. Options expire on either the 15th of January, April, July, or October. The seller of an option must furnish security for 30% of the underlying value of the shares by way of those shares and the remaining 70% in other securities or money.

Settlement of options is organized in a similar way to off-the-floor trading. The trading bank acts exclusively as principal in relation to the investor. After the option is exercised, delivery of the shares usually takes place two days after the transaction.

REGULATIONS AFFECTING NEW ENTRANTS TO THE MARKETS

In West Germany, all firms trading in securities must be members of a Stock Exchange. Official Exchange Brokers, the Freimakler, and banks are the only members of the Stock Exchanges.

Each West German Stock Exchange has a Managing Committee (Börsenvorstand) set up under the internal regulations (Börsenordnung) governing the operation of the Stock Exchanges. The Board is also responsible for issuing regulations governing the operation of the Stock Exchanges, the admission of members and the admission of companies to listing.

Member firms are not required to provide annual financial statements to the Stock Exchange, but Exchange Brokers must report their turnover to the managing committee of the Stock Exchange. Banks are governed by the law concerning credit transactions, and do publish their turnover annually in their balance sheet. A broker's obligation to publish is not uniform, and is fixed by the board of the respective Stock Exchange.

Membership Requirements. It is not necessary to purchase a seat on the German Stock Exchanges but there are licensing requirements which must be fulfilled. To become a member, a firm is required to have sufficient resources, as defined in the Börsengesetz (Stock Exchange Law), as well as display the ability to discharge obligations under the Stock Exchange contracts. Exchange Brokers also must fulfill the same conditions as well as furnish security between DM50,000 and DM100,000. The Freimakler must meet specified liquidity requirements. Since 1985, foreign banks have been admitted to the Stock Exchange.

OUTLINE OF CORPORATE AND INDIVIDUAL TAX CONSIDERATIONS

Residents

Government Bonds—Current Income. Interest income is fully taxable under German law as ordinary income. There is currently no withholding tax on interest from government bonds, although from January 1, 1989 all fixed income investments, except certain savings accounts, will be subject to 10% withholding tax.

Government Bonds—Capital Gains.

Individuals. No capital gains are deemed to arise on the sale of securities unless the assets were held for trade purposes or on a short-term speculative basis (less than six months). In the latter case full income tax is levied.

Corporations. The normal tax rate (56% or 36%) is applicable on capital gains realized by a corporation. Trade tax (average 17.5%) is also due, but it is a deductible trade expense.

Equities—Current Income. Dividends paid by a German company are liable to a withholding tax at 25%. All taxpayers must include dividends received in their taxable income, gross of the withholding tax (25%) and the underlying tax (36%), which are then deducted from the ultimate tax liability.

Equities—Capital Gains. The same rules apply as for Government bonds.

Traded Options and Financial Futures. Profits/gains arising on traded options and financial futures are tax-exempt if realized in the private sector and taxable as normal rates if realized in the business sector.

Nonresidents

Residents of countries with which Germany has concluded a treaty are generally not taxable in West Germany unless the trade or business is carried on through a permanent establishment there. This applies to interest, capital gains, and property tax on the securities themselves. Treaties may reduce the rate of withholding tax on dividends to 20% or 15%. Residents of countries without a double tax treaty with Germany are liable to a final withholding tax at 25% which is deemed to discharge the total German income tax liability. The underlying corporation income tax (36%) is not deductible. This applies only to dividends. In the case of individual shareholdings of over 25%, capital gains are taxable for nonresidents if more than 1% of the total shares are sold in one calendar year.

Stamp Duty

Stamp duty is levied at 0.1% on purchases of government bonds, 0.2% on purchases of other bonds and 0.25% on purchases of other securities. Financial futures are not subject to stamp duty.

Property Tax

All securities are included in the basis of computation of property tax. For nonresidents property tax only arises on equities where at least a 10% ownership exists.

PROSPECTIVE DEVELOPMENTS

Discussions are underway to provide small and medium-sized companies with a second tier regulated market on West Germany's Stock Exchanges. Admission requirements will include less stringent requirements for public reporting, smaller minimum share issues, less widespread shareholding and lower admission costs than for the full market. This will draw some companies away from the OTC markets, and attract new companies to the stock market. A second tier market will also provide additional legal safeguards to investors who wish to trade in such smaller companies. Trading in such companies through the OTC and bond markets is not currently covered by the provisions of Stock Exchange Acts and regulations.

West Germany's eight Stock Exchanges have approved a plan to enhance their coordination and efficiency as a result of growing competition from abroad. Among the changes planned is the establishment of an association based in Frankfurt which will assume the tasks presently duplicated by the eight markets and handle legal issues. It is also planned to use one major computer center to process securities transactions.

It is anticipated that a German Options and Financial Futures Exchange (GOFFEX) will be introduced to the securities market in the near future.

A new withholding tax law on most savings and investments was announced in October 1987 and a draft bill, which will lay out the broad lines of the proposed 10% tax due from 1989, should be ready by March 1988.

HONG KONG

Spicer & Oppenheim
Contact: Nick Heywood-Waddington, Tel: 5-210421

Since 1986, Hong Kong has had a single unified Stock Exchange called The Stock Exchange of Hong Kong Limited, formed by the merger of the four exchanges that previously existed.

Size

Market statistics for The Stock Exchange of Hong Kong Limited for 1987 are as follows:

	Equities	Warrants	Debt Securities	Financial Futures
Turnover (HK$ millions)	354,048	17,283	75	3,611,474
Market capitalization as of 12/31/87 (HK$ millions)	419,612	.... Not available		
Number of securities as of 12/31/87		Total = 412		

There are 791 members of The Stock Exchange, of which about 80 are corporations and the rest are individuals.

All firms trading in Hong Kong securities must deal through members of The Stock Exchange.

There is no over-the-counter market in Hong Kong.

It is possible to trade in some of the larger Hong Kong securities on the London Stock Exchange. Similarly, some overseas equities are listed on

61

The Stock Exchange of Hong Kong. However, there are no formal links with overseas markets in terms of trading or settlement.

There is a small local bond market for locally issued bonds. There is no international market. A number of firms deal in international bonds in Hong Kong on the overseas markets. There is no other significant trading outside the formal markets.

The Hang Seng Index is the most widely observed indicator of stock market performance in Hong Kong. The Index is based on 33 companies in different industry sectors, weighted by market capitalization and is thus strongly influenced by large capitalization stocks.

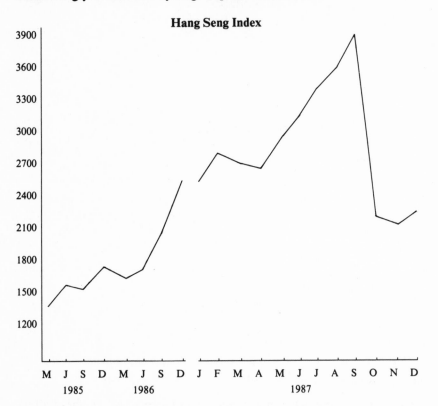

Hang Seng Index

OVERVIEW OF THE BOND AND EQUITY MARKETS

Structure

All securities listed on The Stock Exchange of Hong Kong Limited are traded under common execution, settlement, and clearance procedures.

Trading hours on The Stock Exchange floor are 10:00 to 12:30 and 14:30 to 15:30, Monday to Friday, except Wednesday when the market is closed in the afternoon.

There are no time limits for off-floor trading. The deals transacted off the floor are treated as trades for the following day for the purposes of reporting and settlement.

No statistics are available for the proportions of floor and off-floor trading.

There is no requirement for separation of function between member firms, and member firms do not have any obligations to trade or make markets.

Execution

A computerized trading system was introduced in April 1986 when the new Exchange opened. Transactions are carried out by floor-traders on behalf of their member firms. The trade can be conducted by the Exchange's internal telephone system or face-to-face on the floor. When the transaction has been completed, the security name, quantity, price, and the code numbers of the buying and selling brokers must be input into the computer by the seller within 15 minutes. The buyer must then check these details. The last 20 transactions are displayed on the wall-board.

The following information is publicly available for each stock listed: the day's highest and lowest price; the previous day's closing price; and turnover by quantity and value.

There are no limits on daily permissible price movements in stocks, although the Stock Exchange may investigate significant price movements.

Shares can be traded in board lots or odd lots. Board lots vary from 200 to 5000 shares, although 1000 shares is the most common size. Odd lots are usually traded at a small discount on the board lot price, unless the seller can make up a board lot from fractions.

Settlement and Clearing

Settlement takes place on the business day following the transaction. Delivery of shares usually takes the form of a share certificate and a stamped transfer deed. Physical delivery is always against cash, and delivery of a certificate must normally be effected by 15:45 on the business day following the transaction. In the event of delayed settlement, the buyer has the right to "buy in" against the seller but this right is hardly ever exercised.

Even though registers are computerized, registration is still a lengthy process and may take up to six weeks. During this time, the registered owner is unable to deliver the stock in compliance with the 24-hour settlement rule and is effectively unable to sell. To avoid this problem, individuals normally keep stock in "street names," that is, in the name of a broker, registering it in their own name only when a dividend is to be paid or a rights/bonus issue will take place.

At present there is no central clearing system, although this is being considered.

Market Characteristics

Commission Rates. Commission rates are negotiable, but stockbrokers are not allowed to charge less than the lower of HK$25 or 0.25% of the total consideration.

Stamp duty is levied on both the buyer and seller of equities at the rate of 0.3% on consideration. In addition, a transfer stamp is charged at the rate of HK$5 per transfer deed. Brokers are often able to parcel a number of board lots on to one transfer deed and pay HK$5, but they charge the customer HK$5 per board lot, so making a small turn on their transfer stamp account.

A transaction levy of 0.025% on consideration is also payable on purchases and sales.

Margin Trading. Margin trading is practiced, although statistics as to volume are not available. There are no fixed margin requirements and so the amount will be based on a normal commercial credit decision. The average loan is up to 50% of the collateral value, although it may sometimes be higher for blue chip stocks. Securities firms mostly finance their margin lending by bank borrowing.

Foreign investors may deal on margin, but this is rare, since only local established traders can usually persuade the securities firms to put up a margin.

All settlements must be cash against delivery (CAD) in full.

Stock Borrowing. No official facilities exist for stock borrowing. Stock is only lent by banks and securities firms which have stocks on their own books. They may lend it to borrowers who can prove their right to title for undelivered stock and also prove that their need is only temporary while stock is out for registration.

It should be noted that the Securities Ordinance does not allow short positions, and that there is a current dispute with the Stamp Office as to whether duty is payable on stock borrowing.

Investor Protection

Reporting requirements state that dealing slips must be prepared and contract notes issued for every deal. Contract notes must be kept for two years and client records for six years. Information such as price and volume showing high/low and closing prices is publicly available for each stock on a daily basis. There is a Stock Exchange Compensation Fund which is formed from deposits with the Securities Commission made under S.104 Securities Ordinance. A guarantee fund requires each Stock Exchange firm to deposit HK$50,000 for each individual stockbroker admitted as a member.

This Fund will pay out compensation, up to a limit of HK$2 million per stockbroker involved in any one default, to customers who have suffered monetary loss as a result of a member's default.

The Commissioner for Securities may investigate any transactions. Persons convicted of improper trading practices like creating false markets, making false or misleading statements about securities and so forth are liable on conviction to a fine of HK$50,000 and to imprisonment for 2 years.

The insider dealing tribunal may inquire into insider dealings and report them to the public. However, insider dealing is not a criminal offense in Hong Kong.

New Issues

The 1987 figures for new issues were as follows:

Equities	Number (to 11/30/87)
By introduction	8
By offer	11
By scheme of arrangement	9
Total	28

Prices of new issues are negotiated by the lead managers with the company concerned in consultation with the Listing Committee of the Stock Exchange; the timing of an issue is negotiated between the Stock Exchange and the lead managers.

New issues are registered with the Office of the Commissioner for Securities and Commodities Trading.

The underwriting rates vary according to the length of exposure of the underwriters but they are usually between 0.75% and 1.25%.

FUTURES AND OPTIONS TRADING

Options trading is not permitted on The Hong Kong Stock Exchange.

The financial futures market is organized by the Hong Kong Futures Exchange Limited. A stock index futures contract based on the Hang Seng Index was introduced in 1986 and this is the only financial future presently traded, although there are other commodity futures traded. Turnover in 1987 was 3,611,474 contracts.

Trading, settlement and delivery on the Futures Exchange are as follows:

- Hang Seng Index futures contracts orders are passed to the trading floor through a member of the Futures Exchange. Membership of the Exchange is divided between general clearing members, clearing members, and nonclearing members.

- General clearing members can clear their own trades and also trades done by other members. They are presently required to have a net worth of HK$5 million but this must be increased to HK$15 million by March 31 and to HK$25 million by December 31, 1988.

- Clearing members can clear their own trades only. Their net worth requirement used to be HK$2 million but has been raised immediately to HK$5 million and will be raised again to HK$10 million by December 31, 1988.

- Nonclearing members may only deal on their own account. Their net worth requirement is presently HK$2 million and will be raised to HK$5 million within 12 months.

Traders in nonfinancial future commodities have not been required to increase their net worth though this will be reviewed in 6 months' time. Their net worth requirement accordingly remains HK$2 million for individual clearing members and HK$5 million for general clearing members.

80% of the net worth is required to be in the form of paid-up capital. 20% can be in the form of reserves or subordinated loans.

- When a broker receives an order from a client, he will notify the floor representative on the trading floor to look for a buyer or seller either by open outcry or through a board trading system. Alternatively a broker can ask other authorized full members or market members to trade on behalf of his client.

- When a delivery month expires, the contracts will be settled by cash.

There are no links with overseas options/futures markets.

REGULATIONS AFFECTING NEW ENTRANTS TO THE MARKETS

The regulatory authority in Hong Kong is the Office of the Commissioner for Securities and Commodities Trading which is the executive arm of the Securities Commission, a statutory body which determines all policy matters relating to the securities industry in Hong Kong. The main statutory rules affecting the securities industry are the Securities Ordinance, the Protection of Investors Ordinance, the Stock Exchanges Unification Ordinance and the Securities (Accounts and Audit) Regulations.

There are few restrictions on trading except the prohibition of going short. There are presently no specific requirements relating to the repatriation of income for foreign-owned organizations.

The requirements for market entry by corporations and individuals are as follows:

- All dealers and directors of dealing corporations must be registered with the Securities Commission.
- Both individual and corporate members are allowed.
- A body corporate is eligible for membership if the only business carried on by it is that of dealing in securities and "those activities normally ancillary to a stock-broking business."
- Individual members must be of good character and integrity. Corporate members must be of good financial standing and integrity.
- Members must have been in Hong Kong, or have been ordinarily resident in Hong Kong for five of the seven years preceding application for membership. However, the Commission may on written application by the Stock Exchange authorize admission of an applicant if in the opinion of the Commission he is a person of good reputation experienced in dealing in securities.
- An applicant must also demonstrate that he has maintained a net capital of not less than HK$5,000,000 for corporate membership or HK$1,000,000 for individual membership. Net capital is defined as the excess of approved assets over ranking liabilities.
- A registered dealer is also required to maintain a liquidity margin of not less than 10% of the minimum net capital requirement at all times. Liquidity margin is defined as the excess of liquid assets over ranking liabilities.
- Members must give a HK$500,000 guarantee or participate in the Fidelity Fund by depositing HK$20,000 in cash to compensate

members suffering pecuniary loss as a result of the default of any other member. A defaulting member is liable to compensate the fund for any amounts paid out by it for claims relating to his conduct.

Membership is gained by purchase of an "A" share in The Stock Exchange of Hong Kong Limited. The cost of an "A" share is currently between HK$150,000 and HK$200,000.

Dealers are required to file a copy of their annual accounts with the Commissioner for Securities and the Stock Exchange. They are also required to submit a quarterly Return of Net Capital and Liquidity Margin to the Stock Exchange.

There are no specific regulations which apply to foreign entrants to the market.

OUTLINE OF CORPORATE AND INDIVIDUAL TAX CONSIDERATIONS

There is no concept of residence for Hong Kong tax purposes, so residents and nonresidents are taxed to the extent that they have a source of profit arising in Hong Kong from a trade or a business carried on there, a Hong Kong sourced salary or, in some circumstances, interest arising there.

Securities houses are not subject to special treatment by the Hong Kong revenue authorities.

Government Bonds—Current Income

Interest on government bonds is tax-exempt for all taxpayers.

Government Bonds—Capital Gains

Any profit or gain realized on the sale of government bonds is tax-exempt.

Equities—Current Income

Dividend income paid by a corporation which is chargeable to profits tax is not taxable in Hong Kong in the hands of the recipient.

Equities—Capital Gains

There is no tax liability on capital gains on the sale of equities. However, if the taxpayer is deemed to be a habitual trader, dealing profits will be assessable to profits tax at 18% for corporations or personal income tax for individuals on a sliding scale to a maximum of 16.5%.

Traded Options and Financial Futures

Profits/gains on offshore traded options and financial futures are not liable to tax unless the tax authorities regard the purchase and sale of these as constituting trading, in which case profits will be subject to tax.

Stamp Duty

Hong Kong has a stamp duty of 0.6% on securities transactions.

PROSPECTIVE DEVELOPMENTS

The Exchange has planned to provide new or enhanced facilities in the following areas:

- On-going enhancements to the trading system which essentially will enable the brokers to trade more efficiently and provide the public with more up-to-date information about the market.
- A stock information data base containing up to ten years of trading information and limited trading data from the previous four exchanges. The availability of such information will enable the Exchange to provide more historical data to the public and allow it to carry out its trading surveillance function.
- A central clearing and depository system. At present The Exchange is considering a number of proposals. It is intended that a system will be available within the next 12 to 18 months.
- A report on the idea of a second-tier market is being prepared by a working party for submission to the Securities Commission.
- A back-up center for emergencies is being built by The Exchange at a cost of HK$20 million.
- The Exchange is trying to forge closer links with the international market. It has linked up with the London Stock Market for the exchange of closing prices of selected Hong Kong securities traded in the United Kingdom.

A 90-days interest futures contract was intended to be launched in December 1987, but this has been delayed for some six months.

HONG KONG

In April 1986, restrictions governing bank-related brokers were introduced for a trial period of 18 months. It was forbidden for bank-related brokers to trade among themselves; to conclude direct business transactions; and to deal on their own accounts as principals to their clients. These rules were withdrawn on October 2, 1987.

INDIA

Sharp & Tannan

Contact: H. K. Bilpodiwala (Contact Partner), Tel: (22) 204 77 22/23

There are 15 Stock Exchanges in India. They are located in Bombay, Calcutta, Delhi, Madras, Ahmedabad, Bangalore, Hyderabad, Indore, Cochin, Kanpur, Patna, Pune, Ludhiana, Gauhati, and Mangalore. They all have uniform dealing and settlement periods. Major Stock Exchanges are also electronically linked by means of monitor screens in the trading rooms showing the movements on the other Exchanges.

Participation in the Indian securities markets is prohibited for persons who are not of Indian origin—both as investors and dealers, although recently an investment fund (which is not quoted on the Indian Stock Exchanges) open to non-Indians has been formed.

Since the Bombay Stock Exchange accounted for approximately 80% of the total value of trading in the Indian Market in 1986, this review is primarily concerned with that Exchange.

Size

Volumes of trading on the Bombay Stock Exchange for the calendar year 1987 are as follows:

	Equities	Fixed Interest & Preference Shares	Debentures/ Bonds
Turnover (Rs. millions)	73,135	- - - - - - - 14,270 - - - - - - -	
Number of trades/bargains (millions)	188.25	N/A	N/A
Number of securities	2,482	280	817

71

As of December 31, 1987, there were 515 members of the Bombay Stock Exchange all of whom were individuals. No member firms were part of an international group.

Although all firms trading in securities are not necessarily members of the Stock Exchange, all dealing is only through members.

There is no over-the-counter market, and there is no significant trading outside of the formal markets.

There is neither off-shore trading of domestic equities nor domestic trading of overseas equities, and there are no links with overseas markets.

The main index is the Reserve Bank of India All-India Ordinary Share Price Index, covering 32 weighted industries and 438 securities in the five major Exchanges. Recent movements on this index have been as follows:

The Reserve Bank of India Index

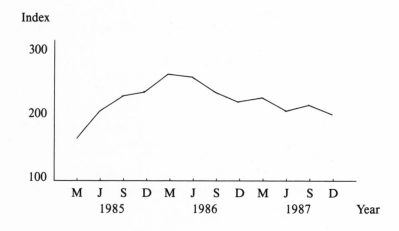

OVERVIEW OF THE BOND AND EQUITY MARKETS

Structure

Separate markets exist for dealings in gilt-edged securities (i.e., government bonds) and shares. Dealing hours are 12:00 to 14:00 for shares and 12:00 to 15:00 for gilts. All trading in shares is on the floor of the Exchange.

There is no required separation of function between member firms, and all members can act both as agent and principal. Under the

Securities Contracts Act, a member can only enter into a transaction with nonmembers as a principal if the written consent or authority of such person has been obtained. Although Stock Exchange by-laws state that the price at which a transaction is completed should be fair and reasonable there is no obligation upon member firms to make continuous markets.

Execution

Prices on the Bombay Stock Exchange are determined by a bid-offer process. Bids and offers are made by open outcry at the designated trading post on the auction market floor. There are no formal limits on daily permissible price movements.

A Sauda (Transaction) list containing particulars of each transaction including the number of shares and price is reported to the Stock Exchange every evening by the members.

A computerized daily dealing list is available by 18:00 every evening and the Stock Exchange Daily Official List of share valuations is available at 11:00 on the subsequent day.

Shares can only be traded in round lots, which are usually 50 shares for securities with a nominal value of Rs. 10, and 5 shares for securities with a nominal value of Rs. 100. Only a handful of quoted shares have a nominal value which is other than Rs. 10 or Rs. 100.

Settlement and Clearing

Each dealing period lasts between 2 and 3 weeks, and delivery of shares takes place at the end of the dealing period when member firms are required to deposit all shares sold through them at the Exchange. The Exchange acts as a clearing house, and upon receipt of shares by the Exchange, they are then delivered to the buying broker, who in turn delivers them to the buyer.

Monetary settlement usually takes place one week after physical settlement when each member is informed of his net dues/receivables from the Stock Exchange Clearing House as a result of trading in the previous dealing period.

Market Characteristics

Commission Rates. Commission rates are negotiable between the buyer/ seller and the broker up to the official maximum rate of 2.5% of the contract value. Another cost is stamp duty at 0.5% of the nominal value for fixed interest securities and the market value for equities, which is paid by the purchaser.

Margin Trading. Margin trading is permissible only for specified equity shares. Margins are specific amounts set by the Exchange authorities and are dependent on volatility. Badla settlements (or contango) are made at the end of the clearing period for those who wish to carry over their purchases or who are short of securities to deliver, these settlements being reversed at the commencement of the subsequent clearing period. Money brokers (badlawallas) charge for the deferred settlement facility offered. Securities firms also have overdraft facilities secured on their nontraded investments.

There are no facilities available in India for borrowing of stock.

Investor Protection. Investor protection is not yet very effective. In late 1987, the Finance Minister announced that the government was preparing legislation to establish a Securities and Exchange Commission to regulate the country's stock markets.

There are no written guidelines or regulations with regard to insider dealing and share transactions by individuals or companies with privileged or price-sensitive information. There are also no restrictions on directors dealing in shares belonging to them or to their companies, except that under general law no officer of a company is entitled to use any information known exclusively to him to his own advantage.

However, there are some investor protection codes as follows:

- Members cannot act as principal in transactions with investors unless they obtain the investors' permission in writing, and specify on the agreement/contract that they are acting as principals.
- A Customers' Protection Fund has been established in the Bombay Stock Exchange to compensate the clients of a defaulting member for his losses, up to a maximum limit of Rs. 10,000, in respect of genuine investment business.
- An Investors' Services Cell which responds to complaints and grievances of shareholders and investors has been formed at the Bombay Stock Exchange to attend promptly to complaints from investors either against a company or a stockbroker.

New Issues

The figures for new issues for the calendar year 1987 for the Bombay Stock Exchange are as follows:

INDIA

	Equities	Debentures	Public Sector Bonds
Numbers	151	23	5
Value (Rs. billions)	4.0	2.6	11.1

New issues are underwritten and managed by brokers, banks, and financial institutions appointed by the issuer. Brokers from other Exchanges are also appointed to market the issue. Underwriting rates are negotiable, subject to a maximum of 2.5% of the amount underwritten.

All issues are registered with the Controller of Capital Issues, and the Government of India must approve the terms.

The issue price has to be confirmed by the Controller of Capital Issues who will insist on nominal values for newly formed companies and a premium based on capitalization of past profits for established companies.

The timing of new issues is influenced by the existing state of the capital market and the prevalent interest rates.

FUTURES AND OPTIONS TRADING

Options trading and trading in financial futures is banned by the Securities Contracts (Regulation) Act 1956, which regulates the workings of the Stock Exchanges. Notwithstanding this, a certain amount of option transactions are carried out by individual negotiation between brokers inter-se, and between brokers and individual investors. These are based on gentlemen's agreements and are not legally enforceable.

REGULATIONS AFFECTING NEW ENTRANTS TO THE MARKETS

Membership Requirements

The Central Government (Ministry of Finance) regulates the procedures for the recognition of stock exchanges, their management, and their power to make rules, bylaws or amendments. Recognized Stock Exchanges therefore have to adhere to the Government regulations.

The main statutory regulations are:

- The Securities Contracts (Regulation) Act, 1956
- The Securities Contracts (Regulation) Rules, 1957

75

A Securities House cannot be incorporated in certain Stock Exchanges (including Bombay) and partnerships should contain at least one partner who is a member of the Stock Exchange. An individual member can set up a sole-proprietorship security house. No foreigner is permitted to become a member of an Exchange.

No repatriation of income from India is permissible.

Membership of the Bombay Stock Exchange is available to individuals who pass the requirements of a screening committee and a final committee. The criteria for eligibility are the individual's wealth and the minimum educational qualification of a bachelor's degree. The latter requirement is waived if the applicant has been apprenticed under a member.

Capital, Liquidity, and Audit Requirements

There are no liquidity requirements, but members are obliged to maintain a security deposit with the Stock Exchange.

Potential members of the Bombay Stock Exchange wishing to trade on the Exchange floor have to pay Rs. 750,000 for the purchase of a seat and an additional Rs. 250,000 as a security deposit.

Members also have to possess adequate working capital and an office space in the financial district near the Stock Exchange, from which to operate.

All members are required to submit their annual audited accounts to the Stock Exchange.

OUTLINE OF CORPORATE AND INDIVIDUAL TAX CONSIDERATIONS

There is no corporation tax in India, as companies pay income tax on profits chargeable under the heading "Income from Business or Profession." Securities houses cannot be corporations, as membership of Stock Exchanges is only open to individuals.

- An individual member would show his commission income, trading income, and underwriting income as part of his business income assessed under the heading "Income from Business or Profession."
- No capital gains tax would apply as the income from purchase and sale of securities will be considered as trading income.
- However, in the case of nontrade investments held by members in the long-term period, members have the option to show interest and dividends received as Income from Other Sources, and the Capital Gains

arising on their disposal as a separate source in their returns of income. The following tax rates are applicable:

- Income tax rates for individuals: Range from 25–50%
- Income tax rates for registered firms with income from a profession where all individual partners being members are also separately assessed on their net income from the partnership: Range from 4–22%
- Income tax rates for registered firms not comprising solely of members where all individual partners are also assessed separately on their net income from the partnership: Range from 5–24%
- Income tax rates for trading/investment companies in which the public are not substantially interested, where shareholders are also assessed separately on dividends received: 60% of the net total income

Nonresidents

Foreign entrants are debarred from entering the market. However nonresidents of Indian origin are allowed to make limited investments in quoted securities.

PROSPECTIVE DEVELOPMENTS

It is proposed to allow Indian banks and financial institutions to become members of the Stock Exchanges, as a substantial volume of the trading is undertaken on behalf of institutions whose funds are invested in quoted equities and fixed interest securities.

The government is considering the regularization of option dealing in quoted securities.

The Stock Exchanges are proposing to set up trading markets in bonds/fixed interest securities on the floor of the Stock Exchange.

Individual Stock Exchanges are proposing to set up training institutes for member brokers to educate them on portfolio management and the rendering of investment advice.

INDONESIA

Drs. S Reksoatmodjo & Co.
Contact: William Macdonald, Tel: (21) 327860

Indonesia's only Stock Exchange is in Jakarta. It handles the trading of all Indonesian securities and is operated by a government agency, Badan Pelaksana Pasar Modal (BAPEPAM), or the Capital Market Executive Agency. A Stock Exchange had been established in 1912 by the Dutch, but the effects of World War II and, later, the nationalization of Dutch business led to the Exchange being almost unused. It was not until 1977 that the Indonesian Stock Exchange (ISE) opened under the guidance of the new BAPEPAM and President Soeharto's "New Order" government.

Size

There are approximately 40 securities companies operating in Indonesia. Twenty-nine are banks and banking institutions, and the remainder are either investment or financial services companies. PT Danareksa, a state-owned mutual fund, controls approximately 55% of all listed shares. Direct investment in Indonesian shares is prohibited for foreign investors, except for investment in specifically approved projects, although foreigners are allowed to purchase bonds.

The market statistics for ISE for 6 months ended 6/30/87are as follows:

Sales trading volume ('000 shares)	722
Sales trading value (R million)	1,372
Number of securities	27

The ISE's primary index is the Composite Share Price Index. It uses August 10, 1982 as its base and is calculated using all listed shares.

OVERVIEW OF THE BOND AND EQUITY MARKETS

Structure

The ISE currently lists 27 companies, 18 of which are affiliates of the major multinationals which have a proportion of their shares owned by Indonesian nationals in accordance with local laws. The basic distinction between the ISE's primary and secondary markets is the trading system. A call-over system is used for new issues (for six days), while more actively traded stocks trade through a continuous system which operates under the control of a BAPEPAM official, the call manager. Only listed securities may be traded on the Exchange, and there is no organized market for unlisted shares. Listed bonds may be traded on both the Exchange and through the over-the-counter (OTC) bond market.

The Indonesian government recently studied the feasibility of creating an over-the-counter market for listing small capitalization companies and a second-section for the ISE was also considered, but although the possibility is now recognized in the relevant law, no implementation plan has yet been announced.

PT Danareksa, the state-owned mutual fund, issues and sells certificates (or units) which are offered to the general public through branches of state banks and private brokers or dealers.

The ISE's trading sessions are from Monday to Friday between the hours of 10:00 and 12:00.

Execution

In the case of the call-out system of execution the call manager announces each security in turn and determines the dealing price by means of ascertaining the orders from the Exchange members. Prices are determined twice a day using this method. Dealing priority is given to the member making the first buy/sell bid. After this initial period, brokers and dealers use the continuous system. This operates on a board-trading basis, whereby any security can be traded at any time—there is no committed marketmaking responsibility although PT Danareksa will intervene by buying or selling to assist the maintenance of a steady market.

Settlement and Clearing

There is no central clearing operation in Indonesia and therefore settlement takes place directly between the original parties. Settlement and physical delivery must take place within 14 days of dealing.

INDONESIA

Market Characteristics

Commission Rates. BAPEPAM fixes commissions for both stocks and bonds at 1% of the transaction value. Additionally, investors must pay a stamp duty of R1000 per transaction.

Margin Trading. Margin trading is permitted but very rare. Short selling is not allowed.

Investor Protection. BAPEPAM requires that listed companies submit financial statements no later than 120 days after their year-end. Companies must also inform BAPEPAM within 30 days of any significant event materially affecting operations. All financial reports filed become public information available through BAPEPAM.

To protect the interests of public investors, BAPEPAM is able to suspend trading in the stock of a company and, in extremis, to delist its shares. The Indonesian system of investor protection relies for the most part on the company's Articles of Association, with BAPEPAM playing a supervisory role by monitoring the trading of listed securities on the Exchange. The Ministry of Finance has issued decrees to prohibit insider dealing.

No fund exists to provide compensation to investors who incur losses resulting from fraud or default by either brokers or dealers.

New Issues

No new companies have been listed on the Exchange since the end of 1984. The market has been depressed due to a general economic downturn in Indonesia.

Any new issues must be approved by BAPEPAM. A company seeking a listing must have a paid-up capital of R200 million, and must have maintained a return on equity of at least 10% for the last two consecutive years. BAPEPAM also requires that the company's financial statements be audited by certified public accountants for the two previous years with no qualifications on the last year's statements, The listing documents are public information and can be obtained from the agency. New shares receiving BAPEPAM approval must be listed on the Exchange at least 90 days after the approval date.

Domestic commercial banks can now underwrite equity issues, a recent liberalization. PT Danareksa serves as the underwriter of last resort; by law, it has the right to purchase at least 50% of any issue.

FUTURES AND OPTIONS TRADING

There are no futures or options markets in Indonesia.

REGULATIONS AFFECTING NEW ENTRANTS TO THE MARKETS

The Indonesian Stock Exchange is run and regulated by BAPEPAM. The Ministry of Finance also plays a major regulatory role. Only members of the ISE who are licensed by the Ministry of Finance may trade securities. Under guidelines established in 1983, Stock Exchange members can only act as either brokers, or as dealers, but not both. In order to ensure this separation, BAPEPAM monitors trading on the Exchange.

Stock Exchange members are banks, financial institutions, or brokerage firms. In 1986, the members consisted of 6 state banks, 6 private banks, 9 nonbank financial institutions, 1 investment company, and 7 brokerage firms.

Trading upon confidential or unpublished information and market manipulation are prohibited and subject to administrative and criminal penalties.

At present, foreign investors cannot directly own Indonesian stocks. Foreign investors are limited to direct investment in pre-approved industrial or economic projects. They may, however, purchase bonds in the over-the-counter market. The Investment Coordinating Board (Badan Koordinasi Penanaman Modal or BKPM) oversees all foreign investors. BKPM requires that all direct foreign investment be made in "foreign capital investment companies" which are joint ventures with Indonesian investors. For the most part, there are no restrictions on the movement of funds in and out of Indonesia, unless the funds are proceeds from the sale to an Indonesian citizen. Since 1986, foreign investment companies may be started with up to a maximum 95% foreign stake. The law requires, however, that this stake be reduced to 49% within 10 years of the company's start-up date.

OUTLINE OF CORPORATE AND INDIVIDUAL TAX CONSIDERATIONS

Indonesia levies a withholding tax of 20% on dividends paid to foreign shareholders from pre-approved projects unless a tax treaty between

Indonesia and the shareholders' country exists and it stipulates otherwise. All securities transactions are subject to a stamp duty of R1000.

Withholding tax of 15% is deducted for dividends paid to local individuals or corporations. Dividends are taxed at the marginal rate of 35% as income of individuals or companies. There is an exemption where the receiving company (other than a bank or financial institution and not an individual) owns at least 25% of the paying company's shares and there is "an economic relationship in the course of business." There is no capital gains tax and gains on sales of shares are treated as part of taxable profit in the case of a corporation and as income in the case of an individual.

PROSPECTIVE DEVELOPMENTS

In 1986, the Indonesian equity market was, in the words of one analyst, "virtually moribund." The market is very limited and thinly traded. Its current depression is mainly due to the country's economic decline (slumping world oil and commodities prices), high interest rates, and economic and tax policies unfavorable to equity investment. The government apparently plans to spur its capital markets through liberalization policies which could include foreign investment in a fund co-sponsored by PT Danareksa, but to date, very little action has been taken in comparison with other Southeast Asian markets.

However, major changes are in progress including the introduction of an OTC market, easing of listing rules and permission for foreign investment. Implementing regulations and timetable are not yet forthcoming.

IRELAND

Oliver Freaney & Company
Contact: Noel Fox, Tel: (01) 688644

The Irish Stock Exchange is located in Dublin and forms part of the Stock Exchange of the United Kingdom and Ireland.

Size

The 1987 market statistics for the Dublin Stock Exchange are as follows:

	Equities	Government Overseas Bonds
Turnover (IR£ million)	4,260	33,525
Number of trades/bargains ('000)	255	50
Market capitalization as at year end (IR£ million)	3,936	11,730
Number of securities as at year end	Total = 101	

There is a significant amount of off-shore trading of domestic equities since the largest quoted Irish companies, such as Allied Irish Banks, Bank of Ireland, Smurfits, and Waterford Glass, have a dual quote on the Dublin and London markets.

The level of off-shore trading in gilts (government bonds) has risen dramatically in 1987, partly as a result of interest rates being higher in Ireland than in other member states of the EMS.

Since the Irish pound severed its links with sterling in late 1978, Irish nationals are prohibited by Exchange Control Regulations from investing overseas unless they had such investments in 1978. The sales proceeds of any sale of United Kingdom stock must be either repatriated or reinvested within 3 months.

Irish financial institutions are also restricted in the level of foreign investment held in their portfolios. The government has consistently sought extension of time at EEC level in relaxing its Exchange Control Regulations. It is intended that no such restrictions will be placed on persons involved in the new financial center (refer to 4 in *Prospective Development*).

The Stock Exchange is intending to introduce an official index of stock market performance shortly, but at present the indices produced by a broking firm, J&E Davy, are used most commonly.

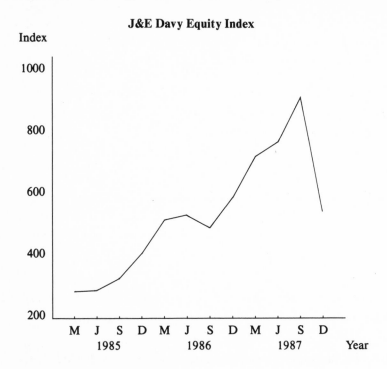

J&E Davy Equity Index

OVERVIEW OF THE BOND AND EQUITY MARKETS

Structure

The Dublin Stock Exchange has a similar structure to the London Exchange, except that it is on a much smaller scale with both a main listing and an unlisted securities market or second-tier market.

In 1986, the Small Companies Market (SCM) was set up by the Exchange to attract companies with a turnover of less than IR£4 million; this limit is however, a guide and not absolute. At the present time there are seven securities listed on the SCM.

Equity trading on the Dublin Stock Exchange is in practice carried out in a similar way to London with a trading floor and member firms who can act both as agent and principal. The Government Broker is the only market maker in Irish gilts. On the instructions of the Department of Finance he leads the market in both offering and buying stock on a continuous basis. All gilts trading takes place on the Stock Exchange floor.

Trading hours on the Stock Exchange floor are 9:30 to 11:15 and 14:15 to 15:30. Off-floor trading takes place all day (particularly with access to the London-based screen trading system), with no set closing time although this is usually between 18:00 and 20:00.

The proportion of on-floor and off-floor trading is not available. However, large institutional transactions in equities take place off the floor.

Execution

Equity trading on the Exchange floor is by the call-over method, whereby securities are called over twice daily at 9:30 and 14:10 to determine the appropriate price level at which buyers and sellers can be matched. Off-floor trading is carried out by telephone. Clients' orders are completed by dealing with other brokers or with London market makers. The equity market is order-driven rather than price-driven.

There are no limits on daily permissible price movements.

Requirements for transaction reporting trading information, lot sizes, and settlement and clearing procedures are the same as for the United Kingdom Stock Market.

Market Characteristics

Commission Rates. Commission rates chargeable on equities are negotiable, typically ranging from 1.65% down to 0.5% for larger transactions. However, commission rates on gilts remain fixed, although a 35% reduction on minimum commissions was announced in March 1987. The current rates for gilts range from 0.52% to 0.006% depending on the size of transaction and the remaining life of the stock.

Stamp duty is payable by the purchaser on the transfer of shares, at a rate of 1% on equities, although there is an exemption for positions sold within the same account period.

Margin Trading. A market for margin trading has not been developed, although brokers are permitted to finance the purchase of securities by clients on a secured basis.

Stock Borrowing. The facilities available for stock borrowing are the same as those in London, but are rarely used.

Investor Protection. The Irish surveillance system is the same as that operating in London, whereby every share dealing transaction is checked by computer to ensure that the best price has been obtained. Investors are protected against the failure of a broking firm by the same compensation fund as in the United Kingdom, up to a limit of £250,000 per customer. The absence of a law against insider trading is considered a weakness, but a bill is now before parliament to outlaw this practice.

New Issues

The 1986 figures for new issues were as follows:

Equities	Amount Raised IR £ Million
Official market	161.8
USM	25.0
Mineral exploration	2.8
	189.6
Gilts	974.0
Total	1,163.6

The procedures adopted for new equity and bond issues, and the underwriting rates applying, are the same as those used in the United Kingdom. New issues must be registered with the Irish Stock Exchange.

FUTURES AND OPTIONS TRADING

There is at present no separate market in futures or options within Ireland, although Irish stockbrokers do have access to the markets in London.

REGULATIONS AFFECTING NEW ENTRANTS TO THE MARKETS

The regulatory authority in Ireland is the Irish Stock Exchange, which is constituted under Irish law, and is part of the International Stock

Exchange of the United Kingdom and Ireland. The Minister for Finance approves Regulations submitted by the Exchange.

The restrictions placed on securities houses for market entry are no different from those operating in London—in particular members of the Exchange can be controlled by outsiders. There are no restrictions on repatriation of income.

Membership requirements are similar to those operating in London, but any member wishing to deal in gilts must obtain a gilt license from the Minister for Finance. In reality no member could survive on the Exchange without such a license since the volume of equity trading by itself is too small to support a member.

The costs of joining the Exchange and the reporting requirements are as listed in the chapter on the London Stock Exchange.

OUTLINE OF CORPORATE AND INDIVIDUAL TAX CONSIDERATIONS

Residents

Individuals. Individuals domiciled in Ireland are liable to income tax on all income wherever arising; nondomiciled individuals are liable to income tax on remittances of foreign income and on all Irish source income.

Companies. Resident companies are liable to corporation tax on their worldwide income including capital gains.

Dividends

Dividends from Irish-resident companies in general carry a tax credit, normally 35/65. In the case of companies qualifying for the 10% rate of corporation tax (principally manufacturing and certain financial services) the tax credit is 1/18. An individual is assessed on the aggregate amount of the net dividend plus tax credit. The imputation system, whereby Advance Corporation Tax (ACT) is paid over on payment of a dividend, now ensures that the tax credit has been paid by the distributing company. The method of taxation of foreign dividends varies and depends upon whether a tax treaty with the country of payment exists. In general, where a treaty exists relief is given by reference to the underlying tax suffered by the payer of the dividend. In other cases, it is by means of credit.

Dividends paid by Irish-resident companies are not liable to corporation tax in the recipient company. There is no ACT charged on dividends or other distributions from a 75% subsidiary to its parent company, provided the parent company is resident in a country which has a tax treaty with Ireland.

Dividends received from abroad are, broadly speaking, taxable. Relief is given for foreign tax suffered, either as a deduction or a credit, depending on the treaty concerned.

Interest

Interest from which tax is not withheld at source is normally assessable on the amount of interest received during the year preceding the year of assessment. Interest in the years of commencement and cessation is taxed on a current basis. This method applies to individuals only; companies are assessed on an actual basis.

Capital Gains Tax

Capital gains are taxed at the following rates:

Gains on assets held for less than one year	60%
Gains on assets held for 1–3 years	50%
Gains on assets held for over 3–6 years	35%
Gains on assets held more than 6 years	30%

Indexation on gains applies from the later of the date of purchase or April 6, 1974.

Wealth Tax

There is no wealth tax in Ireland.

Exchange Control

There is Exchange control in relation to payments in and out of Ireland, and Central Bank approval must be obtained for such payments. In relation to minor payments the clearing banks act as agents, but in relation to substantial payments approval will only be forthcoming if the payments are for valid consideration.

Nonresidents

Individuals are only liable to tax on income arising in Ireland.

Nonresident companies are liable to corporation tax on trading profits and other income derived from an Irish branch.

Other income arising in Ireland is subject to income tax and not to corporation tax. Interest received by nonresidents is subject to withholding tax, although this tax may be reduced by double tax treaties.

Capital Gains Tax. Nonresidents are exempt from capital gains tax on quoted shares. However, capital gains tax is chargeable on gains derived from unquoted shares which derive the greater part of their value from such land, minerals, or exploration and exploitation rights in the state, and gains realized in respect of assets used or held for the purposes of an Irish branch or agency.

Shares sold on the Smaller Companies Market (SCM) between April 6, 1986 and April 5, 1989 incur a tax liability at a rate of 30% regardless of the period of ownership.

The index factor for shares held in 1974 for 1987/88 is 4.756. In relation to development land in the State or shares deriving their value from such land, the current use value at the date of purchase is indexed. The balance is allowable as a deduction without indexation.

The rate of tax on development land in Ireland or shares deriving their value from such land is as above except where the assets are held for more than three years. In such cases, the rate is 50%.

Exchange Controls

Although Ireland has Exchange controls, capital, and profits from business ventures can be repatriated to nonresidents without difficulty.

PROSPECTIVE DEVELOPMENTS

The introduction of the Financial Services Act in the United Kingdom has resulted in the need to discuss with the Irish Stock Exchange how best to amalgamate the U.K. legal requirements with current Irish practice.

Other prospective developments include:

1. *Exchange Control.* The government has partially removed the Exchange control regulations on individuals investing abroad with effect from January 1, 1988. This is the first step in a gradual removal of all Exchange controls and the target is to complete this between 1990 and 1992.

2. *Futures Market.* There are three separate proposals under active consideration in relation to the establishment of a futures market. These are:

- E.M.E.—European Mercantile Exchange
- I.F.O.X.—Irish Futures and Options Exchange
- Stock Exchange

E.M.E. is a proposal by Irish-Americans and will copy the pit system as used in Chicago. It is intended that currencies, interest rate futures and non-Irish pound contracts will be the main market. Seventy seats costing IR£10,000 each have been sold with a proposal to sell 200/300 more at £25,000 each in April 1988. It intends to be operational by early 1989.

I.F.O.X. plans to use a screen-based system. It intends to sell 20 seats at IR£50,000—IR£60,000 in March 1988 and be operational within four months. Initially the Exchange will handle financial futures including IR£/US dollar futures at units of $50,000 and is expected to be operational by the end of May.

The Stock Exchange options market is expected to be operational by the end of May. It is likely to concentrate on equity options using a telephone-based system with dealers advising the Exchange, which would then display the position on Topic. The cost of a seat is not expected to be more than IR£10,000 with participants mainly stockbrokers and institutions.

Initially the I.F.O.X and Stock Exchange will be dealing in separate areas. However, it is already acknowledged that a merger may be desirable at some future date, but it is not expected in the short term.

3. *Privatization.* It is expected that a small number of Irish semi-state-owned companies may come to the market. The principal company being discussed is Irish Life Assurance Company Limited. This is due to its past trade record and the fact that at present it is restricted in the United States because it is a semi-state-owned company.

4. *International Financial Services Center.* Both of the new markets referred to above will be part of the Customs House Financial Center recently set up in Dublin by the government.

In view of the level of interest shown internationally it is expected that this new center will develop further. The incentives offered include:

(a) 10% Rate of Corporation Tax—guaranteed until the year 2000

(b) Extensive Double Taxation Treaties

(c) No Exchange Control Regulations

ITALY

Consulaudit S.a.s. - Arietti & Co.
Contact: A. Arietti, Tel: (02) 870141

There are 10 Italian Stock Exchanges of which the largest is located at Milan and accounts for some 90% of the total national volume of share trading. The other important Exchanges are located at Rome, Turin, Genoa, Florence, and Naples. None of these Exchanges is formally linked for the purposes of dealing or settlement.

All Exchanges are members of the National Association of Italian Exchanges, except for Milan. Because Milan is by far the most significant Exchange, this chapter is principally devoted to its method of operation.

Size

Trading statistics of the Milan Exchange for 1987 were as follows:

	Equities
Turnover	Lire 42,000 bn
Number of trades/bargains	not applicable
Market capitalization (as at 12/31/87)	Lire 142,000 bn
Number of securities (as at 12/31/87)	329

There are approximately 230 stockbrokers in Italy of which 115 are members of the Milan Stock Exchange. All firms trading in securities must be members of the Stock Exchange.

There is a second-tier market in the major Exchanges, which is known as Il Mercato Ristretto. At present, trading takes place once a week, although an early move to daily trading is expected. Il Mercato Ristretto

91

has similar requirements to the main market, except that there is a lower minimum net assets requirement and a lower level of shares held by the public. There is also an unofficial Third Market for newer or smaller companies which is not subject to any regulation.

Domestic trading of overseas equities is discouraged by the requirement that the investor is required to place a deposit, interest free, with the Bank of Italy of 15% of the bargain value which therefore makes such trading uncompetitive with the home market. There is no significant off-shore trading of domestic equities.

There are no trading or settlement links with overseas markets although proposals are currently being studied for a link by Milan with the Stock Exchanges at Turin, Lyons, Geneva, and Barcelona.

The greater part of the business in equities and bonds is transacted outside the Exchanges and within the banking system. Total published volumes of trades transacted on Exchanges represent less than 50% of total equity trades and 2% of total bond trades.

The generally accepted index used to indicate overall market price movement on the Milan Exchange is the Milano Indice di Borsa (MIB). A history of its movements is as follows:

Milano Indice di Borsa

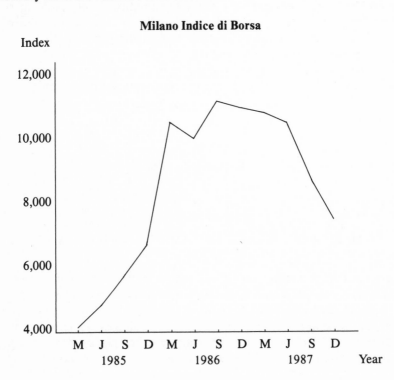

OVERVIEW OF THE BOND AND EQUITY MARKETS

Structure

All listed securities are traded in the same way.

Official trading hours of the Milan Exchange are from 10:00 to 13:45 each day although these hours may be varied depending upon the level of trading activity. Il Mercato Ristretto is open for trading each Wednesday commencing at 16:30.

The only members of the Exchange are the stockbrokers, who are prohibited from dealing on their own account. Much of the investor activity is directed through the Italian banks, who then place their orders with the brokers.

Dealings outside the Exchange generally operate for much longer hours than the official Exchange; in the first half of 1987 one bank commenced for a short time, 24-hour trading, a move which seemed to have support of other banks if not of the brokers and is perhaps an indication of future flexible and longer trading hours on the official Exchanges.

Execution

Only stockbrokers or one of a maximum of seven qualified dealing representatives may deal on the floor of the Exchange. Dealing takes place on a trading post system at one of eight posts (or corbeille).

There is one official price fixing made each day in all securities. Additional fixings are made throughout the day for leading equities. After the closing of the Exchanges, banks and brokers trade by telephone, based on prices as at the close of trading.

Price details are available through the Stock Exchange EDP center in real time. Two national agencies, Radiocor and AGI, along with two international communications networks, Reuters and Telekurs, are linked into the Exchange's system.

There are no designated limits on daily permissible price movements in stocks, however a member of the executive committee or another delegated stockbroker is in attendance at the corbeilles during trading hours. They have the right to intervene at any time to control prices in the case of any irregularity or abnormal situation.

Minimum trading lots have been set for all listed stocks and range from as low as 25 shares to as high as 50 thousand shares per stock. These minimum lots are varied annually by the CONSOB (Commissione Nazionale per le Societa e la Borsa) dependent on the underlying share price.

Bargains in equity odd lots are usually dealt through the banks rather than on the Exchange.

Bonds are dealt in multiples of minimum lots set on the basis of a percentage of their par value which is normally at least Lire 1 million.

Settlement and Clearing

Security transactions are settled by one of two methods, as follows:

Forward deals (one stock market month forward)

- listed stocks
- convertible securities

Cash deals

- fixed interest securities
- unlisted securities—Mercato Ristretto
- listed foreign shares

Notwithstanding the above, the CONSOB may restrict all transactions in a particular share to cash trading when market conditions require. Cash deals require settlement three days after the transaction date.

Forward deals are transacted and settled based on a mid-month to mid-month period with actual settlement for all deals in that period at the end of the second month. Compulsory margins are required on the purchase of equities and range from 30 to 100% of the value of the transaction, at the discretion of the CONSOB, while shares sold must be deposited with an Italian bank.

Simultaneously with the giving of a purchase order, a temporary deposit of the specified sum is made with an authorized Italian bank. Banks' dealings are exempt from this requirement. In the case of a nonresident selling through a broker or institution who is not authorized, he must arrange for the securities to be delivered directly to the clearing house (Stanza di Compensazione).

In Milan and the other major Exchanges, sales and purchases of listed securities are cleared through Bank of Italy clearing houses in each center. These clearing houses are linked with centralized depository systems, either Monte Titoli for listed shares and certain bonds, or Bank of Italy for State securities.

Banks and stockbrokers which participate in the clearing systems transfer eligible securities by book entry.

Market Characteristics

Commission rates are fixed as follows:

Shares	0.7%
Bonds	0.3%
Government stock	0.15%

There are no scaled fees or special rates for large orders. Stamp duty rates apply per 100,000 lire as follows:

	Transaction Type	
	Cash	Forward
Shares	150 Lire	225 Lire
Bonds	45	72
Government stock	24	72

International deals normally attract an all-in fee of 0.8%.

New Issues

There were 29 new issues made during 1987.

The CONSOB has set down new procedures for the placement and public offer of shares, bonds and stakes in public banks. Specifically the new regulations require the issuing of a prospectus and the advertising of public offers. The results of a placement and the type of subscriber must be reported to the regulatory body where they are placed through a consortium of brokers. CONSOB must be informed by the consortium before a placement of the category of interested investor, the terms of the operation, the number and identity of subscribers and how many shares are to be allocated to each.

Investor Protection. In order to compensate investors in the case of default by a broker, several deposits are required to be made by brokers as a guarantee. The deposits are required to be made with:

- Bank of Italy
- Executive committee of the relevant Exchange

In addition to this relatively low level of protection, the National Association of Stockbrokers is building a voluntary guarantee fund.

Other than this, there is relatively little protection for investors in the form of supervision of listed companies and so forth.

FUTURES AND OPTIONS TRADING

The Stock Exchanges contain quite active options markets. Option contracts can be for one, two, or three month periods but are normally traded

95

from one month until the next. The options declaration day is set two days prior to the end of the stockmarket period.

The main options traded are call (dont) and straddle (stellage) options; whilst put options are available, they are rarely traded.

The margin required is based on the current market or striking price on the day on which the contract is bought. The CONSOB has set minimum variations in the striking prices. The commission charged on call options is approximately half of that charged on normal transactions. No stamp duty is payable. There are no links with overseas markets. Nonresidents are not permitted to trade in options.

REGULATIONS AFFECTING NEW ENTRANTS TO THE MARKETS

The industry's regulatory authorities are:

- CONSOB, the National Commission for companies and the Stock Exchange, which is the national securities regulatory body.
- The Executive Committee of the Stockbrokers of each Stock Exchange. This is the technical body responsible for the daily organization of each Stock Exchange.

There are two types of membership open to a broker/dealer depending upon the business conducted:

- Agenti di Cambio—brokers or market markers who do not deal with clients.
- Commissionaire di Borsa—broker/dealers who trade on their own behalf or on behalf of third parties.

To obtain membership of an Exchange (Commissionaire di Borsa) a broker must comply with the following:

- Be an Italian national.
- Operate as individual firms with unlimited liability.
- Make the requisite deposits at the Bank of Italy and at the Executive Committee of Stockbrokers.

At present there is no restriction on foreign investment in Italy. Dividends, interest, royalties, and service fees may be repatriated provided they have been subjected to withholding tax.

Members of the Agenti di Cambio are public servants and become members by passing a public examination. Membership of the Commissionaire di Borsa can be purchased from the Commissionaire di Borsa for approximately Lire 650 million.

There is no minimum capital requirement for brokers, but for broker/dealers it is Lire 500 million.

There are no periodic financial reporting requirements for brokers although broker/dealers require annual audited financial statements and semi-annual unaudited financial statements both of which are available for public inspection.

OUTLINE OF CORPORATE AND INDIVIDUAL TAX CONSIDERATIONS

Residents

Corporations. Income and gains from shares and investments are subject to national tax, IRPEG, at 36%. Certain interest and premiums from public securities issued before September 19, 1986 are not subject to tax.

Corporations are also subject to local tax, ILOR, on income and gains at 16.2%, but dividends and any other income arising from participations in companies are not subject to ILOR.

A tax credit for company tax suffered is given on dividends, and offset against the final tax liability. Credit is also given for the 10% withholding tax imposed on dividends paid by Italian companies to resident shareholders.

Individuals. A resident individual is subject to national tax (IRPEG) and a local tax (ILOR) on income received. Capital gains on disposals of shares in listed companies are taxed as income if more than 2% of the company's shares are disposed of.

Gains on shares of an S.p.A or an S.r.l are taxed if more than 10 or 25%, respectively, of the company's shares are disposed of.

National tax (IRPEG) for individuals is levied at rates ranging from 12 to 65%. ILOR is levied at a flat rate of 16.2%, as for corporations.

Nonresidents

Italian dividends paid to nonresident shareholders are subject to withholding tax of 32.4%, unless reduced by a tax treaty. Shareholders who can prove that they have paid tax on the dividend in their own country may claim a refund of up to two-thirds of the withholding tax.

Interest on securities is also subject to 32.4% withholding tax if the securities are issued to a nonresident. Bank account interest is subject to withholding tax at 25%.

PROSPECTIVE DEVELOPMENTS

Plans are currently being made to introduce continuous trading of equities in Milan. Further to this a computer system "Borsamat" is being developed with three main goals:

- To assist the convergence of all orders on the trading floor
- To provide a system to permit intermarket trading and allow for the prompt checking of transactions
- To provide more and better information to participants in the market

Proposals are currently being debated to extend capital gains tax to shares as well as bonds.

The CONSOB has requested that new laws be introduced in an effort to eliminate insider trading.

Fixed commissions are under threat and it is anticipated that floating commissions will be introduced.

It is anticipated that, early in 1988, the Italian government will begin the long-awaited overhaul of the Treasury market. New regulations are expected to replace the complicated method of calculating stamp duty. Existing stamp duties differ depending on the type of issues exchanged, the maturity of the security and the parties involved.

JAPAN

Spicer & Oppenheim
Shinko Audit Corporation (Representative Firm)
Contact: Gareth Jones or Tohru Takihi, Tel: (03) 475 1711

There are eight Stock Exchanges in Japan, of which Tokyo, Osaka, and Nagoya are the largest. They account for 83%, 13%, and 3%, respectively, of all Japanese Stock Exchange business. The remaining five, Kyoto, Hiroshima, Fukuoka, Niigata, and Sapporo, each handle less than 1% of total turnover.

The 1987 market statistics for trading on the Tokyo Stock Exchange are as follows:

	Equities	Fixed Interest	Government/ Overseas Bonds	Financial Futures
Turnover (Yen trillions)	254	53	50	2
Market capitalization at 12/31/87 (Yen trillions)	337	12	117	—
Number of companies listed at 12/31/87	1,620	—	—	—

The Securities and Exchange Law requires each Japanese Stock Exchange to be organized on a membership basis. These members trade securities on each Exchange and membership is restricted to securities firms. As at the end of 1987 there were 92 Exchange members, of whom 6 were foreign-owned. In December 1987 the TSE invited a further 22 securities firms to apply for membership. Of these 22, 16 are foreign-owned. They

99

are expected to commence business as members of the TSE from May 1988 onwards.

Firms trading in securities in Japan need not be members of the Stock Exchange, but they must be licensed by the Ministry of Finance (MoF).

Members of the Japan Securities Dealers Association and commercial banks licensed for government bonds form the over-the-counter (OTC) market. In terms of volume, share transactions are almost 15 times greater on the Stock Exchanges than those made through the OTC, although 93% of all bond transactions are conducted on the OTC. They are traded either between securities firms and investors or between the securities firms themselves.

Off-shore trading of domestic equities is not yet significant.

Domestic trading of foreign stocks in Japan is also not sizeable. Turnover of foreign stocks listed on the TSE increased threefold to Yen 3,469,228 million in 1987, reflecting the increase in the number of listed foreign corporations from 52 to 88 by December 1987 and the growing interest in foreign stocks among Japanese investors.

In terms of links with overseas markets the International Securities Clearing Corporation (ISCC) of America is at present discussing the idea of co-operative custody account services with the TSE's subsidiary, the Japan Securities Clearing Corporation (JSCC).

There is no other significant trading outside the formal markets described above.

The Nikkei Dow Average Share Price Index is the best-known Japanese index and is an index of 225 shares listed on the first section of the TSE. (See graph on page 101.)

However, its reliability as a market indicator is reduced by the fact that it is an arithmetic average measure. To remedy this defect, the TSE Stock Price Index (TOPIX) was introduced, which is a weighted average of all the shares listed on the first section of the TSE.

There is also an index for bonds, the Nikkei Bond Index, and for stocks listed on the second section of the TSE together with a number of indices defined by industrial sector.

OVERVIEW OF THE BOND AND EQUITY MARKETS

Structure

Listed securities on the TSE, Osaka Securities Exchange (OSE) and Nagoya Stock Exchange (NSE) are allocated to one of two sections on the basis of share-trading volume, dividend history and number of

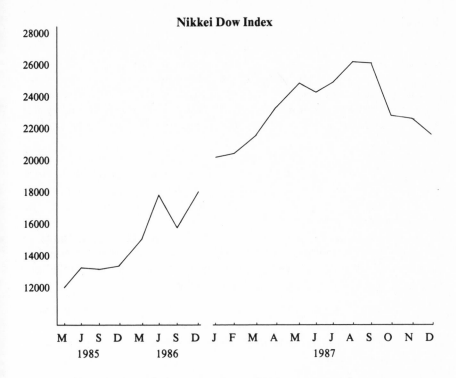

Nikkei Dow Index

shareholders. The first section, for larger companies, has over 1100 stocks listed, representing over 95% of total market capitalization and the second section contains over 400 stocks. There is a separate section for foreign stocks.

The membership of each Stock Exchange is divided into three categories: regular members, Saitori members, and special members. Regular members engage in the buying and selling of securities on the Stock Exchange, either for their own clients (corporate or individual) or on their own account. Saitori members act as intermediaries between the regular members for securities transactions, but they are not allowed to trade on their own account. The third category is composed of members specializing in handling transactions on the TSE or OSE for orders that cannot be handled on the regional Stock Exchanges.

The official hours at present for trading Government bonds, convertible bonds, warrant bonds and equities on the TSE, OSE, NSE, and Kyoto Stock Exchange are 9:00 to 11:00 and 13:00 to 15:00, Monday to Friday. On Saturdays there is a morning session, except on the second and third Saturdays of the month when the markets are closed. The majority of trading takes place on the floor.

Execution

Securities companies are obliged to trade listed securities on an Exchange except under certain specified circumstances. Those specified circumstances include trading by member companies on other Stock Exchanges of which they are members (the four largest securities firms are all members of a number of U.S. Stock Exchanges including the New York Stock Exchange) and block trading outside floor trading hours.

On the TSE, OSE, and NSE, trading in first section stocks is by auction through a Saitori member who matches bids and offers according to rules on price and time priority. Trading takes place at posts which are assigned securities on the basis of the category of business in which the listed companies are engaged.

All transactions are carried out under one of the two methods of auction—Zaraba method and Itayose method. The Zaraba method is used for transactions occurring during the trading day and is carried out on the principles of open auction, for example:

1. Price priority whereby the selling (buying) order with the lowest (highest) price takes precedence over other orders

2. Time priority whereby an earlier order takes precedence over other orders at the same price

The Itayose method is employed to determine opening prices. All orders reaching the floor before the opening are treated as simultaneous orders and each buy order is compared with sell orders until its quantity and price are matched by a sell order.

The five other Stock Exchanges effect transactions in a similar manner, but without the assistance of Saitori members.

As all member firms must conduct business via the Saitori on the three main Stock Exchanges, all orders must, by definition, be exposed to the market. Last trade prices are immediately displayed electronically to securities firms and news offices. The Japan Securities Dealers Association publishes the bid and offer prices of selected heavily traded issues daily on the basis of information provided by the securities firms.

Apart from the 250 most active stocks, which are traded on the TSE floor, trading in all other domestic stocks is conducted by computer. Transaction details are input to the computer and the Saitori clerks at the TSE then match the buying and selling orders on the display screen. When a trade is completed, the result is transmitted to the members placing the order.

Trading in second section stocks is carried out electronically rather than through Saitori. Trading on the OTC is at net prices with the members dealing as principals.

The TSE's computerized Market Information System provides movement by movement price information and trading volume of every stock to the floor of the Exchange and to the offices of the securities firms. This system is also connected with the media and information vendors.

Information on price and bargain size of each security is also made publicly available in the main daily newspapers.

There are price stabilization rules which restrict the maximum daily price change to Yen 2 thousand, in respect of shares with a previous day's closing price of Yen 10 thousand or more, and a reducing scale of maximum movements for prices below Yen 10 thousand. Different price stabilization procedures apply to new issues.

Domestic shares are normally traded in lots of 1000 shares. Foreign shares are traded in lots of 10, 50, 100, or 1000 shares, according to their market prices.

Settlement and Clearing

Almost all transactions are settled on the third business day after execution. Securities firms must settle on that day and business days include Saturdays, except when the Stock Exchange is closed.

There are three other settlement methods:

- Cash transactions are settled on the day of execution or the following day.
- Special agreement transactions are settled within 14 days of execution. (This method was established for overseas investors, although it is not in operation at present.)
- When issued transactions, that is, trades in new shares, are settled on the date fixed by the Exchange.

The TSE introduced a central clearing system in 1971. Clearing on the TSE is by book-entry transfer through the JSCC. This company only deals with stocks listed on the TSE but proposals are currently under consideration which will extend the range of stocks it handles and allow it to act as a nominee name for purposes of registration with the issuer.

A complete book-entry transfer system is currently being planned. It is hoped that it will be implemented within 5 years.

Commission Rates. General brokerage commission rates are fixed. On equities they range from 1.2% on trades up to Yen 1 million down to

0.15% on trades over Yen 1 billion. On straight bonds (government, public and foreign bonds), the rates range from 0.8% down to 0.05% and on convertible bonds from 1% down to 0.15%.

Members of the Japan Securities Dealers Association, including licensed branches of foreign houses in Japan, and Stock Exchange members pay commission at 50% of the above general rates. Firms which are not members of a Stock Exchange in Japan are obliged to reimburse the members through which they deal with 20% of commissions they receive. Foreign securities firms without branches in Japan pay commission at 80% of the above general rates.

Transaction Taxes. Sales of securities are subject to a transaction tax. The base of this tax is the actual price of sale. The different rates for sales by dealers on their own account and by others are as follows:

	Dealers	Others
Straight bonds	0.01%	0.03%
Convertible bonds and warrants	0.09%	0.26%
Equities	0.18%	0.5%

Similar transaction taxes are imposed on the settlement of futures contracts.

Margin Trading. Margin trading is permissible on first section stocks. The minimum margin requirement varies with the type of collateral and is currently 70% for equities and between 80–95% for bonds. It may be lodged in either cash or securities. Under the Securities and Exchange Law the legal minimum margin requirement is 30%, but the ruling rate may be varied overnight according to the Ministry of Finance's view of market conditions. Margin accounts must be settled within six months of the date of contract. The securities houses' lending is financed either by matching trades, lending from own accounts, or borrowing from a securities finance company. There are 3 such finance companies which, in turn, borrow from call-brokers, using the securities deposited as collateral.

The primary activities of securities finance companies include lending, through the settlement agency of the Stock Exchange, funds or securities to regular members of the Stock Exchange for settling the account of margin transactions, as well as bond trade financing and bond financing for individual customers. They also offer a general lending service to make loans to securities firms or their clients against the collateral of stock certificates.

Foreign investors may only conduct transactions for limited purposes such as hedging.

JAPAN

Investor Protection. The MoF has responsibility for all aspects of the securities markets in Japan and issues securities firms with separate licenses for broking, dealing as principal, underwriting, and retail distribution. The majority of the Japanese securities firms are licensed for dealing as principal, broker and/or retail distribution only. Sixty-six regular member companies are also licensed as managing underwriters.

To minimize conflicts arising from multiple capacity, a securities firm may not act as principal and agent in the same transaction and may not lend on margin for the purchase of any security for which that firm is underwriter for a period of six months after becoming an underwriter.

The correct operation of the pricing system on the floor of each Exchange is also checked on a continuous basis by Exchange Supervisors.

There is no insurance or compensation fund for investors.

New Issues

The 1987 figures for new issues on the TSE are as follows:

	Domestic	Foreign
Number	37	36

Issues are now made predominantly on a market pricing basis. Under market pricing, no subscription rights are granted to the existing registered shareholders. Shares issued are distributed either through a public offering or through a third-party allocation by granting subscription rights to a selected person or persons.

Money is raised in the bond markets as follows:

1. Public bonds issued by the government, public local bodies, and public agencies

2. Bonds issued by long-term credit banks (the Industrial Bank of Japan, the Long-Term Credit Bank of Japan, and the Nippon Credit Bank) which are referred to as financial debentures

3. Yen-denominated bonds issued by Japanese companies, principally by private placement

4. Yen-denominated bonds (Samurai bonds) issued by nonresidents (mainly foreign government organizations)

5. Foreign currency-denominated bonds (Shogun bonds)

Government bonds are registered with the Bank of Japan while other bonds are registered with a banking institution specifically designated by the Ministry of Finance, on an issue-by-issue basis.

When a bond is offered for subscription by a large number of unspecified investors, securities companies usually organize a syndicate for the purpose of underwriting. For corporate bonds a syndicate consists exclusively of securities firms, typically between 10 and 30.

The terms and conditions of a bond issue are negotiated by the underwriting syndicate and the issuer. However, from November 1987, the government has begun to introduce a limited auction system for shorter term government bond issues and 20% of the total issue of 10-year government bonds, which themselves constitute 60% of the total government bond issue, is now allocated by this method.

Commissions for underwriting bond issues generally range from 1% to 5%. Typically, issues are priced at 3% to 5% below the market.

FUTURES AND OPTIONS TRADING

In 1985 the TSE started futures trading on the standardized 6% 10-year long-term Japanese government bond. The market has grown dramatically, and in 1986 the total number of contracts traded represented 89% of the cash market in government bonds. Twenty-year government bond futures are also expected to be traded during 1988.

Trading on the Tokyo futures market can be carried out by both its existing "regular" members and by non-members which meet the TSE's special requirements. These traders are known as "special participants." The delivery date is the 20th of each contract month (i.e., March, June, September, and December). Five contract months are traded at any one time. There is a daily price movement limit of Yen 1 million per contract. The margin requirements for customers are the greater of 3% of the nominal transaction value or Yen 6 million, and for members and special participants 2% of the nominal transaction value.

In June 1987, the OSE started trading in a stock futures index (Stock Futures 50) based on a portfolio of Japan's 50 leading stocks. Settlement day is the 15th of each delivery month. The minimum margin is the greater of 9% of the sales value of the contract or Yen 6 million.

REGULATIONS AFFECTING NEW ENTRANTS TO THE MARKETS

Regulations affecting securities firms are established by the Ministry of Finance and the individual Stock Exchanges. The Securities Bureau, which is part of the Ministry of Finance, administers all matters relating to the securities markets. There are six sections within the Securities Bureau: the Co-ordination Division, the Securities Companies Division, the Capital Markets Division, the Secondary Markets Division, the Corporate Finance Division, and the Inspection Division. There are three additional bodies, namely the Securities Exchange Council, the Business Accounting Deliberation Council, and the Certified Public Accountant Examination Commission, which are also charged with the supervision of the securities industry. In addition, there are nine Finance Bureaus, which are local organizations responsible for securities administration.

The Japan Securities Dealers Association, to which all securities companies belong, aims to enforce fair business practices and protect the public investors. It provides voluntary regulation of member securities firms.

The main statutory regulations affecting the securities industry are contained in the 1948 Securities and Exchange Law. Article 65 of this Law separates securities and banking business in a similar way to the U.S. Glass-Steagall Act.

Securities Branch Requirements. Applications by foreign securities firms for a license to establish a branch office in Japan are lodged with the MoF. All applicants must have corporate status. Separate licensing is required for principal trading, agency business, underwriting, and public distribution. A separate license is also required for each branch. A license is not required by foreign securities firms establishing a representative office, providing only research facilities or other information services, but such firms must notify the MoF prior to setting up or discontinuing such an office.

The MoF thoroughly screens applications for branch status on the basis of three principal criteria:

1. Sufficient financial standing. The minimum capital requirement varies with the particulars of the license. For firms applying to manage underwriting syndicates and to undertake public distribution and/or principal dealing or agency business, the minimum capital requirement is Yen 3 billion. For managing underwriters only, the minimum capital requirement is Yen 1 billion and for sub-underwriter status it is Yen 200 million. The minimum capital requirement for other licenses is Yen 100 million on the TSE or OSE, Yen 50 million on the NSE, and Yen 30 million elsewhere.

Forecasts of expected revenues and expenditures must be submitted to the MoF to ensure that they are reasonable.

2. Adequate knowledge and experience, together with sufficient trust of the community. Experience is defined by having at least three years of continuous trading history in the applicant's home country and in the same activity applied for.

3. Market and economic conditions. The MoF must judge a particular application to be necessary in the light of the general state of securities markets in Japan and by reference to the existing numbers of Japanese securities companies and of foreign securities companies' branches.

There are a number of restrictions on licensed securities branches in Japan, one of which prohibits them from engaging in anything but securities business. In the case of foreign groups, whose range of activities would contravene the separation of function regulations within Japan, it may be necessary to arrange for an outside shareholder to hold part of the equity of the company establishing the branch. In addition, any transfer or acquisition by transfer of a branch license must be approved by the MoF, which will also re-evaluate licenses when control of the company changes.

Regular supervisory reporting throughout the year is required by the MoF and the Bank of Japan in accordance with ministerial ordinance, and approximately 45 different types of reports are involved. An unaudited annual business report in prescribed format must be lodged with the Ministry within two months of the end of September each year. From 1989, this reporting date is expected to move to the end of March, in line with other types of financial institution. MoF may also require to see audited accounts of the company which has established the branch and also group consolidated accounts on an annual basis. MoF inspectors may visit a branch at any time to perform an inspection audit on any aspect of its activities and these wide powers are used quite frequently.

Each branch must also meet certain financial requirements. In the case of performance bonds, the branch must deposit a sum equivalent to 10% of the minimum capital requirement or Yen 10 million, whichever is the greater. Due to the effect this has on return on capital employed, up to 20% or Yen 5 million is offset by a contract to pay the MoF in lieu of a physical deposit. In addition, 5% of profit at the close of an accounting period must be placed in a doubtful debt reserve. A reserve for losses arising from securities transactions is also required at an amount which varies in relation to the volume of trading. Assets to the value of reserves against losses, plus debts other than liabilities owing to head office or overseas, must be held in Japan.

Membership of a Stock Exchange requires the purchase of a seat. Since 1949, the TSE has only granted new seats on two occasions—in 1985 and in December 1987. New seats made available at this latter date are each reputed to have a purchase price of up to Yen 2 billion.

Alternatively, membership can be gained by the purchase of an existing Stock Exchange member firm. However, MoF permission would be needed for the new owner to continue operating as a member.

The OSE adopts a more liberal attitude to membership, and in April 1987 the number of seats for brokerage houses was increased from 58 to 82, including two foreign securities firms.

OUTLINE OF CORPORATE AND INDIVIDUAL TAX CONSIDERATIONS

Residents

Bonds—Current Income. Interest received by companies is taxed at normal corporate tax rates. Individuals can elect for tax to be deducted at source at 35%, in which case no further tax is payable, or have tax deducted at 20% and the gross amount aggregated with other income and taxed at marginal rates against which the 20% is credited.

Individuals who were not taxed previously on income arising from government bonds having an aggregate face value of up to Yen 3 million per person (the so-called Maruyu system) suffer a flat 20% withholding tax on such income (which is not aggregated) from April 1988. Tax exemptions remain for elderly, handicapped, and widowed persons.

Bonds—Capital Gains. Capital gains are taxed as income for companies.

Equities—Current Income. The same rules apply to individuals as for bonds. Dividends received by domestic companies from Japanese corporations are not taxable, but if dividends received exceed dividends paid, 25% of the excess is added to taxable income.

Equities—Capital Gains. The same rules apply to companies as for bonds. Individuals pay no tax where gains arise from less than 30 transactions in a year involving less than 120,000 shares of Yen 50 par value or sales of less than 120,000 shares of Yen 50 par value of the same class in one company. These exemptions for individuals also cover gains from most bonds.

Nonresidents

Individuals and companies are taxed on interest and dividends from Japanese companies at a withholding rate of 20%, which is subject to modification by tax treaty.

PROSPECTIVE DEVELOPMENTS

There is a trend towards the gradual liberalization of the Japanese capital markets, notably with respect to the permitted activities of banks and brokers in the bond market and the recent admittance of further foreign securities houses as TSE members. The Ministry of Finance may also allow somewhat greater access by foreign firms to Government Bond underwriting, changing slowly from a syndication issue to an auction system.

It is planned to create a comprehensive Tokyo financial futures market comparable to London and Chicago. As part of this, the introduction of a Traded Options market is regarded as a possibility in the foreseeable future, and the addition of currency and U.S. treasury bond futures contracts and stock index futures to the Tokyo market is expected from late 1988 onwards.

The market in Yen-denominated short-term domestic commercial paper is also expected to develop, having been relaxed in December 1987 with both securities companies and commercial banks permitted to participate. Further steps are expected to be taken by the MoF in the near future to ease restrictions on the issue of domestic corporate bonds. Further selective reductions in brokerage commission rates may also occur.

The problem of insider trading has recently become more of an issue in Japan and a general tightening of the existing rules is expected.

However, the process of liberalization is presently at an early stage and is closely controlled by the MoF. Any significant changes to Article 65 of the Securities and Exchange Law is unlikely to be contemplated unless and until the Glass-Steagall Act is also modified.

SOUTH KOREA

Samduk Accounting Corporation
Contact: Byong Nam Kim, Tel: 735 0241

The Korea Stock Exchange (KSE), located in Seoul, is Korea's only Exchange. It handles the trading of all Korean securities and is a nonprofit corporation, 68% owned by the government, with the remainder in the hands of the 25 securities companies. The KSE was established in 1956 by the government to help finance the reconstruction necessary after the Korean War.

Size

There are 25 member firms trading on the KSE.
The 1986 market statistics for the KSE are as follows:

Stock Trading Volume (million shares)	9,276
Trading Volume Value (Won billion)	9,596
Total Market Value (Won billion)	11,994
Number of listed companies	355
Number of listed bonds	3,812

The Exchange's primary index is the Composite Stock Price Index. It incorporates all listed stocks and is set to a base in 1980.

Composite Stock Price Index

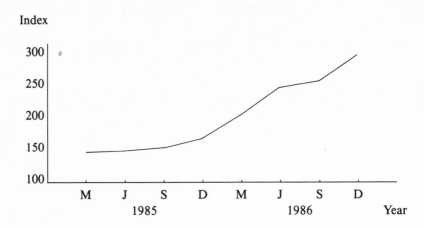

Index

OVERVIEW OF THE BOND AND EQUITY MARKETS

Structure

The KSE is divided into two sections. Companies listed on the first section must have declared a dividend on at least two occasions during the three previous years' accounting periods, and the ratio of after-tax profit to capital must be 5% or more in the last business year. Additionally, the companies' shares must be listed for at least six months, and no less than 40% of their share capital must be freely traded and held by more than 300 shareholders. Companies not satisfying these criteria are traded on the second section. Shares listed on the second section may be promoted to the first section when they satisfy the necessary requirements.

There is no over-the-counter market.

Trading sessions are held daily from Monday to Friday between the hours of 9:40 and 12:00; and 12:30 to 15:20; and on Saturday from 9:40 to 12:00.

Execution

Transactions on the KSE take place through one of the 25 member firms. Korean securities firms act as brokers but may also buy and sell as principals for their own account. Customer orders are electronically transmitted to the trading floor by the securities firm where they are routed to the appropriate trading post by the firm's floor representative. The KSE functions on a continuous trading auction basis, whereby an auctioneer matches the best bids and offers to determine price. Opening prices are determined by reference to all bids and offers in the first five minutes of the trading session.

The KSE is highly automated with current market prices immediately available to the public through the Korea Securities Computer Corporation (KSCC), an on-line computer service.

Equities trading takes place in lots, either 100 shares or 10 shares according to whether the nominal value is less than or greater than W5,000. Bonds are normally traded in units of W100,000. Trading of odd lots is not permitted on the KSE.

Settlement and Clearing

Transactions are handled as either regular-way or cash transactions; the distinction between the two being the settlement date. Regular-way transactions are settled on the second business day following the contract date. Settlement for cash transactions is due on the day of the transaction.

Equity instruments such as shares and investment trust certificates are traded as regular-way transactions, while bonds are traded in either manner.

The Korea Securities Settlement Corporation (KSSC) serves as the Exchange's clearing agent. Securities firms must pay the net balance between their purchases and sales to the KSSC in cash and/or securities. The KSCC then settles its account with the securities company likewise on a net basis. A book entry clearing system is employed which is operated by KSSC, although securities can also be registered in either the customer's name or the dealer's name. The KSSC also functions as a transfer agent, along with two banks, because listed companies are required to have a transfer agent.

Market Characteristics

Commission Rates. For equity transactions, brokerage commission rates are fixed, based upon sales value. The following rates currently apply:

Transaction Value	Commission (%)
Up to W1,000,000	0.9
W1,000,000–W5,000,000	0.8 plus W1,000
W5,000,000 and over	0.7 plus W6,000

Additionally, any part of an order that is not a multiple of 100 shares is charged a 2% brokerage fee. The government also levies a 0.2% securities transaction tax on sales except when the share price falls below par value and in the case of securities sales by investment trusts.

Debt securities and investment trust transactions are subject to a commission rate of 0.3% of market value.

Margin Trading. Margin trading is permissible on the KSE, with margin financing available from the Korea Securities Finance Corp (KSFC) and the major securities houses.

New Issues

New issues for 1986 were as follows:

	Market Value (W billion)
New listings	43.1
Listed concerns	797.7
Total	W 840.8

New issues must be approved by the KSE and the Securities and Exchange Commission (SEC). After approval is granted, the newly listed company enters a listing agreement with the KSE that requires it to observe various Stock Exchange regulations.

Korean shares are either bearer or registered shares and all have a nominal value. Shareholders of common shares are entitled to nominal voting rights, usually one vote per share. Common, cumulative and participating preferred shares are the equity instruments most commonly traded. Companies may also list convertible bonds on the KSE. Deferred shares are not available on the KSE, but they are legally recognized.

Foreign companies may not be listed on the Exchange.

Investor Protection. Under the Securities and Exchange Law, listed companies are required to file annual and semi-annual financial reports with the SEC and the KSE. In addition, companies must file a report if the company undertakes any significant investment or action such as a joint venture, off-shore loan, transactions exceeding 10% of paid-up capital, and acquisitions or more than 20% of another company's stock. Mergers and acquisitions are closely regulated since the law requires special shareholder resolutions stipulating two-thirds majority approval. Insider trading is also prohibited; in particular, employees and officers of securities companies, the KSE, and the regulatory agencies may not trade listed securities in either their own name or via a third party for their own account—except under certain special circumstances.

No direct compensation fund exists for investors who incur losses due to fraud or default by traders. The KSE, however, grants shareholders second preferential rights in an insolvency, and operates a fund to make good losses arising from execution errors. All members of the Exchange contribute to the compensation fund by means of a levy of 0.001% on the value of all transactions.

FUTURES AND OPTIONS TRADING

There are no future or options markets in Korea.

REGULATIONS AFFECTING NEW ENTRANTS TO THE MARKETS

All companies trading in securities listed on the KSE must be members of the Exchange. As members, securities companies become part owners of the Exchange and are subject to regulation by the SEC, the Ministry of Finance and the KSE.

Exchange membership is limited to Korean nationals and all foreigners are prohibited. The Korean government grants seats to prospective members free of charge, but members must purchase a specified number of KSE shares as required by the Ministry of Finance. There are no specific minimum capital, solvency, or insurance requirements.

The principal regulations governing the industry are:

- Securities and Exchange Law of 1976
- The Commercial Code
- Foreign Capital Investment Act
- Foreign Exchange Control Law
- Securities Transaction Law

These statutes cover all aspects of the industry from listing and reporting requirements to insider trading. The KSE's own regulations include a "limit-up mechanism" which restricts daily price rises to a variable percentage of the stock's value. The MoF also intervenes in the Exchange's operation using less explicit methods, such as making recommendations to securities houses on when and how to stabilize the market, and issuing Monetary Stabilization Bonds.

Foreigners were, until recently, prohibited from direct investment and stock ownership in Korea except as stipulated by the Foreign Capital

Investment Act. Foreign investors, however, have been allowed increased access to Korea's capital markets through investment trusts run jointly by Korean and overseas securities houses, and in recent months have been permitted limited direct investment rights in certain securities.

OUTLINE OF CORPORATE AND INDIVIDUAL TAX CONSIDERATIONS

Residents

Under the Korean Corporation Tax Law, corporate income taxes are levied at the rate of 20% to 30% for listed companies, and 33% for large unlisted companies. Dividend and interest income from listed companies are subject to a 10% withholding tax for minority shareholders, and 10% withholding tax, and taxation on aggregate income, for majority shareholders. Dividend and interest income from unlisted companies are subject to a 25% withholding tax, and taxation on aggregate income, for all shareholders.

Nonresidents

Foreign investors approved by the MoF are subject to taxation on dividends, interest, and capital gains based upon treaties on a country by country basis. The maximum tax rate for dividends and capital gains for foreign investors is 26.875%.

Transfer Tax

Transactions on the KSE are subject to a securities transfer tax of 0.2% for listed securities, and 0.5% for unlisted securities.

PROSPECTIVE DEVELOPMENTS

It is generally believed that in the near future the Korean government will extend direct investment privileges in the capital markets but no definite date has been set.

LUXEMBOURG

Fiduciaire d'Organisation et de Revision Fernand Faber
Contact: Claude Faber, Tel: 2 56 26

The Luxembourg Stock Exchange (LSE) was incorporated in 1927 and has become one of the world's most important centers for listing Eurobonds. The operation, administration and management of the LSE is carried out by a joint stock company, Société Anonyme de la Bourse de Luxembourg which is 80% owned by the state savings bank and 20% by the public.

Size

There are some 45 banks and 20 brokers who are members of the LSE. The trading statistics for the LSE for 1986 are as follows:

	Stock and Shares	Bonds	Collective Investment Undertakings
Turnover (in million FLUX)	5,397	18,800	1,758
Market capitalization as at year end (in billion FLUX)	6.37	25.46	1.133
Number of securities as at year end	219	4,000	300

117

LUXEMBOURG

OVERVIEW OF THE BOND AND EQUITY MARKETS

Structure

There is no separation of function between member firms in trading.

Only regular members approved by the LSE are authorized to deal in securities on the LSE. Qualified credit institutions and stockbrokers are members of the LSE.

An over-the-counter (OTC) market exists and several of the banks have large holdings of foreign securities and bonds which are traded on the OTC market. Some firms have also become large market makers in OTC securities both in domestic and foreign stocks. There are between 20 and 30 domestic securities traded regularly on the OTC for which orders are placed primarily through the domestic bank branches.

No trading or settlement links exist with overseas markets.

The majority (in excess of 90%) of trading is in bonds particularly in Eurobonds and a large portion of that in equities takes place off the Stock Exchange.

Trading sessions are held on working days from 10:45 to 13:15.

Execution

The LSE operates on the open outcry basis. Any member who wishes to trade must announce his intention to do so. The members present reach agreement as to a price, which is the price at which the largest number of securities can be traded.

Settlement and Clearing

Since 1969, the financial institutions in Luxembourg have benefited from the incorporation of an international clearing system, CEDEL, which is used for nearly all international bonds. Transactions on the Exchange are all settled through CEDEL or through the Chambre de Liquidation, which is controlled by LSE. Settlement is against cash payment through the clearing house.

Market Characteristics

Commission Rates. The basic brokerage rate is 0.5% for bonds and 0.8% for equities with a minimum of FLUX 250 and a maximum of FLUX 250 thousand brokerage per contract.

Decreasing brokerage fees are applied to contracts in excess of FLUX 2.5 million for bonds and FLUX 5 million for stock and shares. No other tax (e.g., stamp duties) is due.

Margin Trading. There is no margin trading on the LSE.

Investor Protection. There is no compensation fund for investors, nor are there any regulations prohibiting insider dealing (although civil actions may be brought).

New Issues

The 1986 figures for new issues on the LSE are as follows:

	Equities	Bonds	Investment Funds
Number	36	1,169	129
Value (in millions FLUX)	460,506	5,270,864	278,781

The issue and listing of securities is governed by the Grand Ducal Decree of March 22, 1928 and by the provisions of Chapter V of the Governing Rules of the LSE.

Every application for listing must be submitted by at least one member of the LSE and must be accompanied by the prescribed documentation. The Stock Exchange Commission will prepare a file about the new issue and transmit it to the Board of Directors of the LSE.

The issuer must also prepare a prospectus covering the application for listing. This must be approved by the Luxembourg Monetary Institute before it can be published.

There are two types of listed securities: fixed-income and variable-income. Fixed-income securities are quoted and dealt in the currency of issue. Furthermore, they are listed in terms of percentage of their nominal value and accrued interest is paid to the seller. Variable-income securities cover foreign and local equities, foreign and local Collective Investment Undertakings and Certificates representing Foreign Equities.

Following enactment of a law in 1983, a new type of investment known as a collective investment underwriting has considerably expanded in Luxembourg, and trading of some securities is now available on the LSE.

FUTURES AND OPTIONS TRADING

There are no futures or options markets in Luxembourg. Nevertheless there are brokers who deal on the EOE in Holland or LIFFE in London.

REGULATIONS AFFECTING NEW ENTRANTS TO THE MARKETS

All firms trading on the LSE have to be approved members of the LSE, whether they are a bank or a broker. Membership of the LSE can only be granted to a natural person or a legal entity which wishes to incorporate as a stockbroker in Luxembourg or as a bank authorized to operate under the control of the Luxembourg Monetary Institute.

The LSE is organized by the law of December 30, 1927, by the charter of incorporation of the Société Anonyme de la Bourse" and by a set of internal rules and regulations (Règlements d'Ordre Intérieur de la Bourse). All regulation must be approved by ministerial decree. The Board of Direction of the Société Anonyme de la Bourse de Luxembourg is assisted by a Government Commissioner.

Membership Requirements. Membership to the LSE can only be obtained by duly authorized brokers and credit institutions. It is not possible to purchase a seat on the LSE. Membership costs FLUX 50 thousand a year. In the case of natural persons they must fulfill the following criteria:

- Be resident in Luxembourg
- Be more than 25 years old
- Have the necessary professional skills

In the case of a legal entity the minimum capital requirement is FLUX 5 million. There are no liquidity requirements but all members are obliged to provide a surety (with a minimum of FLUX 2.5 million) to cover their commitments to the Société Anonyme de la Bourse.

OUTLINE OF CORPORATE AND INDIVIDUAL TAX CONSIDERATIONS

Corporations

Income Tax. With respect to corporations engaged in the trade of business of securities, profits arising therefrom are treated as part of business income and are taxed as ordinary income. The company's profits are subject to a corporation tax at a rate up to 38% for 1987 and 36% for 1988. In addition a special contribution to the unemployment fund is levied, which amounts to 2%.

Capital Taxes. Capital taxes, including annual subscription tax (0.36% for a joint stock company) and trade tax on capital, are levied on an annual basis on the capital of the company (an adjusted net asset value is used for trade tax purposes). Property tax is also levied on the company's net assets.

Individuals

Income Tax. With respect to individuals engaged in the trade of business of securities, profits arising therefrom are taxable if the securities have been sold less than six months after their acquisition (operation of speculation). If the gain is realized on securities held for more than six months the realized profit is tax-free. The maximum rate of taxation applicable to speculation profits is 28.5%.

Property Wealth Tax. Individuals resident in Luxembourg are subject to a property wealth tax on their net worldwide assets at a rate of 0.5% p.a. subject to an allowance of FLUX 100 thousand for the taxpayer, his spouse and each child. For wealth tax purposes, securities are evaluated at their estimated market value.

PROSPECTIVE DEVELOPMENTS

There are no changes currently anticipated for the activities of the Luxembourg Exchange.

MALAYSIA

Ahmad Abdullah & Goh
Contact: Michael K. J. Goh, Tel: 3-2922937

There is one Stock Exchange in Malaysia, located in Kuala Lumpur. Despite an official separation since 1973, the Stock Exchanges in Malaysia and Singapore continue to be closely linked. A large number of stocks listed in Singapore are Malaysian companies, and Singapore investors are major traders of Malaysian stocks. Since 1986, the Malaysian government has instituted new laws designed to increase stock market supervision and to allow greater Central Bank and foreign participation in the market.

Size

There are 50 member firms on the Kuala Lumpur Stock Exchange (KLSE).

In 1987, licenses were issued to the 3 largest local banks to conduct stock broking businesses. These new member firms are expected to commence business on January 1, 1988.

In addition, a number of member firms were incorporated in order to increase capitalization in stockbroking firms.

The market figures to 6/30/87 for the KLSE are as follows:

	All Securities
Turnover (M$ billion)	6,721
Number of trades/bargains (billion)	4,079
Market capitalization (M$ million)	102,007
Number of listed securities	290

MALAYSIA

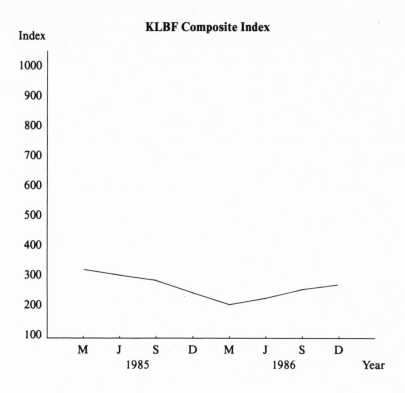

STOCK PRICE INDEX

The most commonly used stock price index is the KLSE composite index.
Recent movements are as follows:

OVERVIEW OF THE BOND AND EQUITY MARKETS

Structure

KLSE rules permit dealings in the following securities:

- Securities which are quoted on the Official List of the Stock Exchange.
- Treasury bills, loans, short-term securities, and other obligations issued by the government of Malaysia or the government of any other country.
- Securities which have been granted quotation on a recognized Stock Exchange or by a recognized Stock Brokers Association.
- Unit trusts managed in Malaysia.

123

MALAYSIA

Government securities are, however not currently traded on the KLSE. Institutional investors either trade these through discount houses or arrange private deals themselves. Individual investors account for only a small proportion of total trading in government securities.

It is estimated that off-shore trading of Malaysian equities is equivalent to 20% of total market trading. Outside the KLSE, investors are known to trade actively on the Singapore and Hong Kong Stock Exchanges. No over-the-counter market exists in Malaysia, other than for government securities.

All securities on the KLSE are traded in the same manner. The trading hours on the Stock Exchange are Monday to Friday, 10:00 to 11:00, 11:15 to 12:30, and 14:30 to 16:00. An estimated 80% of total trade occurs on the Stock Exchange floor.

Execution

The price for each transaction is determined by a bid-and-offer system. Shares are traded either in round lots of 1000 or in odd lots, although KLSE plans to allow shares to be traded in round lots of 500. The transaction information, which includes the name of the security, the brokers involved, the quantity, and the price, must be reported to the KLSE.

The information made publicly available by the next day includes the last sale of each stock at the close of business on the KLSE, price changes, volumes dealt, and the year's high and low prices.

Settlement and Clearing

The KLSE operates a computerized clearing system through a separate company called Securities Network Services Sdn. Bhd. (SCANS). This provides delivery and settlement services for the investing public and member firms.

Two types of delivery systems are currently used, namely Ready Bargains, with a two-week trading period and the Delayed-One-Month (DOM) Bargains. Investors can choose to trade under either of the two systems, and their choice must be indicated in the contract note.

The following features apply in the Ready Bargains System:

- The calendar year is divided into trading periods of one week each.
- A trading period consists of five business days or less if there are any public holidays in the trading period.
- All securities shall be delivered on any business day but not later than 15:00 on:

—Wednesday of the week following the trading period when clients are selling;

—Thursday of the week following the trading period when brokers are dealing with SCANS;

—Friday of the week following the trading period when SCANS is dealing with buying brokers

Under the DOM system, each trading period begins on the 15th day of one month and ends on the 14th day of the following month. SCANS will accept delivery of securities sold, only after the trading period has ended but not later than the following dates:

- Client to broker—the third business day after the end of the trading period
- Broker to SCANS—the fourth business day after the end of the trading period
- SCANS to broker—the fifth business day after the end of the trading period

The KLSE Committee may declare any listed securities as "designated securities" if it believes there has been manipulation or excessive speculation in such securities. The consequence of such a designation is that immediate delivery then applies to transactions in such securities. The KLSE Committee only withdraws the designation if it concludes that the securities are free from manipulation or excessive speculation.

Under immediate delivery, a client who sells shares must deliver them to the broker before 15:00 on the following business day to enable the broker to deliver them to SCANS on the second business day. In turn, SCANS will deliver them to the buying broker on the third business day, in all cases following the date of contract.

The KLSE rules specify that where settlement is between two brokers, payment should be no later than 11:00 on the day after physical delivery. Where customers are concerned, brokers may withhold the release of securities until cleared funds have been received. Where the customer is selling, he will be paid no later than two days after the physical delivery.

Market Characteristics

Commission Rates. Commission rates on ordinary stock and preference shares generally range between 0.5% and 1.5% depending on share price and delivery procedure, subject to a minimum of M$5. Commission rates for those stocks quoted in other currencies are 1% for ready contracts or

1.5% otherwise. Rates for government and municipal bonds are generally 0.375%.

For transactions in overseas securities, the commission is either at the rates applied by the recognized overseas Stock Exchange, or the rates stated above, whichever is higher. Other costs of dealing include a clearing fee of .05% of the value of the transaction, a contract stamp of 0.1% payable by buyers and sellers, and a transfer stamp of 0.3% paid by the buyer.

Margin Trading. Margin trading is permitted by the KLSE. Margin averaging 50% of the value of the security is normally required, and margin lending is financed mainly from bank borrowings and/or internal funds. The KLSE does not specify rules for handling margin accounts but leaves the individual securities firm to specify the rules depending on its relationship with its clients.

There are no official facilities available for stock borrowing, although they exist in practice. It may be an offense under the Securities Industry Act 1983 (Securities Act), which states that a person shall not sell securities to a purchaser, whether as agent or principal, unless he has a presently exercisable and unconditional right to vest the securities in a purchaser.

Investor Protection. Brokers can act as principals in all transactions, subject to disclosure obligations. A broker shall not, as principal, deal in any securities unless he first informs the person with whom he is dealing that he is acting in the transaction as principal and not as agent. A broker who fails to comply commits an offense under the Securities Act.

The Securities Act also has provisions covering, among other things, the issue of dealer licenses to approved applicants, the maintenance of proper accounts and records, the conduct of securities business (disclosure of interest, short selling), trading in securities (false trading, stock market manipulations, misleading statements), and investigative powers.

Each member firm of the KLSE is required to submit to an annual financial audit by an approved company auditor. In addition, member firms are required to furnish annually to the Committee, a statutory declaration stating that no securities received by it, from, or on behalf of a nonmember for safe custody or sale have been dealt with other than in accordance with the nonmember's instruction. In the absence of the instructions, such securities are held by it, or lodged with its bank, for safe custody only.

The KLSE is self-regulating and issues rules on permitted dealings, conduct of business by member firms, maintenance of proper records, disciplinary powers, fair settlement price in cases of default, etc.

MALAYSIA

Members of the KLSE must contribute an initial amount of M$10,000 and a subsequent annual amount of M$5,000 to the KLSE Fidelity Fund. The Securities Industry Act includes regulations relating to the Fund which exists to compensate those who suffer loss from any defalcation or default committed by members of the KLSE. The Act empowers the KLSE Committee to use monies from the fund to enter into insurance contracts indemnifying the Stock Exchange. These contracts may be entered into in relation to members generally, or in relation to any particular members. In addition, members themselves may have their own indemnity insurance.

New Issues

The 1986 figures for new issues on the KLSE are as follows:

Number   6 companies
Value   M$776.8 million

The KLSE's rules on underwriting state that the approval of the KLSE Committee is required when a rights issue is to be undertaken by a member firm jointly with an outside company or individual. In all rights issues the underwriting agreement between the company and its underwriters must be lodged with the Stock Exchange.

The underwriting agreement is a private arrangement between the underwriter, a merchant bank or securities firm, and the company. There are no fixed underwriting rates, but they typically range from 0.5% to 1.75% of the issue price. The underwriter will normally assist the client in obtaining approvals from the relevant authorities, especially the Foreign Investment Committee (FIC) or the Capital Issues Committee (CIC).

Proposals must be submitted to the CIC by:

- All public limited companies incorporated in Malaysia for any new issues to the public, together with rights or bonus issues and other capital reconstructions and the like.

- All public limited companies incorporated outside Malaysia which intend to issue or offer securities for sale to the public or to list such securities on an Exchange prior to the registration of prospectuses with the Registrar.

- All public limited companies incorporated outside Malaysia which are already listed on a Stock Exchange, for the listing and quotation of any additional securities.

The CIC will coordinate and schedule the timing of issues if there are several proposals at a particular time.

The FIC's function is to regulate the acquisition of assets, mergers, and takeovers of companies and businesses, whether by Malaysian or foreign interests.

A recent development was the introduction of a code on takeovers and mergers in April 1987. All takeovers or mergers must now be approved by the Panel on Takeovers and Mergers.

After satisfying the requirements of either the CIC, FIC, or Panel on Takeovers and Mergers the company must register forms and prospectuses with the Registrar of Companies. The Malaysian Industrial Development Finance Berhad (the government-sponsored development finance institution) is then appointed to manage the public issue, including the distribution of application forms and the allotment of shares. A requirement of the New Economic Policy is that all companies must make a special issue of shares to the Bumiputra Community (i.e., the native Malays). Under this policy, the government aims by 1990 to achieve transfers in ownership such that the Bumiputra own 30% of the equity capital, other Malaysians own 40%, and foreigners own 30%.

FUTURES AND OPTIONS TRADING

There are no futures or options markets in Malaysia.

REGULATIONS AFFECTING NEW ENTRANTS TO THE MARKETS

In carrying out the business of a broker or dealer in securities on the KLSE, members may trade as partnerships or companies. All partners or directors of a member firm must hold a personal membership of the Stock Exchange.

The main regulatory authorities are the Registrar of Companies, CIC, FIC, and the KLSE, and the chief statutory regulations are the Companies Act 1965, as amended, and the Securities Act.

Membership Requirements

A person may only carry on the business of dealing in securities if he holds a dealer's license issued by the Registrar of Companies. An applicant for membership of the Stock Exchange must also:

- Be at least 21 years of age
- Be a citizen of Malaysia, subject to a provision where a non-Malaysian may be admitted to membership if the Committee recommends this to the Minister of Finance
- Have had acceptable experience
- Pay an entrance fee
- Have not been suspended or expelled from the Exchange

The entrance fee payable to the Stock Exchange is M$10,000 and there is an annual subscription fee of M$4,800. In addition, members must contribute an initial amount of M$10,000 and M$500 annually to the KLSE Fidelity Fund.

The sole business of a member firm must be that of a stockbroker or dealer in securities, and no partner or director may engage in any other business without the prior approval of the Committee. He may, however, hold shares or be a director of a company provided he does not actively engage in the executive management of such a company without prior approval of the KLSE Committee.

Liquidity Requirements

Each member firm must maintain one of the following liquidity levels, whichever is greater:

- Not less than M$100,000 for each partner or director of a member firm, and M$50,000 for each dealer's representative in the member firm
- An amount that is equivalent to four times the monthly net commission earned

In addition to this requirement, a member firm with limited liability must have a paid-up capital of not less than M$2 million.

Representation by Members of Foreign Stock Exchanges

Under the KLSE rules, a foreign person, but not a company, may be admitted to membership of the KLSE if the Committee recommends this in writing to the Minister of Finance. Such a person can only remain a member if he deals in securities as a director and shareholder of a member firm along with Malaysians who are also members. In addition, the foreign broker's participation shall be restricted to not more than one-third of the total paid-up capital of the member firm; however it is unlikely that foreigners will be admitted to membership of the Exchange at the present time in view of the demand from Malaysians.

OUTLINE OF CORPORATE AND INDIVIDUAL TAX CONSIDERATIONS

Residents

Government Bonds—Current Income. Interest paid or credited to any individual or company in respect of government bonds is taxable unless otherwise provided for under the terms of the issue.

Government Bonds—Capital Gains. Gains on the sale of government bonds are not subject to tax unless the disposer carries on the business of dealing in these bonds.

Equities—Current Income. Dividends paid to individuals are taxable at their respective scale rates of tax. Dividends paid to companies are taxable at 40%. Tax is deducted at source and tax relief for this sum so deducted is given to the recipient upon filing of taxation returns. Where the tax of an individual is less than 40%, a tax refund would be made.

Equities—Capital Gains. Share transfer tax (STT) at 2% on the gross consideration is levied on the disposal of shares in a land-based company (LBC), if at the time of the sale the shares are not listed on a Stock Exchange in Malaysia or elsewhere and if the disposal values or the aggregate disposal values within 12 months are M$5 million or more.

Nonresidents

Government Bonds—Current Income. The same comments as above for residents apply.

Government Bonds—Capital Gains. Gains on the sale of government bonds by nonresidents are not subject to tax unless the disposer carries on the business of dealing in these bonds.

Equities—Current Income. Dividends paid to nonresident individuals or companies are subject to income tax at a rate of 40%. No personal reliefs are given to nonresident recipients who are taxed at a flat rate of 40%. Apart from the tax at source of 40%, there are no further taxes applicable.

Equities—Capital Gains. The same rules apply as for equity-current income.

Stamp Duty

Stamp duty is payable by both buyers and sellers at 0.1% of contract value, rounded up to the nearest dollar. No stamp duty is payable on government bonds.

PROSPECTIVE DEVELOPMENTS

The rules and regulations of the KLSE are currently in the process of being revised. It is not known when changes will be implemented.

NETHERLANDS

Horlings, Brouwer & Horlings
Contact: Eppo Horlings, Amsterdam, Tel: (020) 769955

The Netherlands' sole Stock Exchange, located in Amsterdam, is the oldest established Stock Exchange in existence. The Amsterdam Stock Exchange (ASE) handles the trading of all Dutch securities. It is self-regulating, and is administered by the "Vereniging voor de effechenhande" (VVDE).

The 1986 market figures for the ASE are as follows:

	Equities	Fixed Interest	Government and Overseas Bonds	Traded Options
Turnover (Dfl million)	153,757	27,700	76,251	6,464
Number of trades/bargains	- - - - 257,710 - - - -		N/A	
Market capitalization (Dfl million)	183,492	46,400	146,700	N/A
Number of securities	629	- - - - 1,422 - - - -		27

There are approximately 150 member firms in the ASE. All firms trading in securities must be members of the Stock Exchange.

Domestic trading of overseas equities has become increasingly significant, while there is also significant off-shore trading of Dutch equities in London and New York.

Bond and equity trading is conducted on one of three markets:

- The official market comprises approximately 2000 securities, 70% of which are domestic and foreign bonds, the remaining 30% being Dutch and foreign shares.

The listing requirements for the official market are a minimum capitalization of Dfl 30 million and all of the stock made available for purchase.

- The second market, known as the parallel market, is intended to facilitate entry for smaller companies. The trading rules are similar to those of the official market, and the prices and turnover are published on a special page of the official list. In recent years, the parallel market has grown considerably to a turnover in excess of Dfl 5 billion.

The listing requirements are less stringent than for the official market, in particular the company need only have a minimum capitalization of Dfl 2.5 million and only 10% of the shares need to be held by the public.

- The unofficial market, which is relatively inactive, involves trading in companies which are not officially quoted but in which dealing is carried out according to the regulations of the Exchange. Eurobonds are also traded but only in odd lot amounts (smaller than US$100,000). For all transactions daily prices and volumes are published.

ASAS. In 1980, the Amsterdam Stock Exchange began trading in original American shares under the ASAS system (Amsterdam Security Account System). All settlements and transfers are done by book entry only. The major advantages of the system are the absence of costs associated with bearer certificates and the application of settlement practices of the home market, resulting in less than $\frac{1}{4}$-point difference between the Amsterdam and home-market prices. ASAS was extended to original U.K. shares in 1986, and in 1987 to Japanese and Canadian Stocks.

STOCK PRICE INDEX

The generally accepted index used for monitoring price trends is the ANP/CBS index. In recent years, movements have been as shown on the graph on page 134.

OVERVIEW OF THE BOND AND EQUITY MARKETS

Structure

Trading on the floor takes place from 10:00 to 16:30, Monday to Friday, and accounts for the vast majority of total trade. In an evening session, which runs from 16:30 to 22:00, trading occurs in the more active domestic

NETHERLANDS

Amsterdam ANP/CBS General Share Price Index

Index

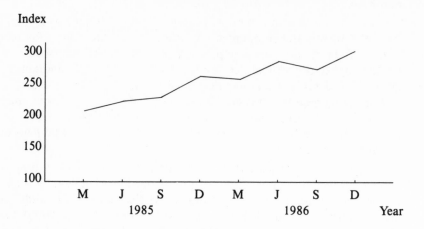

securities as well as securities quoted on foreign Stock Exchanges. Trading in these securities is timed to coincide with trading on the New York Stock Exchange. The Exchange operates on the trading-post system (known in the Netherlands as "Hoek" or corner). The open outcry method is used for very active stocks. Members can act both as an agent and principal on their own account.

Members are divided into two categories: banks/brokers and "Hoekmen." The latter are competing market makers who cannot deal with the public but, instead, act as intermediaries between banks/brokers on the floor of the Stock Exchange.

The banks and brokers are obliged to pass their client orders on the official market to a Hoekman, who is responsible for a market in an assigned group of securities, and has an obligation to make a continuous market. The Hoekmen have a role somewhere between that of the New York specialist and the London market maker, although their intermediation is not required for the parallel market.

However, for block transactions with value more than Dfl 1 million (shares) or Dfl 2.5 million (bonds), trading is effected through the Amsterdam Interprofessional Market System.

Amsterdam Interprofessional Market System, AIM. This system was introduced by the Amsterdam Stock Exchange in May 1987. Banks and brokers are allowed to negotiate with clients and make transactions on a net basis (without charging a commission). Transactions between banks and brokers must be channeled through the Hoekman on the central

134

market, which effects a functional link between AIM and the existing market. In introducing the system, the Amsterdam Stock Exchange was satisfying the wish of institutional investors to operate actively in the professional market.

At the end of each day an official daily list of official rates and turnover is produced. If prices change by more than 10% for no obvious reason trade may then be stopped and only indicative prices are given. Trading may also be suspended in other cases. Shares can be traded in round lots.

Settlement and Clearing

Settlement of bond and equity transactions requires delivery within 10 days.

A computer-based clearing system (Effectenclearing) is used. For each party dealing on the Stock Exchange, a summary for each security is produced showing all purchases and sales. The balances show the securities which must be received or delivered through the central securities clearing system. This system is also used for financial settlement. Increasingly, participants are able to make use of a certificateless, book-entry transfer system.

Market Characteristics

Commission Rates. Banks and brokers charge standard commissions according to fixed minimum scales established by the Stock Exchange. These range from 0.36% to 1.5% for bonds and 0.7% to 1.5% for shares, depending on the value of the transaction. Hoekmen are paid a nominal amount by the bank/broker out of the commission charged to the client.

In general, rebates may be granted for transactions in shares of Dfl 1 million and more and in bonds of Dfl 2.5 million and more.

When transactions are settled in AIM, a fixed commission is not prescribed. In addition, a transfer stamp duty of 0.5% is payable on all purchases, up to a maximum of Dfl 1200.

Margin Trading. Under Dutch law, one is not permitted to buy securities with borrowed money. Securities may, however, be used to secure a loan so that margin trading is to some extent possible and foreign investors may deal in this way.

It is possible to buy or sell shares for delivery at a later date. The total open positions are published monthly. The banks and certain institutions engage in stocklending with the Hoekman as well as with members of certain Overseas Stock Exchanges, with up to a limit of 70% of the securities pledged.

Investor Protection. Separation of capacity between banks/brokers and Hoekmen is rigidly enforced on the ASE. The VVDE has a Complaints Committee (Klachtencommisie Effectenbedrijf) consisting of external legal experts and an Ethical Committee which can discipline members by fining or suspending them.

A Guarantee Fund exists to protect clients' funds indirectly by providing a source of financing should members of the Stock Exchange become insolvent. Each member firm is required to submit a balance sheet and profit and loss account quarterly as part of the solvency requirement.

From January 1, 1987, a code against insider trading came into effect. In addition, a bill submitted by the Minister of Finance has made insider dealing a criminal offense. The code is similar to the U.K. Insider Dealing Act of 1986.

New Issues

The 1986 figures for new issues are as follows:

	Fixed Equities	Government Interest	Bonds	Foreign Issues Bonds
Number	41	10	38	19
Value (Dfl millions)	2,543	15,123	6,134	3.881

Equity and bond issues are underwritten and managed by the banks. A bank can take over or guarantee the entire issue and earn fees for this service. Alternatively a bank can act purely as a selling office for the issue, leaving the underwriting risk with the company. Price is usually determined by negotiation between the bank and the company.

All proposed bond issues, other than convertible bonds, must be registered with the Dutch Central Bank which maintains a calendar of such issues and determines when the bonds can be issued. The Dutch Central Bank normally approves the issuing of shares, although this is not a formal requirement. Formal ministerial approval is required for each new issue whether on the Official or Parallel Markets.

Current underwriting rates are 0.625% for bonds, and 0.8% of the issue price for shares on the Official Market. On the Parallel Market the rate is 1% of the share issue price.

FUTURES AND OPTIONS TRADING

Options trading takes place on the European Options Exchange (EOE) in Amsterdam.

Membership. Some 200 companies and persons are registered as members of EOE. There are 7 types of members of the Exchange:

Public Order Member (POM)

A Public Order Member is entitled to accept orders from public investors (nonmembers) and to have these orders, or orders for his own account, executed by a floor broker on the floor of the EOE.

Public Order Correspondent Member (POCM)

A Public Order Correspondent Member is also entitled to accept orders from investors or for his own account, but only for execution through a Public Order Member acting as intermediary.

Floor Broker/Specialist (FBS)

A Floor Broker/Specialist is entitled to trade for own account and is responsible for creating a continuous two-way market in classes to which he is assigned.

Market Maker (MM)

A Market Maker is only entitled to trade for his own account. He is obliged to make a market in one or more option classes to which he is assigned.

Floor Broker (FB)

A Floor Broker executes orders on the floor of the EOE for other members (or for the account of the members of participating Exchanges) or for his own account.

Off-floor Trader (OFT)

An Off-floor Trader is entitled to have orders for his own account executed on the floor of the EOE by a floor broker.

Clearing Member

A Clearing Member is entitled to settle transactions effected on the floor of the EOE through the intermediary of a clearing organization recognized by the EOE with which he is associated.

The following options are available:

1. Dutch stock options, on the major domestic securities. In 1987, EOE was the first Options Exchange in the world to introduce stock options with a duration of 5 years. The level of volume in these new series proves that they are an important contribution to the range of option tools and they are now available on AKZO, Philips, Royal Dutch, and Unilever.

2. Options on the EOE Dutch Stock Index, which were introduced during 1987.

3. Currency options, mainly on the dollar/guilder, precious metal options and bond options.

Futures

Until 1986, there was no financial futures market, but on November 28, 1986 the Financiël Termijnmarkt Amsterdam (FTA) was established. It is wholly owned by EOE, and was founded to establish a regular trade in financial futures in Amsterdam. The opening of the financial futures market took place on June 19,1987, in guilder/interest futures, and there is also a very modest trade in gold futures.

REGULATIONS AFFECTING NEW ENTRANTS TO THE MARKETS

All firms trading in securities listed on the Official and Parallel Markets must be members of the Stock Exchange and, if they are not also members of the VVDE, must be licensed under the Securities Trades Act.

The main regulatory authority is the VVDE which is referred to as "the holder of the Exchange." In practice the VVDE and ASE are not always fully distinct from each other. The VVDE sets rules for dealing and gives advice to the Minister of Finance who formally decides whether a security is to be admitted. The VVDE regulates securities activities by ensuring that all members operate in a single capacity. It is also responsible for setting rules and producing the daily list (prijscourant) and for imposing sanctions on members.

There are no restrictions on the legal formation of securities firms but there is a minimum capital requirement of Dfl 1 million for banks which trade in securities and Dfl 250,000 for nonbank organizations. The major banks are subject to banking rules which require a minimum capital of Dfl 5 million. There are liquidity requirements for members not subject to banking regulations (the latter are subject to Central Bank liquidity requirements). Experience is also a requirement.

Membership Requirements

Membership of the Stock Exchange does not require the purchase of a seat. To become a member one has to apply to the Association for Securities Trade and comply with its requirements. These include the minimum capital requirements stated above and a certain level of securities expertise. There are no restrictions on the legal form of a member. Membership is of two types: corporate members (brokerage firms/banks) and personal members who represent the corporate members on the floor. Entry fees are Dfl 15,000 for corporate members, and Dfl 7,000 for personal members. Annual membership costs Dfl 2.5,000 for each corporate member and each personal member, with the exception of the first personal member associated with each corporate member.

Every member must report on solvency and liquidity every three months. There are no additional regulations applying to foreign entrants to the market.

OUTLINE OF CORPORATE AND INDIVIDUAL TAX CONSIDERATIONS

Residents

Government Bonds—Current Income. Interest income is fully taxable at normal rates as part of total income.

Government Bonds—Capital Gains. For individuals, capital gains arising from the sale of securities are tax-exempt. Corporations are liable to tax at a normal rate (42%) when the gains are realized.

Equities—Current Income. Both individuals and corporations are liable to tax on dividend received at normal rates. On payment of a dividend, a company is required to withhold 25% dividend tax which the taxpayer can deduct against income tax ultimately payable. For corporations, dividends and capital gains arising from investments in companies are exempt from corporate income tax if at least a 5% shareholding is held from the beginning of the tax year.

Equities—Capital Gains. The same rules apply as for Government Bonds, although corporations are exempt from tax on capital gains arising from investments in companies where at least a 5% shareholding is held from the beginning of the tax year.

Traded Options. Profit/gains realized by individuals are tax-exempt. Corporations are liable to tax at a normal rate.

Nonresidents

Government Bonds—Current Income. Interest income paid to nonresidents is taxable in the Netherlands only if the activity is attributable to a Dutch permanent establishment. There is no withholding tax on interest paid to nonresidents.

Government Bonds—Capital Gains. Similarly no tax on capital gains arises in the Netherlands on the securities sold unless the business is carried on through a Dutch permanent establishment.

Equity—Current Income. In the absence of specific rules in the tax treaties, individuals who have a substantial interest (33% or more) in a Dutch company are subject to 20% tax in the Netherlands on dividends and capital gains arising from their substantial shareholding. All dividend payments made to nonresidents (corporations or individuals) are subject to a withholding tax of 25% or a lower rate applicable to residents of treaty countries.

Equities—Capital Gains. For individuals, capital gains are taxable in the Netherlands only in the case of a substantial interest as defined in the previous paragraph. Nonresident corporations are subject to Dutch tax only if capital gains are attributable to a permanent establishment.

Traded Options

Profits/gains are not taxable in the Netherlands unless the income is attributable to a Dutch permanent establishment.

Stamp Duty

Stamp duty is levied on purchases and sales of securities at 0.12%, limited from January 1, 1987 to a maximum of Dfl 1200 per transaction.

PROSPECTIVE DEVELOPMENTS

Amsterdam Stock Exchange

There is expected to be major growth in the processing of net transactions by the use of AIM.

Both brokers and Hoekmen have a perceived need to gain more capital for net transactions and financing positions. This may lead to links with major banks, as in the United Kingdom.

European Options Exchange

During 1986, EOE concluded negotiations with the American Stock Exchange (AMEX) in New York, on the listing of EOE options on the U.S. Major Market Index. The two Exchanges signed a letter of intent in June 1986.

EOE, AMEX, and OCC (Options Closing Corp, Chicago) have completed the technical and legal preparations and parties involved are now awaiting the approval of the Dutch Supervisory Commission, and the U.S. Securities Exchange Commission. The trading in Major Market Index Options was started on August 29,1987.

NEW ZEALAND

Kirk Barclay
Contact: Owen Pierce, Tel: (09) 792 950

New Zealand's four regional Stock Exchanges are located in Auckland, Wellington, Christchurch-Invercargill and Dunedin. These regional Exchanges are linked in operation to form The New Zealand Stock Exchange (NZSE) which is regulated by the Sharebrokers Amendment Act, 1981.

Market activity on the NZSE for the year ended December 31, 1987 was as follows:

	Equities	Bonds and Fixed Interest
Turnover – value (NZ$billion)	4.46	
Turnover – volume (billion shares)	2.4	Information not
Market capitalization (NX$billion)	40.49	available
Number of securities	719	

There are a total of 95 members of NZSE who operate from the regional Exchanges as follows:

Auckland	34
Wellington	32
Christchurch/Invercargill	18
Dunedin	11
Total	95

All firms trading in securities on the NZSE must be members of it. There is significant off-shore trading of the major domestic equities particularly in Australia, but there is no significant trading of overseas equities/bonds domestically. There are no links with overseas markets in terms of trading and/or settlement.

No significant trading exists outside the formal markets and in particular no over-the-counter market exists in stocks not listed on NZSE.

Performance of Exchange Traded Securities. The NZSE does not publish an index which is indicative of the full range of traded securities, but several indices exist which measure the performance of various sectors. One of the more significant is the Barclays Industrial Index, a daily weighted capital index which comprises 40 major New Zealand companies.

Barclays Index

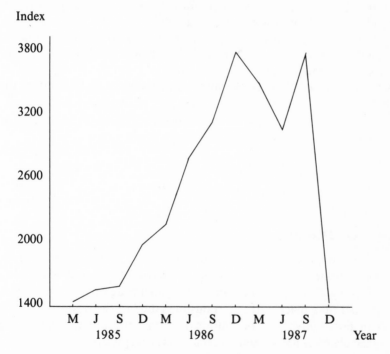

OVERVIEW OF THE BOND AND EQUITY MARKETS

Structure

The NZSE is divided into two boards, the long-established Main Board and the newly established Second Board. The Second Board began

143

operations in November 1986 to trade the securities of smaller companies which do not qualify for Main Board listing. The hours of trading on the floor are 9:30 to 11:15 and 14:15 to 15:15.

Members may act as both agents and principals in their dealings on the NZSE. There are no obligations on market-making members to make continuous markets.

Execution

The procedures for execution are identical for all the regional Exchanges. Details of trades in the morning and afternoon sessions are reported to the regional Exchange within an hour of trading. The details which are required to be reported are: description, volume, price, whether the sale was made on the floor or not and special sales.

The market price of shares are determined by an open-outcry market conducted on a trading post system. No limits exist on daily permissible price movements in stocks.

Shares are normally traded in round lots, dependent on the value of the shares:

Price	Lot Size
1c – 25c	2000
26c–50c	1000
51c–$1.00	500
$1.01 and over	200

Settlement and Clearing

Investors are required to settle trades on receipt of the contract note. Within the broking community, trades are settled on an individual basis by the delivery of the relevant transfer documents against payment. Settlement must take place within ten business days of the trade, otherwise buying in procedures will be enforced against the seller. There is no centralized clearing house, and all securities are registered in the name of the beneficial owner, unless he makes use of the nominee services provided by the banks.

Market Characteristics

Commission Rates. Commission rates are negotiable but generally are in the following ranges:

Value of Trade	Commission
NZ$ 0 – 5,000	2.5%
5,000 –50,000	1.5%
50,000 and over	1.0%

Margin Trading. Margin trading is permitted based on variable margins which are defined in the terms of agreement and are generally set at 20%. Securities firms generally finance their margin lending through a finance house and/or bank borrowings. Short selling is not permitted.

Investor Protection. The NZSE Fidelity Fund provides financial assistance to persons who have suffered a pecuniary loss from a share dealing transaction as a result of a member being unable to meet his financial obligations, subject to a limit of NZ$20 thousand per individual and NZ$500 thousand for any one failure.

In addition to this, the NZSE inspector receives a copy of the monthly accounts for each firm. The inspector also reports annually on the activities of each member firm, and can make spot checks on any member firm. There are no legal restrictions on insider dealing, although the listing requirements restrict dealings by officials of a company.

New Issues

New issues during 1987 were as follows (equities):

	Number
New Zealand companies	65
Overseas companies	58

A company seeking an official quotation for its securities must meet the Exchange's official listing requirements.

The issuing broker must have authority to act from the NZSE prior to the issue commencing. Both underwriting and commission rates are negotiable.

FUTURES AND OPTIONS TRADING

Options

There is as yet no organized market for trading options. Instead, they are issued by the companies and are freely traded in the same way as ordinary shares. The market is relatively new and approximately 20% of the companies on the Exchange offer options.

Futures

A financial futures market exists and is conducted by the New Zealand Futures Exchange (NZFE), which is a self-regulatory body. The following instruments are traded, as well as certain physical commodities:

- Barclays Share Price Index Contract
- 5-year Government Stock Futures
- 90-day Bank Bill Futures

The NZFE is owned by its trading members and a separate institutional body known as the Clearing House maintains the financial viability of the market, by standing between each counterparty and thereby guaranteeing settlement of all contracts. There are 17 trading members, who are subject to separate membership rules—essentially minimum net capital of NZ$350,000 and purchase of membership.

Rules of Operation

Trading. Due to the geographical dispersal between brokers, trading is conducted through a computerized order matching system known as the ATS. Trading is conducted daily and bid/offer quotes are available continuously. Each client pays a deposit to open a contract and margins may be required depending on the movement of the relevant futures contract.

Settlement. For the stock index future, settlement is by reference to the value of the index at the end of the final dealing period. The cash settlement day of a contract will be the second business day following the final day of trading in a cash settlement month. For the interest rate futures, settlement is by delivery of an appropriate instrument.

There are no trading links with overseas futures markets.

REGULATIONS AFFECTING NEW ENTRANTS TO THE MARKETS

New Zealand regulatory authorities are the Securities Commission, Commerce Commission, Justice Department, and NZSE. The statutory regulations which govern the securities industry are the Securities Act, Sharebrokers Act, and Companies Act.

NEW ZEALAND

Membership Requirements

All firms trading in securities must be members of the NZSE. A company shall be admitted as a member if the following broad rules are complied with:

- A majority of the Directors are individual ordinary members of the Exchange.
- At least 50% of the voting shares are registered in the name of and beneficially owned by individual ordinary members of the Exchange.
- The issued and paid up share capital of the company is at least NZ$500 thousand (shortly to be increased to NZ$1 million).
- The Managing Director is an individual Stock Exchange member.
- It holds a Sharebroker's license.
- The Articles of Association comply with Stock Exchange Regulations.

To become a personal member of the NZSE the following rules must be complied with:

- 3 years' experience in the industry.
- Possession of a Sharebrokers' license.
- Evidence of qualifications—passes in NZSE exams.
- References and nominations by other members.
- Balloting by members to decide admission.

There are no prohibitions on overseas ownership of stockbroking firms, up to the 50% level permitted for outsiders.

As noted, firms have to file monthly and annual accounts with the NZSE inspector, but the only solvency or net capital requirement is to have net worth of NZ$500 thousand (shortly to be increased to NZ$1 million).

OUTLINE OF CORPORATE AND INDIVIDUAL TAX CONSIDERATIONS

Corporations

A company not resident in New Zealand is liable to tax only in respect of income derived from New Zealand. A company resident in New Zealand is assessable on all income, whether derived from New Zealand or elsewhere, subject to the provisions of the Income Tax Act of 1976.

NEW ZEALAND

A company is deemed to be resident in New Zealand if it:

1. is incorporated in New Zealand;
2. has its head office in New Zealand

A single flat rate of tax is levied as follows:

Resident Companies	48%
Nonresident	53%

From the income year commencing April 1, 1988 rates proposed are:

Resident Companies	28%
Nonresident	33%

Individuals

Individuals are subject to tax in New Zealand at rates ranging from 15 to 48%. The 48% level applied to incomes over NZ$30,000.

From October 1, 1988 the maximum rate of tax for individuals will be 33%—applying to incomes in excess of $30,875.

Residents

Government Stock—Current Income. The interest on government stock is normally assessable in the year of earning.

Equities—Current Income. Presently dividends received by an individual shareholder are liable to tax at marginal tax rates. In the case of a dividend derived by a company, unless it is a specified preference dividend, it is excluded entirely from the company's assessment.

Government moves on international tax reform propose that foreign dividends received by New Zealand resident companies (where the New Zealand company holds less than 10% of the paid-up share capital) will be taxable from April 1, 1988. Where the New Zealand resident company holds in excess of 10% paid up share capital, the foreign dividend will remain exempt, but the New Zealand company must withhold taxes which will be credited against the New Zealand shareholder's mainstream tax liability.

A fully integrated dividend imputation system is proposed from April 1, 1988. Companies will maintain an imputation credit from which dividends (grossed up) can be paid. The imputation credit will not be available to nonresidents.

Equities—Capital Gains. No specific capital gains tax currently exists in New Zealand. However, the Inland Revenue considers that if a profit or

148

gain derives from the sale of shares which were acquired for the purposes of resale at a profit, any such profit will be taxable.

Financial Futures. For futures contracts entered into after 20:00 on October 23, 1986 tax will be charged on the gain under the accrual rules. Income will be assessable without regard to the contracting person's motive in entering the contract. Losses realized or unrealized will be deductible and unrealized profits assessable.

Nonresidents

Government Stock—Current Income. Nonresident withholding tax is not payable on income derived from stock or debentures issued by the New Zealand government, the interest on which is payable out of New Zealand.

Equities—Current Income The nonresident withholding tax is imposed on nonresidents deriving nonresident withholding income from New Zealand at the rate of 30% of the gross amount of dividend payments unless modified by a double taxation agreement. In effect for those countries with a double tax agreement with New Zealand, the rate will be 15%.

Interest Income. Nonresident withholding tax is also imposed on nonresidents deriving interest income from New Zealand. It is levied at the rate of 15% of the gross amount of the payment. For those countries with a relevant double tax agreement the rate of withholding tax on interest payments to nonresident individuals is reduced to 10%.

Capital Gains Tax. No capital gains tax currently exists.

Other Taxes. Financial transactions are exempt from the Goods and Services Tax (GST).

Stamp Duty

Stamp duty is payable on purchases of securities at the rate of 40c per $100 worth of consideration.

PROSPECTIVE DEVELOPMENTS

Since 1986, the NZSE has been engaged in a staged implementation of a computerized system to automate most, if not all of the work involved in the buying and selling of securities.

The NZSE is also proposing to introduce certificateless trading in the next few years. Currently the NZSE Automation Project is being developed to introduce broker accounting using the comprehensive Kismet database. Eventually it is hoped that the system will have the capacity to carry certificateless registration information, interbroker communication, and screen assisted trading.

The Securities Commission is seeking to implement legislation during 1988 to outlaw insider trading.

A full system of the imputation of tax on dividends is to be introduced in 1988.

PORTUGAL

CONSULTEAM - Consultores de Gestão, S.A.
(Prepared in co-operation with Banco Português do Atlantico)
Contact: Jose Paiva Novo, Tel: (1) 543 770

There are two Stock Exchanges in Portugal—one in Lisbon and one in Oporto. The Lisbon Stock Exchange accounts for more than 80% of total securities trading in the country. The Oporto Exchange is small but growing and many companies are quoted on both Exchanges. The contents of this chapter are applicable to both Exchanges unless otherwise indicated.

The market figures for the Lisbon Stock Exchange in 1987 were as follows:

	Equities	Bonds (Public and Private Companies)	Profit Sharing Bonds
Turnover (Esc. billion)	151.9	35.0	4.1
Number of trades/bargains (million)	16.5	16.3	2.4
Market capitalization (Esc. billion)	1,183	491	37
Number of securities	143	229	5

Turnover on the Oporto Exchange reached Esc. 57,761 million for 1987.

About 85% of the bonds traded are public debt bonds issued by the Treasury. Profit-sharing bonds were introduced during 1986 but can be issued only by state-owned companies or companies in which Portugal has a majority holding.

There are nine brokers on the Lisbon Stock Exchange and three on the Oporto Stock Exchange. Between them, they have a legal monopoly on trading.

STOCK PRICE INDEX

The most commonly used stock price index is the BTA share index. Recent movements are as follows:

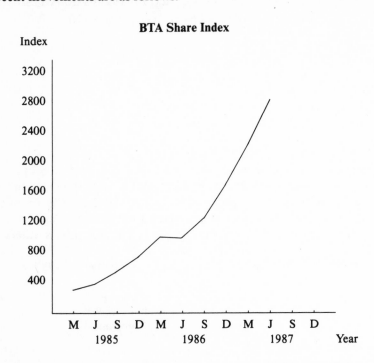

BTA Share Index

New Issues

In 1987, the official market in the Lisbon Exchange recorded the following new issues:

	Equities	Government Bonds	Other Public Sector Bonds	Corporate Bonds	Profit Sharing Bonds
Number	49	12	14	81	29
Value (Esc. billion)	46.4	69.6	87.9	74.8	111.5

Authorization for the issue of shares or bonds by public subscription is granted by the Auditor Geral de Titulos' representing the Minister of Finance. An application to the Treasury Department (Direccão Geral do Tesouro) of the Ministry of Finance, must contain details of the issuer's business, as well as the terms and conditions of the issue.

The Direccão Geral do Tesouro may ask for any additional information deemed necessary. Applications are submitted to the Bank of Portugal and the Executive Committee of the Stock Exchange. The Auditor Geral de Titulos' representing the Minister of Finance may require that it is underwritten before giving authorization for the issue.

Once authorization is granted, the Direccão Geral do Tesouro will indicate the timing of the issue, taking into account the desires of the issuer and the situation in the financial markets.

Issues are normally advertised by a prospectus addressed to the public which will include historical financial data as well as five-year forecasts and general information on the issuer.

The procedures are aimed at guaranteeing not only the financial standing of the issuer but also that a fair issue price is set, timely information is provided to prospective investors and the issue itself is integrated into the market.

Shares are placed at a fixed price and payable on subscription. The underwriters guarantee the issue as appropriate. The delivery of the securities takes place within six months of the commencement of trading, and provisional securities are traded in the meantime. There is no underwriting commission.

There are certain tax incentives available for companies who issue shares. During 1986, there was a 50% reduction of corporation tax for the next three years, in 1987 and 1988, this was reduced to 40% and 25%, respectively. It is these tax incentives which have persuaded a number of family-owned Portuguese companies to come to the market.

OVERVIEW OF THE BOND AND EQUITY MARKET

Structure

The securities market is divided into two main categories, the official market and the unofficial market.

To be traded on the official market, bonds and shares must meet certain minimum requirements. For shares these include a capital requirement of Esc. 20 million for the issuing company; at least 25% of this must be in the hands of the public to allow for a reasonably liquid market in the shares.

PORTUGAL

The unofficial market provides a means of trading in the stocks of companies which do not meet all the requirements of the official market as well as in the provisional scrip of bonds and shares with official listing.

No organized over-the-counter market exists in Portugal, but occasionally trading outside the Stock Exchange is carried out by brokers in both listed and unlisted companies.

Stock Exchange dealings are conducted from 10:00 to 13:00 every Tuesday to Friday. Trade can be in all types of listed and unlisted securities.

Trading of bonds and shares is restricted exclusively to brokers on the Stock Exchanges. Brokers are either individuals or broker companies. Brokers are appointed by the Minister of Finance and must be Portuguese nationals. Banks act only as intermediaries in passing buy and sell orders to the brokers.

Execution

The brokers trade listed securities on the Stock Exchange floor in compliance with the buy and sell orders they receive directly from clients or through credit institutions, usually banks.

Prices are fixed in accordance with a call-over arrangement, whereby all transactions in a stock in any session are transacted at the same price. Exchange rules prohibit variations of more than 15% in consecutive sessions.

Securities have to be traded in minimum lots, defined by the Lisbon Stock Exchange, usually between 10 and 100 shares dependent on share price.

At the end of each working day, a bulletin is published with all the information relating to the transactions made: number of securities traded, prices, quotations of the previous session, and buyer/seller positions at the end of the session.

A statistical bulletin is published at the end of each month with all the information relating to the trading made during the previous month.

After normal business, the so-called "transactions outside Stock Exchange" take place involving both listed and unlisted securities. These transactions normally involve large lots at prices previously set by the contracting parties, although made through the brokers. This off-the-floor trading is often used by large foreign investors because of the semi-liquid nature of the Portuguese market.

Settlement and Clearing

Trading on the Stock Exchange is presently settled by physical delivery though deferred settlements are allowed. The contracting parties have until the sixth working day after the bargain to deliver and settle the trade. As the securities are normally held by investors or kept in credit institutions the process tends to be lengthy. However, to cope with the expanding market it is proposed to introduce a system of book entry transfer supported by the establishment of a central depository.

Market Characteristics

Commission Rates. Investors can deal either directly through brokers or through a bank which will charge its clients variable commissions—0.2% on average—depending on the amounts traded. Brokers commission may be negotiated for transactions above Esc. 50 million. Below this level, commissions are fixed and defined according to the nature of the securities, the type of operations and so forth. Rates vary between 0.1% and 0.6%.

Transactions made on the Stock Exchanges are subject to an additional charge of:

      — Public funds and other bonds   0.025%
      — Shares   0.05%

Margin Trading. Margin trading does not exist in Portugal.

Investor Protection. The Portuguese Stock Exchanges are governed by the Minister of Finance with day-to-day responsibility delegated to the Executive Committee of the Stock Exchange. The Executive Committee of the Stock Exchange ensures that all listed companies meet their obligations for listing. These obligations include a requirement under Portuguese Company law which prohibits insider trading by individuals or companies with privileged information. There is no compensation fund for investors.

FUTURES AND OPTIONS TRADING

At present there are no recognized futures or options markets operating in Portugal.

REGULATIONS AFFECTING NEW ENTRANTS TO THE MARKETS

The activity of Lisbon Stock Exchange is governed by law and controlled by the Ministry of Finance. The day-to-day operations of the Exchange are controlled by the Executive Committee and the Bank of Portugal. All brokers are represented in the Brokers' House (Camara dos Corretores) which plays essentially a consulting role.

Membership Requirements

The appointment of brokers is made by the Minister of Finance. To become a broker an individual must be a Portuguese citizen over 25 years old and pass the equivalent of a "fit and proper" test. There are arrangements whereby certain Brazilian naturalized citizens can obtain appointment by the Ministry of Finance. Each broker must also meet a minimum capital requirement of Esc. 500,000 in case of an individual and Esc.1 million if incorporated as a firm.

OUTLINE OF CORPORATE AND INDIVIDUAL TAX CONSIDERATIONS

Resident and Nonresident

Capital Gains. Individuals are exempt from tax on capital gains while companies are taxed at normal corporation tax rates on any gains arising from the sale of securities, whether resident or not.

Current Income—Government Bonds. Except for certain bonds which are liable to Gift and Inheritance Tax at 5%, individuals are exempt from tax on income received from government bonds. For companies, there is a withholding tax of 10% deducted at source and resident companies are subject to corporate tax, less a credit for the withholding tax. For nonresident companies, the withholding tax is a final tax. The withholding tax may be reduced by double tax treaties.

Corporate Bonds. For individuals, income from bonds issued in 1987 with a maturity date of 8 years or more is fully exempt. Income from bonds issued from May to December 1986 and all 1987 issues with a maturity date of less than 8 years is subject to withholding tax and a Gift and Inheritance Tax of 5%. Income on bonds issued before May 1986 is subject to a Gift and Inheritance Tax at 5%. Similar categories apply for companies but the income is subject to Corporation Tax rather than Gift and Inheritance Tax.

Profit-Sharing Bonds. Individuals have full tax exemption. Companies are subject to withholding tax of 30% and corporation tax, as for government bonds.

Equities. For individuals, income is subject to withholding tax of 12% at source and resident individuals are subject to Income Tax (50% of dividends for 1986 to 1989 are subject to Complementary Tax) less a credit for the withholding tax. For companies, income is subject to 15% withholding tax at source and resident companies are subject to corporation tax, less a credit for withholding tax suffered.

Dividends from a more than 25% subsidiary are exempt from corporate tax if held for more than 2 years or from the date of establishment of the company.

Stamp Duty

There is no stamp duty on purchases and sales of bonds and equities effected on Stock Exchange. Outside the Stock Exchange, transactions are subject to a stamp duty rate of 6%.

PROSPECTIVE DEVELOPMENTS

The Stock Exchanges in Portugal are presently undergoing re-structuring and it is expected that a Central Depository for Securities will be created. This will lead to the lifting of the physical delivery requirements that currently exist and allow for a greater volume of transactions. Broker firms are expected to be in a better position than individual brokers to cope with the growth of the market.

The prospects for growth of the securities market in Portugal are considered to be good, based not only on the emergence of new institutional investors, such as Investment Funds and Pension Funds, but also on the rising interest shown by foreign investors towards the Portuguese market.

New instruments are expected to be introduced shortly, including Convertible Bonds, Certificates of Deposit, and Commercial Paper.

SINGAPORE

Spicer and Pegler
(locally Foo, Kon & Tan)
Contact: Eric Tan, Tel: 336 3355

As a result of the problems associated with the collapse of the conglomerate Pan-Electric Industries, in December 1985, the government introduced the Securities Industry Act, 1986. The introduction of the legislation has effectively provided regulation by which the Singapore Central Bank, through the Monetary Authority of Singapore (MAS), can control the capital market. These regulations cover disclosure of information and control over the conduct of stockbrokers and the investment advisory industry. Legislation and developments in current regulations are still occurring which may further regulate and control the markets. The market has been separated from that in Malaysia since 1973.

Size

Singapore's market ranks as the third largest in the Far East, after Japan and Hong Kong. As at May 1987, there were 24 member firms on the Stock Exchange.

The December 31, 1987 figures for turnover and capitalization are as follows:

	Equities	Debentures, Bonds and Loan Stock
Turnover (S$ million)	22,000	595
Number of trades/bargains	8,800,000	940
Market capitalization (S$ billion)	86	194
Number of securities	321	137

158

On December 31, 1986 there were 317 companies listed on the Singapore Stock Exchange (SSE) of which 123 were Singapore-incorporated companies, 176 were Malaysian and 11 were from other countries.

The most commonly used stock price index is the Straits Times Index (STI) which is based upon the stock prices of 30 companies representing a cross-section of the industrial and commercial companies listed on the SSE.

Recent movements in this index were as follows:

Straits Times Industrial Share Index

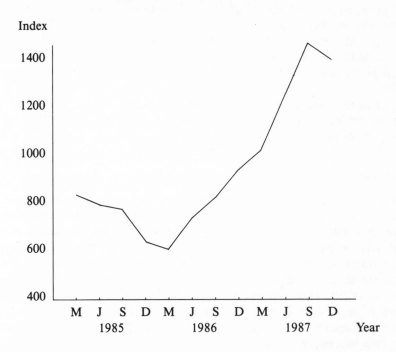

OVERVIEW OF THE BOND AND EQUITY MARKETS

Structure

Singapore has a tiered market with the Stock Exchange dividing the Official List of Companies into two sections—the First Trading Section and the Second Trading Section. Admission to the First Section is dependent on companies meeting minimum criteria with respect to capital, number of shareholders, turnover, and dividends, though the Stock

Exchange Committee may exempt a company which is unable to comply with many of these requirements, after taking into consideration its overall performance.

Approximately two-thirds of the companies listed on the Stock Exchange are included in the First Section with the remainder included in the Second Section. Shares listed in the Second Section may be promoted to the First Section when they satisfy the necessary requirements. The most significant trading difference between the two sections lies in the settlement procedures which are outlined next.

In 1987, the government introduced the Unlisted Securities Market (USM) to promote entrepreneurial growth and activity in the corporate sector. The market is regulated by the MAS and the Economic Development Board. The market, similar to the United Kingdom's USM, will be controlled by a electronic transaction system called SESDAQ which is modeled on the NASDAQ automated quotation system of the USA.

Trading sessions are held daily from Monday to Friday between the hours of 10:00 and 11:00, 11:15 and 12:30 and 14:30 and 16:00. Off-floor trading is permitted.

Execution

Transactions are executed through brokers, who can act as either principal or agent in any transaction, but who must disclose to clients the capacity in which they are acting. The system of price determination uses a call-over system, which involves the central collection of bids and offers to determine the highest bid and lowest offer of any particular stock which are then posted on the electronic board with the names of the relevant brokers. Deals are executed at these bid and offer prices until all orders at these prices have been transacted. The next highest bid/lowest offer prices are then posted and act as the ruling prices for trading until orders are successively exhausted.

For every transaction, information on stock, buy/sell price, volume of transaction and broker is publicly available on the same day. No limitations are placed on daily permissible price movements in securities.

Shares are generally traded in lots of 1000 and 2000 shares. For stock priced above S$10, trading may take place in lots of 100 and 500 shares.

Settlement and Clearing

Details rules regarding delivery and settlement between broker and client are defined in the by-laws.

Settlement procedures differ between securities listed on the First and Second Sections. Those listed on the Second Section are settled on a Ready Delivery basis which requires that all contracts be delivered by Tuesday in the week following the transaction. Settlement Contract trading (suspended 1986) applied only to First Section stocks and required that all contracts done on the 1000 lot board during the month were due for delivery on the last Thursday of each month. All contracts done on the 2000 lot board were due for delivery at mid-month on the dates specified by the Stock Exchange Committee. Shares traded on the First Section could be traded on a Ready Delivery basis if preferred.

Settlement procedures vary depending on the parties involved. When trading occurs between broker and client, if the broker receives a delivery by a selling client on any business day before 12:30, the broker must pay the amount due to the client before 11:00 on the second business day following. Payment by a purchasing client is to be made upon receipt of a debit note or upon notification that the securities purchased are ready for collection. Should the client fail to pay, a broker is entitled to withhold delivery of securities until the client's check in payment has been cleared by the bank.

When trading occurs between brokers, if the purchasing broker delivers shares before 12:30 on any business day they must be paid for before 11:00 on the next business day. Default in payment may give rise to an interest charge of 1% per month and possible action by the Stock Exchange Committee.

Effective from January 11, 1988 the Exchange will buy-in stocks where a selling broker fails to deliver on the settlement date. Stockbrokers may also buy in against clients who fail to deliver.

Since 1978, the Securities and Clearing and Computer Services Plc Ltd (SCCS) has provided an interbroker clearing service. The SCCS will utilize a central depository system in the future to act as a custodian for clients who do not wish to collect their certificates.

Market Characteristics

Commission Rates. The Stock Exchange sets minimum scales of commissions payable by both buyer and seller, which range between .5% and 1% of the contract value. Government securities, bonds, and debentures are charged fixed rates ranging from 0.25–1.0% of the transaction value. For any contract, the minimum brokerage payable is S$5. There are no other material costs of dealing.

Margin Trading. Margin trading is permitted by the Singapore Stock Exchange. There are no compulsory margin requirements, although the Stock

161

Exchange Committee and the Minister of Finance can impose margin requirements under the rules and by-laws of the Stock Exchange and the Securities Industry Act. In practice, margin covers are at the discretion of the brokers. Foreign investors are also permitted to deal on margin.

There are no rules either permitting or prohibiting borrowing of securities.

Investor Protection. The Securities Industry Act 1986 (the Act) provides for investor protection. Under the Act a dealer is prohibited from acting as principal with another person who is not the holder of a dealer's license without disclosing that he is acting as principal. Failure to comply with this section is an offense and entitles the other contracting party to rescind the contract within seven days after receipt of the contract note.

The Minister of Finance is empowered under the Act to establish regulations for the prohibition of trading on or off the floor of the Stock Exchange by stockbrokers or their representatives directly or indirectly for their own accounts or for discretionary accounts.

Under the provisions of the Act, the Stock Exchange has established a fidelity fund to compensate investors who suffer financial loss due to the dishonest misuse of their funds by a stockbroking company or any of its employees.

The Act also requires a broker to segregate his clients' money and certificates in a separate trust account. A dealer company is required to keep a General Scrip Register for recording the receipt and disposal of all securities by the dealer company and a Sale Custody Scrip Register for recording all securities held for such purposes.

Insider trading is a criminal offense with a maximum fine of S$50 thousand or seven years' imprisonment for an individual and maximum fine of S$100 thousand for a company.

The purposes of the Securities Industry Council (SIC), a consultative and advisory body, are:

- To advise the Ministry of Finance on all matters concerning the securities industry, including the administration of legislation particularly relating to protection of investors
- To advise the Committee of the Stock Exchange on matters referred to it and to consider recommendations submitted by the Committee, including listing requirements and suspension and delisting of companies
- To administer and enforce the Singapore Code on Takeovers and Mergers

New Issues

New issues during 1987 were as follows:

	Equities	Debentures, Bonds and Loan Stock
Number	7	4
Issue price	S$700m	S$318m

New issues must be approved by the Stock Exchange and the Securities Industry Council (SIC). New issues can be effected in three ways: a rights issue, allotted to third parties, or an offering for public subscription.

Under the Companies Act, the underwriting commission must not exceed 10% of the total issue value or the amount authorized by the company's Articles of Association, whichever is lower. However, the prevalent rate is estimated at between 1.25% and 2% of total issue value.

FUTURES AND OPTIONS TRADING

The futures market in Singapore is regulated by the Singapore International Monetary Exchange (SIMEX). SIMEX has four main functions:

- Providing facilities (trading floor and an advanced trade matching and clearing system) to facilitate the trading of SIMEX futures contracts
- Establishing and enforcing a set of rules to ensure that all trading is carried on in a regulated manner
- Disseminating market information to all users
- Providing arbitration facilities for disputes that may arise in the conduct of trading

SIMEX financial futures contracts are interchangeable with those traded in the International Monetary Market of the Chicago Mercantile Exchange (CME). SIMEX and the CME have developed a mutual offset system whereby positions established on SIMEX can be closed in the CME. The futures contracts traded on the SIMEX include a Eurodollar interest rate, Japanese yen, and deutschmark, pound sterling, Swiss francs, Nikkei stock index futures, international gold futures, and U.S. treasury bonds. Trading hours are between 9:20 and 13:20.

The SIMEX futures market employs the open outcry competitive system of trading. The best bids and offers are announced publicly along with the actual deals traded. Trading information on price, volume, and open interest is made public. Trades are settled on a daily basis, whereby SIMEX undertakes failed contracts.

The Singapore Stock Exchange provides the only equities options trading market in the Far East at present. Options are written for lots of 1000 shares and are issued with fixed time periods which expire on the last Friday of March, June, September, and December.

The Options Clearing Company, a wholly-owned subsidiary of the Stock Exchange, provides the facilities for the registration and recording of options transactions.

Membership Requirements for SIMEX

There are no citizen or residency requirements for SIMEX other than normal immigration or corporate requirements. There are three types of membership:

- A clearing member, (being a corporate member), holds three seats, exercises full trading rights on the floor, clears trades and accepts customer business
- A nonclearing member, (being a company incorporated in Singapore), holds three seats on the Exchange, exercises full trading rights on the floor and accepts customer business. All trades must be qualified by and cleared by a clearing member, and;
- An individual nonclearing member holds one seat, trades on their own account, and may act for other members. All trades must be confirmed by and cleared by a clearing member.

There is no restriction on foreign ownership of SIMEX seats as long as the foreign company maintains a subsidiary or a branch in Singapore. Membership is also open to foreign individuals.

The open market price of a seat on SIMEX ranges from S$60,000 to S$70,000.

Commission Rates

Commission generally charged by members is US$6 per SIMEX contract.

REGULATIONS AFFECTING NEW ENTRANTS TO THE MARKETS

All firms dealing in securities must be either members of the Stock Exchange or approved overseas representative offices. The regulatory authorities in the market are the Stock Exchange and the government. The main statutory regulations which affect the securities industry are as follows:

1. Self-regulation by the Stock Exchange based on its Memorandum and Articles of Association, Rules and By-laws, Listing Manual and Corporate Disclosure policy.

2. The Securities Industry Act, which is administered by the MAS, includes the following areas:

- The establishment and operation of stock markets which require ministerial approval.
- The licensing of dealers and investment advisers and their respective representative.
- Proper accounts and documents which must be maintained by dealers in securities, including trust accounts which will be subject to audit.
- Investment of stockbrokers' trust funds.
- The establishment and administration of a Fidelity Fund.
- Prohibition of unfair trading, such as insider trading and market rigging.

3. The Singapore Code on Takeovers and Mergers, administered by the SIC, gives guidance on the principles of conduct and procedures to follow in takeovers and mergers.

4. The Companies Act, Chapter 185 and Companies Regulations administered by the Registrar of Companies.

Market entry is governed by the rules, by-laws and requirements of the Stock Exchange. Listed companies must sign an agreement to comply with the requirements of the Listing Manual and Corporate Disclosure Policy.

Membership Requirements

The Stock Exchange has two categories of membership—corporate and individual. In the corporate category, securities firms must be Singapore-incorporated companies with either limited or unlimited liability, whose shareholders (in the case of subsidiaries of local banks, their directors) have been approved by the committee of the Stock Exchange. A limited company must have a minimum paid-up capital of S$2 million or a minimum liquid capital calculated along the guidelines described in the Stock Exchange Rules, whichever is the greater. It must have at least two qualified stockbroking members who should jointly hold no less than 51% of the paid-up capital of the member company.

An unlimited company may be formed by any two stockbroking members of which one must be a qualified stockbroking member. An individual representing a member company must also have a valid dealer's license.

Foreign membership is achieved by holding shares in stockbroking firms which are member companies of the Stock Exchange of Singapore. Foreign ownership can be as high as 49% of the equity of the stockbroking firm. At present, there are seven firms with foreign interests.

Individual members can be the directors and shareholders of the securities firms and are known as stockbroking members. To qualify for admission as a stockbroking member, an individual must be at least 21 years of age, a Singapore citizen or have resided in Singapore for not less than five years, and must hold a professional qualification or have experience which is acceptable to the Committee of the Stock Exchange. A membership application must be proposed and seconded by existing members. A person elected initially becomes a provisional member for three years and thereafter becomes a qualified member. In addition to stockbrokers, dealers' representatives are attached to stockbroking companies and they can also handle the trading of shares. Dealers' representatives may be employed by stockbroking companies or act as agents if they pass the Stock Exchange Dealers' Representatives examination or hold equivalent qualifications acceptable to the Committee.

A member company cannot, without the consent of the Stock Exchange Committee, act as a broker for a company in conjunction with another person which is not a member of a recognized Stock Exchange. It may not have its name appear as a broker or underwriter in any new issue which is underwritten or counderwritten by persons who are not members of a recognized Stock Exchange unless they have been approved by the Stock Exchange Committee. A member company cannot establish a branch office within Singapore unless approved by the Committee.

Corporate membership is obtained by the subscription of one share in the Stock Exchange. Only corporate members may hold shares in the Stock Exchange and not more than one share is to be allotted to a member company.

The costs of joining the Stock Exchange vary according to the category of membership. There is an entrance fee of S$5,000 for individual membership and a monthly subscription fee of S$125. For corporate membership, there is a share subscription price which is revised periodically by the Stock Exchange Committee.

Liquidity Requirements. A member company must ensure that the liquid capital employed in the business is not less that S$100,000 for each dealers' representative (who is not a stockbroking member) during the first years of its operation. From that point on, liquidity can be maintained either at that level or at an amount that is equivalent to four times the monthly net commission earned (gross commission less rebates permitted under the by-laws).

There are reporting requirements whereby a member company must submit a copy of its Memorandum and Articles of Association as well as a copy of its annual return to the Stock Exchange for approval. The annual return must also be filed with the Registrar of Companies. Each member company is subject to an annual audit by auditors approved by the Stock Exchange.

Representation by Members of Foreign Exchanges. Members of foreign Stock Exchanges may establish an approved overseas representative office in Singapore. This does not amount to membership of the Stock Exchange, but is an arrangement whereby the member of a recognized foreign Stock Exchange can establish a branch office in Singapore and deal with members of the Stock Exchange of Singapore through that branch. Branch offices of members of foreign Stock Exchanges which do not have such approved status can only deal with Stock Exchange members as clients. This measure has been introduced in an effort to improve the expertise of the industry and improve Singapore's status as a financial center.

Repatriation of income is permitted as there are no foreign Exchange control restrictions in Singapore. Proceeds arising from the sale of securities may be remitted abroad without any foreign Exchange restriction.

OUTLINE OF CORPORATE AND INDIVIDUAL TAX CONSIDERATIONS

Company taxation applies to all brokers. Deductible expenses include depreciation and interest. Net losses may be carried forward and deducted against the net profits of future years only if the shareholders and their respective shareholdings as of December 31 of the loss year remain the same as those at January 1 of the tax year in which the losses are utilized. Withholding tax, currently at 33% or at treaty rates, applies to royalties, interest, management fees, technical assistance, rentals and directors' fees that are paid to nonresidents of Singapore. An individual (either resident or nonresident) is subject to tax on profits derived from or accrued in Singapore.

Residents

Government Bonds—Current Income. Interest income is generally subject to normal tax rates. Interest derived from specific Government bonds held as investments is tax-free. If the income arised as part of a trade or business, tax is charged at normal rates but a tax credit of 50% is available.

Government Bonds—Capital Gains. There is no tax on capital gains. Profits arising from the sale of securities are taxable when related to a trade or business or when they have an income nature, even though the transaction is not connected with a trade or business. Profits arising from a sale and which have a capital nature are not liable to tax.

Equities—Dividends. Generally dividends received from shares are taxable income in the hands of the recipients unless they are specified as exempt dividends. A tax rate of 33% is deemed to be deducted at source, and a tax credit of 33% is granted against the ultimate tax payable. Dividends derived from foreign shares are taxable only if they are received in Singapore.

Equities—Capital Gains. The same rules apply as for government bonds.

Traded Options—Current Income. Profits arising from transactions in traded options are taxable as income when related to a trade or business or when they have an income nature, even though the transaction is not connected with a trade or business.

Traded Options—Capital Gains. The same rules apply as for government bonds.

Financial Futures

To stimulate the growth of the financial futures market the government has granted SIMEX a five-year tax concession on its income derived from futures activities. Corporate and individual members of SIMEX are taxed at the offshore concessionary rate of 10% on income derived from transactions in gold bullion or in any approved commodity in addition to financial futures on any approved exchange or in any approved market with:

1. An Asian Currency Unit of a financial institution.
2. Another member of SIMEX.

3. A person who is neither a resident of, nor has a permanent establishment in, Singapore.

To the other market users who are not members of SIMEX, the profit/gain is taxable if the conditions described above for government bonds are met.

Nonresidents

Government Bonds—Current Income. Interest on government bonds which are not tax-exempt are liable to 33% withholding tax or a reduced rate under double tax treaties.

Government Bonds—Capital Gains. Singapore income tax is imposed on a territorial basis; a nonresident will be liable to tax on income accrued or derived from Singapore. Therefore tax treatment described for residents is also applicable to nonresidents.

Equities—Current Income. There is no withholding tax on dividends paid to nonresidents. The tax at 33% deducted from payment of Singapore dividends is deemed to be an underlying tax.

Equities—Capital Gains. The same rules apply as for government bonds.

Traded Options. The same treatment as for dividends paid to nonresidents.

Financial Futures

The same rules apply as for residents (see also government bonds, nonresident capital gains).

Stamp Duty

Stamp duty on contract notes is levied on both buyer and seller at the rate of S$1 for each S$1,000 of contract value, and stamp duty on registering ownership of share by the buyer at 20 cents for each S$100 of share value. There is no stamp duty payable on government bonds and financial futures.

PROSPECTIVE DEVELOPMENTS

A second securities market which will be supervised by the Stock Exchange is to be established. This market will serve as an alternative source of long-term funds for young and growing companies which do not yet qualify for listing on the main Stock Exchange.

Apart from member firms of the Singapore Stock Exchange, financial institutions such as banks will also be permitted to deal in this market. A working committee consisting of members of the government, the Stock Exchange and the banking and merchant banking community has been formed to assist with the establishment of this market.

SOUTH AFRICA

Fisher Hoffman & Stride
Contact: Geoff West, Tel: (011) 643 7361

There is one Stock Exchange in South Africa, located in Johannesburg. For the first 50 years of its existence, the Johannesburg Stock Exchange (JSE) was essentially a mining market but this emphasis changed with postwar industrial development. Now mining companies represent less than 20% of the market.

Size

The JSE has 41 member firms, who are able to act both as banker and principal.

The 1987 figures for equities and government bonds are as follows:

	Equities	Gilts and Semi-Gilts
Turnover (R million)	19,471	165,192
Number of trades/bargains (deals)	1,354,582	

Gilts are securities which are issued directly by the government or treasury. A semi-gilt is a security which is issued by a municipality or a quasi-goverment agency, such as the Post Office or the South African Transport Services.

There is significant trading in equities dealt on dual Stock Exchanges, for example De Beers, Minorco and Barlow Rand are all dealt on both the Johannesburg and London Stock Exchanges.

Very few overseas stocks or bonds are however listed on the local Exchange. Overseas stocks or bonds not listed on the local Exchange may only be dealt in subject to Exchange control approval. Such approval is rarely granted except in the case of institutions such as pension funds, assurance companies, etc.

The most representative accepted index is the JSE Actuaries Overall Index, which reflects the performance of the largest companies listed on the Exchange. It is calculated several times each day. Recent figures for the index are as follows:

JSE Actuaries Overall Index

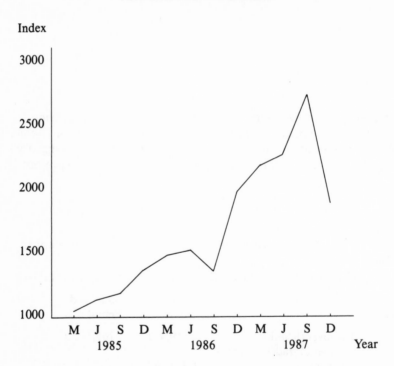

OVERVIEW OF THE BOND AND EQUITY MARKETS

Structure

There is no over-the-counter market, but a second-tier market, the Development Capital Market (DCM), was established in 1984. The DCM is listed as a section of the JSE share market. To date, 85 companies have been listed in this section. Though off-shore trading in South African stocks, especially in gold and mining financials, is the most significant area of trading, there is also considerable activity in government securities.

On-the-floor trading hours are 9:30 to 16:00 for equities and 7:00 to 15:00 for government bonds. Off-the-floor trading can occur any time after hours, but deals must be reported the following day for monitoring purposes.

The majority of total trading occurs on the floor, with only a small percentage occurring after hours. Since there are no "jobbers," there is no separation of function between member firms. However, firms transact business for clients on an agency basis only and are prohibited from acting as principal and agent in the same transaction. Member firms have no obligations for trading, that is, there are no commitments to make prices in a share, except in the case of the broker in odd lots who is a specialist broker.

Execution

There are no trading posts; execution is by open outcry of bid-and-offer prices in front of the relevant section of the trading board.

The price is determined by negotiation for each transaction. For regulatory purposes, reporting requirements state that the Stock Exchange must be notified by both parties of the price of the transaction for immediate recording on the market prices board. Shortly thereafter, full details of each transaction must be submitted by each broker to the Stock Exchange Clearing House. There are no limits on daily permissible prime movements. Shares are normally traded in R100's or multiples thereof, although an odd lot market is available through a specialist broker.

Settlement and Clearing

There is a weekly clearing system whereby net balances in each stock are settled via the Clearing House. The Friday closing prices constitute the settlement price and differences between this and the dealing price, both adverse and favorable, are settled with brokers on the Monday following the transaction. Net balance differences are settled on Tuesday and any balances which may still be outstanding go into the next week for settlement at the new price. Clients must settle with brokers within seven business days. Banks and institutions with R1 million of net assets, where settlement is generally against delivery of the share certificate, are excluded from the seven-day settlement rule.

173

SOUTH AFRICA

Market Characteristics

Commission Rates. Commission rates for equities are fixed, and the current scale ranges from 0.20% to 1.20% depending on the value of the transaction. A rate of 0.6% of the value is applicable to nonconvertible bonds and notes and other fixed interest loans with a fixed rate of dividend.

There are no fixed rates on discretionary managed accounts, the charge being dependent on the performance and value of the portfolio.

Other costs associated with dealing include a basic charge of one cent per share with a maximum of R25 (i.e., 2500 shares) paid to the broker. The buyer also pays a marketable securities tax of 1.5% of the transaction value.

Margin Trading. Margin trading is permissible, but as a proportion of total Exchange volume it is negligible. Brokers must finance margin lending from their own resources. There are no defined rules for settling margin accounts, but double cover must be maintained whereby clients are given margin only up to 50% of the value of the shares pledged. Foreign investors are not permitted to deal on margin. The Clearing House provides a medium through which brokers can borrow stock from other brokers.

Investor Protection. Firms are prohibited from acting as principal and agent in the same transaction. A full-time internal inspectorate with complete access to brokers' records exists within the Stock Exchange. In addition, there is a guarantee fund in case brokers go into liquidation. As a final resort, brokers have joint and several liability.

Reporting requirements require brokers to submit annual and half yearly audited financial statements to the Stock Exchange inspectorate. Brokers are also subject to an additional surprise audit, following which reports are submitted to the Stock Exchange inspectorate. Firms with safe custody facilities are subject to another surprise scrip count by the inspectorate.

New Issues

In 1987, there were 211 new equity issues.

New issues are registered with the Registrar of Companies in Pretoria, and stockbrokers are obliged to create a market.

An offer for sale (i.e., a public offer) is the most common method of issue. Underwriting is usually handled by a consortium of a stockbroker, merchant bank, and sub-underwriters. The stockbroker or merchant bank will usually manage the issue, although DCM issues may be handled by a firm of chartered accountants. The price and timing of the issue are determined through agreement among the stockbroker, merchant bank, and the company. Current underwriting rates are negotiable, but are usually between 1% and 2.5% of the actual capital to be raised.

FUTURES AND OPTIONS TRADING

South Africa has no financial futures market at present, but the establishment of such a market is currently under investigation. Options trading is minor, but a clearing house is being established to cater specifically for this market. South Africa is still in the process of standardizing options documents for trading purposes. To date, these markets deal with options for government bonds, public authority bonds, Krugerrands (gold coins), and shares.

The Stock Exchange is represented on the Reserve Bank Committee which has been established to investigate the introduction and eventual control of an options and futures market. The proposed rules of operation are similar to those for bond and equity markets, but these have not been universally approved, nor do they have government backing.

REGULATIONS AFFECTING NEW ENTRANTS TO THE MARKETS

The JSE, which is controlled externally by the Stock Exchange Control Act, sets rules and regulations for its members. Dealing is between brokers on behalf of the public. Unlike London and New York, there are no jobbers or specialists.

The agencies charged with regulation of the market are the JSE and the Registrar of Financial Institutions. The main statutory regulation is the Stock Exchange Control Act 1985, which places a wide range of restrictions on securities houses. All firms trading in securities must be members of the Stock Exchange.

Membership Requirements

Brokerage firms must have unlimited liability, either in the form of a partnership or an unlimited company. Members of the Exchange must be South African citizens, reside locally, and derive the majority of their income from activities on the Stock Exchange.

Before becoming a member of the Stock Exchange each partner or director must pass an entrance examination and have served a satisfactory probationary period of three to four years. Individual members of the Stock Exchange must also purchase a minimum of three rights at their market price which is currently around R22,000 each. On joining the Stock Exchange, each member must also pay an entrance fee of R5,000, a payment to the guarantee fund of R800 and an annual subscription of R2,000.

Capital and Liquidity Requirements

Minimum capital for each firm is R40,000 for the first two partners or directors and R10,000 for each subsequent partner or director although this is likely to be increased to R40,000 in the near future.

Additional trading liquidity requirements state that transactions deemed to be at risk must not exceed twice the adjusted liquid capital in the firm, as defined by the rules of the Stock Exchange.

OUTLINE OF CORPORATE AND INDIVIDUAL TAX CONSIDERATIONS

Both businesses and individuals are subject to normal tax, ranging from 16 to 50% for individuals and 47 1/2% for companies. Specific rules are:

Residents

Government Bonds—Current Income. Interest income is fully taxable as part of total income.

Government Bonds—Capital Gains. Capital gains are tax-exempt on surpluses of a capital nature unless bonds have been acquired, held and disposed in terms of a profit-making scheme, in which case the surplus on disposal is fully taxable.

Equities—Current Income

Individuals. Dividend income from equities forms part of taxable income, but a percentage of company dividends is allowed as a deduction. The deduction (varying between 33.33% and 100%) is related to the amount of the total income.

Companies. Companies are not liable to normal tax on dividend receipts. They are, however, subject to undistributed profits tax (UPT) at the rate of 33.33% on dividends which are not redistributed by the company during its specified period. The specified period begins six months after the beginning of its fiscal year and ends six months after the tax year end.

Equities—Capital Gains

The same rules apply as for government bonds.

Nonresidents

Government Bonds—Current Income. Interest income received by nonresidents is tax-exempt. No withholding tax is levied.

Government Bonds—Capital Gains. The same rules apply as for residents.

Equities—Current Income (Individuals and Companies)

Dividends received by nonresidents are exempt from normal income tax. Such dividends are, however, liable to withholding tax of 15%. This rate is reduced under certain double taxation agreements to 7.5% or 5%.

Equities—Capital Gains

The same rules apply as for residents.

Stamp Duty

There is no stamp duty on the acquisition or disposal of government bonds. Stamp duty of 1% of the value is payable by the purchaser on the acquisition of equities.

Traded Options and Financial Futures

As these markets are in an embryonic state, no specific tax rules have been laid down.

PROSPECTIVE DEVELOPMENTS

The major development anticipated is the establishment of a Take-Over Panel, whose purpose would be to enforce decisions on mergers and takeovers. It is envisaged that there will be co-operation and discussion between the JSE Committee and the Panel, and the JSE will be represented on such a Panel. The objectives and functions of such a Panel are intended to be incorporated in the Companies Act. Discussions on this Panel are underway and legislation is expected to be introduced in 1988.

Although deregulation is being discussed, it is not likely to have impact on the potential entry of foreign securities houses for several years.

The establishment of a financial futures market is under investigation, and such a market is expected to be established in the near future.

SPAIN

Audihispana
Contact: Jorge Escudero, Tel: (1) 521 91 10

There are four Stock Exchanges (Bolsas) in Spain of which the Madrid Exchange is the largest with around 80% of the total turnover. The Barcelona Bolsa is the second largest, with two smaller Exchanges in Bilbao and Valencia.

The market figures for the Madrid Exchange in 1987 were:

(Pta Million)	Shares	Debentures	Public Securities
Turnover	3,681,763	118,228	105,750
Number of securities	N/A	N/A	N/A

At the end of 1987 the Madrid Exchange had 87 members (stockbrokers).

Indices

The main index on the Madrid Exchange is the general index, which currently comprises 72 securities. Up until the start of 1986, the index was rebased at the end of every year to 100.

Madrid Stock Exchange
Share Price Index

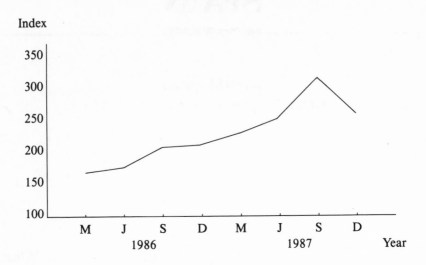

Index

OVERVIEW OF THE BOND AND EQUITY MARKETS

Structure

Stockbrokers on the Madrid Exchange operate purely as intermediaries between buyers and sellers, and therefore not as agents and do not deal on their own account or make markets. Generally, a potential investor will deal through one of the Spanish banks, who are not themselves members of the Bolsa, and the banks then use the stockbroker to match the buyer with a seller on the market. Stockbrokers are prohibited from providing advisory or other services (these being provided by the banks), and from having more than three traders within the firm.

Trading takes place between 9:30 and 12:30, with a later session for the more active securities to coincide with other European and New York markets.

Since late 1986, there has been a second tier market for smaller companies, and these securities are traded in a similar manner to the main market.

The majority of trading is concentrated in the securities of a small group composed mainly of banks and public utilities, including the state-run telecommunications company Telefonica. This narrowness of the

180

market causes some liquidity problems and is seen as a factor holding back the expansion of the Spanish Stock Markets.

Execution

Prices are set based on a call-over system, that is, the matching of sale and purchase orders at pre-specified times on the Bolsa floor. In these periods, transactions may take place at different prices according to the calls of buying and selling brokers or representatives. Prices are determined by brokers "crying out" bids and offers.

Most of the 350 shares listed on the Madrid Stock Exchange are traded according to this call-over system, but 46 registered shares, mainly bank securities, are traded by an auction system, the Sistema de Caja.

Prices are presently quoted as a percentage of nominal value, the minimum unit of change being $\frac{1}{8}$%, although a change to the more normal Peseta-per-share basis is now under consideration. A minimum volume of transactions of 250,000 pesetas or 500 shares is required to move the price. Trading is under the supervision of the Delegate of the Council for Quotations who may intervene to ensure the fairness and liquidity of the market.

On the Madrid Stock Exchange prices may not change from one day to the next by more then 10% for shares, 2% for corporate bonds, and 1% for government securities. Larger variations may take place with official permission.

Treasury bills and commercial paper are traded through a competitive tender. However, before trading the selling brokers communicate their lots to the central computer, which classifies them according to different issues. The auctioneer then offers the lots from the different issues, prices being quoted on the basis of discount from nominal.

The Official List is split between two basic kinds of issues, cotizacion calificada and cotizacion simple, the first one fulfilling the more stringent requirements in terms of frequency and turnover.

Settlement and Clearing

Settlements in Spain are complicated and the increase in business has caused settlement problems, as systems are often slow. However, steps have been taken to simplify the procedures. There are now three types of securities:

1. "New System" Securities which no longer require physical movement in order to change hands, being settled through a "book-entry" transfer

system. Requiring only an exchange of Technical Reference Number between parties involved. No physical delivery to the new owner is needed.

2. "Old System" Registered or Nominative Securities which require physical delivery to the new owner and registration with the issuing company of the new name holding them. It is often not known when the seller, through the distribution system of the Stock Exchange, will be able to produce the securities. For this reason, no exact payment date exists.

3. "Old System" Bearer shares which subject to payment being made, are usually delivered on the Friday of the week following the deal.

Stockbrokers can take direct orders from the public, but most orders are channelled through the banks, or through licensed stockbroker companies (of which there are 14).

New Issues

The 1987 figures for new issues on the Madrid Bolsa were as follows:

	New Companies	Shares	Bonds	Companies Already Listed Public Securities
Value (Pta billions)	386.5	387.0	815.9	1,205.4
Number	18	N/A	N/A	N/A

Market Characteristics

Commission Rates. Trading in shares and bonds is controlled by the 87 Agents de Cambie who notarize the transactions and take a fixed commission in the process.

Brokers' Commission

Shares. For share prices below 500 pts, commission is calculated at a flat rate per share of 0.80 pts or 1.50 pts per share. For share prices over 500 pts commission is calculated at 0.25% of the gross proceeds.

Public debt issued by the state. Commissions range from 0.016% to 0.125%.

Subscription Rights. For rights prices below 500 pts, commission is calculated at a flat rate per share of 0.5 pts, 0.8 pts or 1.5 pts per share. For rights prices over 500 pts commission is calculated at 0.25% of the gross proceeds.

Settlement fees are charged by the Stock Exchange Committee for each bargain ranging from 150 pts to 250 pts.

Stamp duty or "Poliza" is payable on purchases over 2 million pts at 11 pts per each 10 thousand pts consideration.

Investor Protection. Insider trading is not prohibited, and is believed to occur frequently. The Spanish government is currently considering ways of solving this problem but there is strong opposition from within the Exchange itself.

FUTURES AND OPTIONS TRADING

There are currently no futures or options markets in Spain.

REGULATIONS AFFECTING NEW ENTRANTS TO THE MARKETS

Spanish Stock Exchanges are governed by the 1967 General Rule of Stock Exchanges. However, much of the day to day operation of the Madrid Exchange is supervised by the Junta Sindical a regulatory body elected from amongst the members of the Exchange.

The Stock Exchange Council (Consejo Superior de Bolsas) is responsible for the basic control mechanisms in the markets, including ensuring that new shares are registered within 90 days. The Spanish Treasury is also required to approve the issues of new commercial paper.

Any trading in Spanish securities must be certified by a licensed stockbroker (in Madrid there are 87 licensed stockbrokers).

In order to become a member of the Exchange, it is necessary to hold a seat—these are granted to a registered public broker on passing an official examination. At present there are no foreign Exchange members.

No rules are imposed on members of the Stock Exchange concerning net capital or accounts filing as long as the members are individuals.

OUTLINE OF CORPORATE AND INDIVIDUAL TAX CONSIDERATIONS

Spain is trying hard to encourage foreign investment and a number of changes to the tax law have recently been made. At present, foreign individuals may freely purchase and sell securities in Spain as well as repatriate the income from those investments.

All proceeds from investments, including capital gains, profits, and dividends, may be converted into foreign currency and repatriated as long as the original investment was made in foreign currency. No minimum time limit exists as to the period of investment or the currency in which amounts resulting from the sale of the investment may be remitted. However, these remittances are subject to tax clearance. Permission from the authorities is however required when a transaction involves more than 50% of a company's stock. The current tax situation is as follows:

Residents

Resident companies are liable to corporation tax on world-wide income, including capital gains.

Nonresidents

Nonresident companies are liable to corporation tax on income, including capital gains, arising in Spain.

However, a distinction is made between resident and nonresident shareholders. Nonresidents receiving income from a Spanish source are subject to withholding tax at a rate of 18% on dividends and interest income. Such withholding tax is subject to amendment by any double taxation treaties in existence. Capital gains and losses are added or deducted when computing the basis of the tax.

PROSPECTIVE DEVELOPMENTS

The government is currently reviewing the operations of the Bolsa. The proposed changes are many but are expected to include a nationwide Stock Exchange rather than the four separate markets which presently exist. Such a change would probably see the introduction of an overall regulatory body to control the Exchange and to outlaw insider trading.

Other changes would see the introduction of variable commission rates and the removal of the current monopoly held by the Agents.

Continuous trading is expected to replace the current ring (Corros) system in the near future.

SWEDEN

Spicer & Oppenheim

Contact: Peter Oliver (London), Tel: (01) 480 7766

The Stockholm Stock Exchange (SSE) or Stockholm Fondbors, is the only Stock Exchange in Sweden.
Trading statistics of the Exchange for 1986 were as follows:

	Equities	Government Bonds	Other Bonds
Turnover (SEK billion)	226	960	207
Number of trades/bargains	413,000	Not registered	Not registered
Market capitalization (SEK billion)	433	70*	79
Number of securities	161	111	1,573

*Includes SEK 18,500m non-interest bearing lottery bonds

There are 13 banks and 17 brokers on the SSE, although it is not a requirement for all firms trading in securities to be members of the SSE. An active over-the-counter market (OTC) exists which caters for small and medium-sized companies.
Trading statistics of the OTC market for 1986 were as follows:

	Equities
Turnover (SEK million)	2,100
Number of trades/bargains (million)	3,600
Market capitalization (SEK million)	9,239
Number of securities	72

Foreigners trading on the SSE represented in excess of 10% of the turnover of equities. There are 22 Swedish companies listed on one or more of the major foreign Stock Exchanges. It is estimated that London sees a greater turnover in the largest Swedish companies than Stockholm. The strict currency regulations have restricted Swedish investment in foreign equities to SEK 168 million although turnover amounted to SEK 5,500 million. Sweden has laws which, generally, allow foreign ownership. However, should such ownership exceed 40% of equity or 20% of voting power, the company cannot own land nor trade in securities. There are no trading/settlement links with overseas markets.

In excess of 35% of trading in securities in Sweden takes place outside the opening hours of the SSE. In the case of bonds, all secondary market transactions are carried out by SSE members or other brokers from their own trading inventory and thereafter notified to SSE. Other financial instruments such as options and futures are traded by banks and brokers without obligation to report to SSE.

The SSE calculates an index for all registered equities, weighted by the latest price paid and taking into account capitalization changes. Weekly journals Affarsvarlden and Veckans Affarer publicize their own indices, and recent movements on the Affarsvarlden are shown below.

Affarsvarlden All Share Index

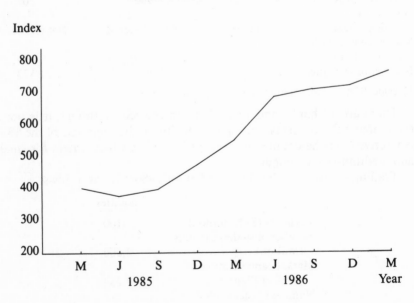

186

OVERVIEW OF THE BOND AND EQUITY MARKETS

Structure

The market is divided into four segments for equities:

- Stock Exchange A1 and A2 lists
- OTC
- Unofficial parallel market

STOCK EXCHANGE A1 and A2 LISTS

The A1 List consists of the 50 leading equities and is only open to the largest companies, with the most widely held equity.

The A2 List comprises all other listed securities—the key criteria for admission to the A2 list being shareholders' funds of SEK 4 million and at least 400 shareholders.

Over-the-Counter Market. This market has been in existence since 1982, to provide a market for companies not able to meet the requirement for listing. Although formed with the assistance of SSE, trading takes place away from the Exchange floor.

Unofficial Parallel Market. This consists of trading in shares both on and off the Exchange floor. Most shares traded are those which are no longer listed on the A1 and A2 lists or those which are closely held and where there is therefore not the volume of sellers necessary for listing.

In the case of bonds there are three categories registered by the SSE but which are traded outside the SSE to a significant extent:

- Government bonds
- Municipal and housing bonds
- Industrial bonds

Other financial instruments also traded outside the SSE are:

- Treasury bills—cash and forwards
- Commercial papers
- Forwards in government and housing bonds

The auction for A1 equities commences at 10:00 and finishes at approximately 11:00. Floor trading commences at 10:00 for equities not auctioned and finishes at 14:30. Off-floor trading generally commences at 8:30 and finishes at 17:00. Approximately 60% of trades are performed on the floor or by auction and 40% off the floor.

In the main, members only act as agents but are allowed to carry a trading inventory to facilitate business. The level of the permitted inventory is based on 4% of turnover and cannot exceed SEK 50 million.

There is no commitment by members of the SSE to make continuous markets, but banks and brokers take on market-making functions according to arrangements made with the issuers of OTC equities and other financial instruments.

Execution

In the case of A1 list equities, prices are initially determined each day by the call-over or auction process, whereby a price at which buyers and sellers are matched is determined for each security in turn, while the prices of all other equities (and the A1 list equities after the finish of the auction) are based on bid and offer.

Transaction reporting regulations require that closing notes be executed by banks and brokers.

Information is available to the public including buy, sell, closing (latest day high and low), and volume which is maintained electronically. The equivalent information is available for the OTC market and for other financial instruments on Reuters screens.

There are no limits on price movements in stocks but large and unusual movements are closely monitored by the SSE and the Bank Inspectors Board (BIB).

Shares are normally traded in multiples of 50 shares with the object that the value of each bargain approximates:

- A1 list SEK 20,000
- A2 list SEK 10,000
- OTC SEK 5,000

Settlement and Clearing

SSE rules require payment 5 days after the date of the transaction. The actual stock however, must be delivered the day after the deal was transacted. There are no formal "book-entry" procedures for share transfer although a bank and state owned organization, VPC, handles the registration and prints new share certificates for the buyer and destroys the old ones. However, banks and brokers which hold client share certificates in safe custody may be registered instead of the owner.

Market Characteristics

Commission rates are negotiable but generally fall in the range 0.5% for bargains of SEK 500,000 or less and 0.3% for bargains over SEK 500,000. There are no commissions on the trading of bonds except for lottery bonds which have a fixed charge per bond.

Margin Trading. An investor may borrow from the broker conducting a transaction, that is, trade on margin. No strict rules apply to the margins required, but the Banker's Union has issued an advisory list of prudent pledgeable share values which require margins of 30–40%. Foreign investors are not permitted to trade on margin.

Stock borrowing/lending is not permitted.

New Issues

Statistics for 1986 are as follows:

1. Equities

	Ordinary Shares	Loan Conversions and Options	Rights Issues
Number of issuing companies			
SSE	8	N/A	9
OTC	6	N/A	3
Value (SEK million)			
SSE	400	72	1,106
OTC	60	N/A	229

In addition to the above:
- New loans convertible to shares amounted to SEK 3,000 million
- New issues to foreign Exchange amounted to SEK 2,366 million

2. Others
- Bonds: SEK 144,373 million
- Commercial papers: Lines granted SEK 29,145 million

FUTURE AND OPTIONS TRADING

Options trading is permitted in Sweden, and both call and put options are available on the major securities as well as index options and certain interest rate options.

There is also a financial futures market which trades in two stock index futures and bond futures.

The Market. Stockholms' Optionsmark and OM Fondkommission AB started in 1985 and is a broker operating under BIB license and inspection. The firm created a marketplace with clearing functions including a guarantee of fulfillment. Operations are based on dealings by terminal and telephone with 32 brokers and market makers. Turnover in 1986 was SEK 10,000 million. The number of equity contracts was 2.1 million with a year-end open balance in excess of 300,000. The number of interest contracts traded during the last quarter of 1986 was 250,000 with an open balance of 70,000.

Sweden Options and Futures Exchange (SOFE) started in 1986, and is broadly backed with ownership by the securities industry. The SSE has an option to acquire the company in 1989. It operates a floor trading system closing at 15:00, not allowing dealings to be registered after that time, it has now acquired one third of the index-based market and is planning to introduce new financial products.

Trading, Settlement, and Delivery. An option contract is for 100 shares, for 6-months duration with three groups rolling in three-month intervals. The underlying shares have to be delivered as security. The options can be exercised at any time in the period, unless they are index-based. Forward contracts have to be fulfilled at maturity. Futures are cleared daily. Interest options are for SEK 1 million for 6-months duration and price is quoted in fixed intervals of 0.2%. The option can only be exercised at maturity.

There are no trading or settlement links with overseas options and futures markets.

REGULATIONS AFFECTING NEW ENTRANTS TO THE MARKETS

The regulatory authorities are:

Bankinspektionen	BIB
Riksbanken	Central Bank

The statutory regulations covering the finance and securities industry are:

- Lag om vardepappersmarknaden—Law on securities' market
- Lag om Stockholms' Fondbors—Law on Stockholm Stock Exchange
- Fondkommissionslag—Law on professional securities trading in own name for others
- Aktiebolagslagen—Company law

Anyone trading professionally in securities as an agent in their own name can only do so with a permit from the BIB, granted basically on discretionary judgment. The formal requirement is that the trader must be a Swedish-owned limited liability company with share capital not less than SEK 500,000 with an authorized public accountant as auditor, or be a Swedish bank.

On a continuing basis, the BIB sets reporting requirements, elects its own auditor and conducts unlimited investigations and inspections. SSE members can only be those having the BIB permit to trade and are admitted on a discretionary basis by the SSE board which also admit individual floor representatives, subject to the purchase of a seat on the Exchange. In surveying price fluctuations, the SSE can require any information needed from members and representatives as well as from registered security issuers. The SSE itself is submitted to BIB surveillance.

Foreigners are only permitted to acquire unrestricted (free) shares in a Swedish company. In order to trade professionally in securities for others in its own name, such a company would not be able to issue free shares carrying more than 20% of voting power. Foreign acquisition of free shares involves obtaining Central Bank permission to transfer funds and government approval for stakes larger than a 10% holding.

Foreigners cannot, without special permission, act as directors of a Swedish company and as a rule not more than one third of directors can be non-Swedish.

Companies Law requires winding up procedures when net assets do not cover half of the capital issued. Share capital issued has to be paid in.

Investor Protection. There is no investor compensation fund, although BIB does receive audited annual accounts and bi-annual financial information. There is no prohibition of insider dealing, although certain insiders are restricted.

OUTLINE OF CORPORATE AND INDIVIDUAL TAX CONSIDERATIONS

Corporations—Residents

Resident companies are liable to corporation tax on their income worldwide, including capital gains arising in Sweden or abroad if that income is transferred to Sweden or in any other way is made available to the Swedish company.

A company that is registered in Sweden is considered to be a resident company.

Taxes Imposed. Companies are subject to a national income tax. Although the Swedish tax rates are high, effective tax rates can be kept low if full advantage is taken of the beneficial tax rules for companies. The tax system has for a long time been used as an instrument in leveling out fluctuations in Swedish and international trade conditions.

Rates of Tax. National income tax is calculated at a flat rate of 52%. In addition, a profit-sharing tax exists which, where applicable, can add approximately 10% to the national tax level.

The profit-sharing tax, in addition to income taxes, is applicable based on the following calculation principles:

• Inflation effects on income are eliminated
• Wages and salaries are deductible at the rate of 6%; if total wages are less than SEK 1 million, the rate is 20%. The amount paid is deductible for income tax computations the year after, thus the effective rate is 9.6%.

Anyone trading professionally in securities:

• Will be fully taxable for realized gains less losses.
• Is permitted to deduct an inventory book reserve, computed as a percentage of the year end inventory of securities. The permissible percentage varies with the security and the taxable entity.

Nonresident Companies

Companies registered outside Sweden are taxed on income realized in Sweden if the company is deemed to have established a permanent place of business in Sweden. Income includes capital gains on business assets and real property in Sweden. Withholding tax is levied on dividends paid at the rate of 30%, reduced by double tax treaties. Sweden does not withhold tax on interest paid to nonresidents.

Individuals—Residents

An individual resident in Sweden will be taxed on all his income and wealth both from Sweden and foreign sources. This is referred to as unlimited tax liability.

Taxes on Income. Income is subject to national income tax levied at progressive rates and local income tax levied at a flat rate set by the local municipalities.

Net income and net losses from all sources are in principle netted off against each other. Any remaining loss may be carried forward and must be utilized within 6 years. Special rules apply when the taxpayer wishes to utilize capital losses.

Rates of Tax. National tax is charged at rates varying from 4.5% to 20%, with additional tax at rates of 5% to 27% on taxable income in excess of SEK 126,000. In computing additional tax, any net loss from other sources is added back to the net income base thus reducing the marginal tax deductions. Local tax rates differ from municipality to municipality, but approximate 30%.

Individuals—Nonresidents

An individual nonresident in Sweden will be taxed on certain income and wealth in Sweden, referred to as limited tax liability. No withholding tax is levied on interest paid to nonresident individuals, but dividends paid are taxed as for nonresident corporations.

Turnover Tax. A turnover tax of 1% arises on the sale of equities and is payable by domestic buyers and sellers. This tax is not applicable to banks and brokers trading for their own account or between themselves for their own clients, but legislation is proposed to include these transactions at half the rate and extend the tax base to nominal securities to a rate of 0.03%.

PROSPECTIVE DEVELOPMENTS

A parliamentary committee has been appointed to review the rules and surveillance of the securities market including SSE, operations of broking entities and insider trading.

A special government appointee is in place to consider the possible transfer of options and futures operations to the SSE as well as the present restrictions on a broker's right to hold equity inventory.

The SSE will, in the autumn of 1988, introduce a new automatic decentralized trading system, which will offer the facility of international trading.

"Book-entry" systems for shares and other financial papers are under investigation.

SWITZERLAND

Experta Treuhand AG
Contact: Pierre N. Rossier, Tel: (1) 201 71 71

Switzerland's seven Stock Exchanges are located in Zurich, Geneva, Basel, Lausanne, Bern, Neuenburg, and St. Gallen. Each Exchange is a separate entity in itself and operates independently, although the Swiss Stock Exchange system is co-ordinated by the Association of Swiss Stock Exchanges. Unless otherwise stated, this chapter is mainly concerned with the details of the Zurich Exchange.

The following statistics relate to the Zurich Exchange for 1987, although it should be noted that they refer only to business on the official Exchange and not over-the-counter trading.

	Equities	Swiss Bonds	Overseas Bonds
Turnover (Sfr million)	636	—	—
Number of trades/bargains ('000)	624	—	—
Market capitalization (Sfr billion) as of 12/31/87	208	103	89
Number of securities as of 12/31/87	454	1,425	870

The Zurich Exchange has 25 members and approximately 211 "off-floor traders." It is important to note that it is not necessary for a firm to be a member of a Stock Exchange to trade in securities although it must be licensed by the Canton to deal outside the Exchange.

Securities trading takes place in three market segments:

- Official Market (Börsenhandel): Trading takes place on the floor of the Exchange amongst its members.

194

- Semi-Official Market (Vorbörse): Trading also takes place on the floor of the Exchange but mostly only for equities in smaller companies not yet admitted to the official Exchange listings.
- Unofficial Market (Ausserbörslicher Wertpapierhandel): This market is conducted by both members and nonmembers, but usually only in equities with low volumes. Both listed and unlisted securities can be traded. There are approximately 200 nonmember dealers licensed to deal in this over-the-counter market (OTC) and it is estimated that there is as much activity on the OTC market as there is on the Zurich Exchange.

There are no trading links or settlement arrangements with overseas markets.

One of the main indices used to indicate overall market price movements is the Swiss Bank Corporation (SBC) All Share Index which quotes indices for stocks across all sectors; indices are also available for the following sectors: banks, insurance, engineering, chemicals, consumers, and power plants.

The movements in the All Share Index over recent years are as follows:

All Share Index

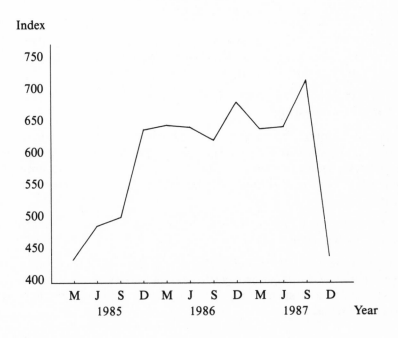

OVERVIEW OF THE BOND AND EQUITY MARKETS

Structure

Securities are traded on the one board at each Exchange. The opening times of the Zurich Exchange are as follows:

- 9:00: Opening of unofficial trading in unlisted securities for Swiss Bonds, Foreign Bonds, and Swiss Stocks.
- 10:30: Opening of official trading in listed securities for Swiss Bonds, Foreign Bonds, Swiss Stocks, and Foreign Stocks.

The market closing time is dependent on the level of activity.

There is no separation of function between member firms acting as principal and agent. Member firms are obliged to have a representative on the trading floor at all times.

Execution

Trading on all Exchanges is broadly similar; the open outcry method is adopted with the members' buying and selling transactions matched on a one-to-one basis thus arriving at the transaction prices. The Exchanges limit the daily permissible movements in stock prices to 10%.

The following transactions information is available daily: stock name, buy/sell price, and volume.

Transactions on the Exchanges are in board lots which depend on the value of the underlying security—ranging from 100 shares (for shares priced below SF5) to 1 share (if priced above SF10,000).

Settlement and Clearing

Settlement is required to take place three business days after the transaction. The procedure is for delivery against payment. Most trades (in bearer stocks) are cleared through SEGA, that is, by book entry; however, registered shares are still physically delivered directly between banks/brokers.

Market Characteristics

Commission rates are fixed, dependent on category, split between Swiss brokers/banks and foreign brokers/banks, and are dependent on value. The precise charging structure is complex, but for the most part rates are between 0.1% and 2.5%.

Margin Trading. Margin trading is permissible and requires approximately 50% margin, the settlement of which will depend on the broker/bank where the account is kept. Foreign investors may deal on margin. Stock borrowing is not permitted.

NEW ISSUES

In 1987 there were 330 new equity issues resulting in proceeds of Sfr33,633 million.

FUTURES AND OPTIONS TRADING

No trading currently takes place but it is expected to commence during 1988. The leading Swiss securities firms are forming an automated futures Exchange to be known as "SOFFEX."

REGULATIONS AFFECTING NEW ENTRANTS TO THE MARKET

The regulatory authorities controlling the Swiss securities market are:

- Cantonal Advisory Commission on Securities Trading
- Association of Swiss Stock Exchanges
- Swiss Securities Trading Commission

Restrictions placed on securities houses in entering the Zurich market require that Concession Holders must be banking institutions domiciled in the Canton of Zurich and incorporated in Switzerland. Further, Concession Holders must be professionally qualified, supported by at least two full members and they may represent foreign companies.

No minimum capital requirements exist apart from the requirement for a deposit with the Canton of Zurich. Funds may be repatriated to overseas shareholders, however they are subject to withholding tax—there are no foreign Exchange controls.

Membership of an Exchange is not by means of the purchase of a seat, but by application to the Canton of Zurich and the Stock Exchange. The cost of membership is Sfr300,000 plus an additional fee based on trading volume.

A concession holder membership in Zurich requires a deposit in kind or securities of Sfr300,000, in addition to the standard deposit with the Canton.

The Cantonal deposit is as follows:

Floor traders (A-members)   :   Sfr30,000
Off-floor traders (B-members) :   Sfr20,000

Special rules apply to off-floor traders that have no capital bases in Switzerland (foreign brokers).

Investor Protection

No procedures other than disclosure and a guarantee fund are adopted to ensure investor protection.

Financial statements from the bank/broker are required to be submitted to the Exchange semi-annually.

OUTLINE OF CORPORATE AND INDIVIDUAL TAX CONSIDERATIONS

Corporations—Residents

Resident companies are, in principle, subject to federal, cantonal, and communal taxes on all their income, including capital gains and net assets.

Due to the country's federal structure taxes are levied by three different authorities: the federal government, the cantons and the municipalities. Basically there are two taxes, income tax and capital tax.

Income Tax

In Switzerland, companies are assessed to federal, cantonal, and communal taxes at rates on sliding scales which are related to earnings intensity (i.e., the relation which assessable income bears to net assets) subject to minima and maxima, for example, 3.63% and 9.8% with respect to the direct federal tax. The tax calculated on this basis, therefore, represents in most cases a basic tax only. The effective cantonal or communal tax which varies considerably according to the taxing authority and totals together some 15–20% at most, is obtained by multiplying the basic tax by a factor (tax multiple) determined independently from time to time by the cantons or municipalities according to their financial requirements for the particular year.

The multiple is expressed either as a percentage (e.g., cantonal tax = 120% of basic tax) or as a simple multiplier (e.g., cantonal tax = 1.2 × basic tax).

Capital

The rate for the direct federal tax is 0.0825% whereas the cantonal rates vary from about 0.04% to 0.7%. These latter rates again represent in most cases a basic tax only. The effective cantonal or municipal tax is derived as described under income tax above.

Nonresidents

Nonresident companies are subject to all the above-mentioned taxes on their income and net assets attributable to a permanent establishment in Switzerland.

Tax is withheld from dividends and interest paid to nonresidents at the rate of 35%, but this rate may be reduced by double tax treaties.

Individuals

Individuals are mainly liable to the income and net wealth tax. The income tax is imposed by the federal government, the cantons, and the communities, whereas the wealth tax is only levied at cantonal and communal level.

The total tax burden from canton to canton and from community to community often vary considerably. The maximum income tax charges lie normally between 35% and 45%, whilst the net wealth tax charges, in an average, amount to 0.76%.

Individuals who are not present in Switzerland for more than 3 months a year and who do not have a home in Switzerland are not subject to unlimited taxation in Switzerland but may have a limited tax liability. Individuals without a limited or unlimited tax liability in Switzerland are subject to withholding tax on dividends and interest, as for nonresident corporations.

Other Taxes

Stamp duty

Issue of Swiss share capital is subject to a 3% duty which in the case of mergers is reduced to 1%. A further stamp tax is due on the purchase, sale, or exchange of Swiss and foreign securities by registered professional security dealers. The rate is 0.15% on securities of a Swiss issuer and 0.3% on securities of a foreign issuer.

TAIWAN

Van Fred & Co
Contact: Van-Fred Long, Tel: (2) 3114040

Taiwan's sole Stock Exchange is located in Taipei. Established in 1961, the Taipei Stock Exchange (TSE) is a private corporation. Private banks and enterprises own 61% of the Exchange, and the remainder is in the hands of the government-owned banks and businesses. A board of directors, composed of 14 members and 3 supervisors, manages the Exchange's operations. The TSE accounts for virtually all securities transactions in Taiwan, except for those made through a small over-the-counter market.

Size

Twenty-eight member companies trade on the TSE. Fourteen members are state-owned banks, and the other 14 are licensed companies. In addition, there are 10 securities investment and trust companies known as traders that may also trade on the Exchange. The 27 members and 12 traders account for all trading volume on the TSE. Direct investment by foreigners is prohibited, although they can invest in certain investment funds.

The 1987 market statistics for the TSE are as follows:

	Equities	Bonds
Share trading value (NT$ billion)	2,669	651
Volume traded (million shares)	76,857	N/A
Number of companies	141	3

The Exchange's primary index is the Taiwan Stock Exchange Index (TSE Index) which is comparable to the U.S. Standard & Poor's Index and

TSE Index

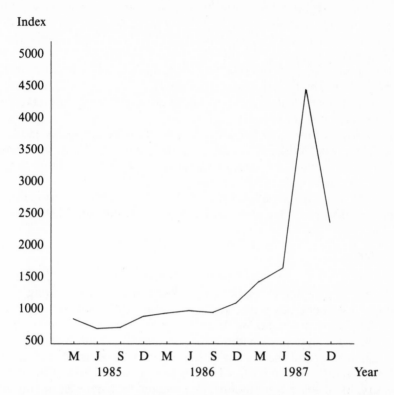

Index

the Tokyo Stock Exchange Index. It is a weighted share price index based on the number of shares outstanding of a wide selection of listed shares.

OVERVIEW OF THE BOND AND EQUITY MARKETS

Structure

The TSE is divided into three categories (sections): A (First), B (Second) and C (Third). Added in July 1984, C was designed to meet the requirements for capital of new high technology ventures. The Exchange categorizes companies based upon paid-up capital, pre-tax net profit, operating income, net worth, number of shareholders, and distribution of shares. The basic difference between categories A and B (virtually all companies) is the paid-up capital requirement which is NT$200 million and NT$100 million, respectively. Companies in Category A fall to Category B if they do not maintain the necessary requirements for four consecutive years; conversely, Category B companies may qualify for A upon meeting the requirements. If companies fail to meet both categories' requirements, they are not de-listed, but become designated as "full delivery" shares. All listed shares trade through the TSE.

Transactions on the TSE take place through the 27 licensed brokers and 12 traders. The licensed brokers can only act as agents for investors, whereas the traders deal on their own account and therefore preserve the liquidity in the market.

An over-the-counter market was established by the Securities and Exchange Commission (SEC) in 1982, but trading is limited to government and corporate bonds and bank debentures. Only securities brokers are allowed to trade over-the-counter.

The TSE's trading sessions are from Monday to Friday between the hours of 9:00 and 12:00, and on Saturday between 9:00 and 11:00.

Execution

The Exchange lists company stocks, government bonds and corporate bonds. Trading of these instruments takes place via the trading post method. Customers may buy shares by placing either a market order (to buy or sell at the best obtainable price) or by a price limit order. The TSE's computer system provides a direct communication link between brokerage offices and the trading posts. A computer-assisted trading facility is currently used to trade all shares except those shares in financial difficulty. Most share transactions are executed by computer operators, who are Exchange employees, and who match the buy and sell orders they receive from the brokerage firms' computers. However, transactions of those shares in financial difficulty are executed by floor specialists who receive the orders from floor representatives of the brokerage firms acting on the individual client's behalf.

The TSE automation program, ordered by the SEC, now includes approximately 111 of the 130 listed stocks. Brokers can now execute their orders and receive rapid confirmations of completed trades. TSE and SEC officials hope to eliminate all stockbrokers on the trading floor in the near future, theoretically reducing the probability of stock manipulation by traders and brokers. Current market prices may be accessed via personal computer and are broadcast by radio stations.

Daily price fluctuation limits are 3% for shares and 2.5% for bonds, except that share transactions greater than 300,000 shares or NT$3 million are also limited to 2%.

In 1979, the SEC's Rule of Certificate Unification standardized the trading unit. Listed companies must now have a NT$10 par value certificate and be traded in a 1000 share board lot. All shares now meet these requirements.

Settlement and Clearing

Transactions are handled as either regular or cash transactions. Settlement of regular transactions is made in cash, and shares are delivered the next business day after the transaction date. Similarly, cash transactions are settled in cash but share delivery takes place on the same day. The Taiwan Securities and Exchange Commission's clearing department processes all deliveries and settlements. Share sales made by brokers and traders are offset by purchases of the issue on the same day and therefore only net balances of securities and cash are computed and paid.

Fuh-Hwa Securities Finance Co. acts as a centralized depository for shares, but deliveries and payments may also be effected directly through brokers.

Fails must be reported in the customer's name.

Market Characteristics

Commission Rates. For equities transactions, brokerage commission rates are fixed at 0.15% of the share's trading value. Commission rates for both corporate and government bonds are fixed at 0.1%. Sellers are subject to a 0.3% tax, but the Ministry of Finance has the right to suspend this tax due to market conditions.

Margin Trading. Available since 1974, margin transactions have become fairly common. The coverage required to trade on margin is 50% on A (first section) stocks and 60% for B (second section) stocks. The margin requirement may be adjusted as market conditions dictate. The only institution licensed to provide margin financing is Fuh-Hwa Securities Finance Co., which can also lend securities to brokers.

New Issues

Over the last several years, an average of just six new listings per year has been granted. The growth in the number of listed companies has not matched the Taiwanese economy's rapid growth. Partly, the lack of listed companies results from a concentration of economic activity in a relatively small number of companies, many of which are state-controlled and not listed. Also, much of Taiwan's economy is in private hands that have a great aversion to the listing requirements requiring detailed financial disclosure and therefore they refuse to list.

All new issues must be approved by the Taiwan SEC. Listed companies are required to enter into a listing agreement with the TSE which is sanctioned by the SEC. Once listed, companies must promptly report any material events affecting their business or affairs in addition to standard annual and semi-annual financial reports.

Taiwanese shares must be in registered form. The most prevalent equity instruments are common shares, although preferred shares also exist. The SEC requires companies to restrict the voting rights of any stockholder owning more than 3% of the issued and outstanding stock.

Foreign companies are prohibited from listing their shares on the Exchange.

Investor Protection. The SEC and TSE require companies to file annual and semi-annual financial reports. They may also compel a listed company to submit financial reports at any time after the company becomes publicly traded. Companies must also report substantial events such as: corporate reorganization; change of directors or key managers; mergers or sales of the substantial assets; and major legal matters. Under the Securities and Exchange Law, the SEC instituted the following significant major investor protection rules:

- Any untrue statements or deceptive practices in the purchase, sale, and issue of securities are prohibited.
- All directors, key employees, and shareholders owning more than 5% of a company's outstanding shares must disclose their holdings; and such entities or persons are subject to the company's claim for any short-term trading profits.
- Manipulative practices are prohibited.
- Disclosure of profits earned by insiders in their trading is mandatory.
- Public companies must be audited by independent auditors.

An amendment to the Law has been proposed which would require persons trading on inside information to disclose profits.

No compensation fund exists for investors who incur losses due to fraud or default by brokers or dealers.

FUTURES AND OPTIONS TRADING

There are no futures or option markets in Taiwan.

REGULATIONS AFFECTING NEW ENTRANTS TO THE MARKETS

In order to trade on the Exchange floor, a securities company must have a contract with TSE and be licensed by the SEC. Exchange membership is limited to Taiwan nationals and to date all foreigners have been prohibited. Foreign broker/dealers must therefore transact all business through a domestic broker or dealer who will charge the standard commission. Membership on the TSE is obtained by purchasing a seat. The minimum capital required is NT$30 million and no insurance coverage is required.

The major regulatory agencies are the SEC which reports to the Ministry of Finance and the TSE. The Securities and Exchange Law is the principal regulation governing the industry. It covers all aspects of the industry from broker/dealer licensing to financial reporting and listing requirements.

The Ministry of Finance prohibits direct foreign investment in listed companies. Foreigners may invest only by purchasing beneficiary shares in funds such as the Taiwan (RoC) Fund which is managed by a Taiwanese fund manager. Other similar funds include the Formosa, Taipei, and Taiwan funds. Additionally, nonresident foreigners and foreign companies without registered domestic offices, may not maintain bank accounts in the country except in offshore banks.

OUTLINE OF CORPORATE AND INDIVIDUAL TAX CONSIDERATIONS

Personal tax rates range from 6% for income under NT$80,000 to 50% for income over NT$3.5 million. Corporate tax rates range from 15% for income in excess of NT$50,000 to 30% for income in excess of NT$500,000.

Under Taiwanese Law, dividends are subject to a withholding tax of 20% and interest of 10%, while capital gains are subject to a 35% tax. The government occasionally announces exemption from the capital gains tax if shares are publicly listed. Currently, a 0.3% transaction tax is levied on securities transactions of all types with the exception of bonds issued by all levels of government. Investment funds with Foreign Investment Approved (FIA) status, such as the Taiwan (RoC) Fund are subject to a 20% withholding tax on dividends rather than the 35% rate normally levied.

PROSPECTIVE DEVELOPMENTS

The SEC has proposed a major overhaul of securities industry legislation which, among other changes, would strengthen disclosure requirements for listed companies and tighten rules against insider trading. Brokers and stockbrokers firms would be allowed to expand their capital base by going public. The proposed changes would also allow foreign investment in the local brokerage firms. No clear details of this proposal have been made public so it seems that implementation is still some time away.

The TSE is continuing its step-by-step computerization program. The system's future enhancements will expand the Exchange's ability to supply the public with accurate data.

UNITED KINGDOM

Spicer & Oppenheim
Contact: Peter Oliver, Tel: (01) 480 7766

The longest established securities market in the United Kingdom is the Stock Exchange which was formed in 1973 by the merger of separate Exchanges in London, Belfast, Birmingham, Bristol, Dublin, Glasgow, Liverpool, and Manchester. As part of the restructuring of the London market, it is now known as The International Stock Exchange of the United Kingdom and the Republic of Ireland (ISE). In 1988, its responsibilities for financial supervision of member firms and client relations are being transferred to the The Securities Association (TSA).

In addition to the other financial markets described below, there are in London commodity futures Exchanges covering metals (hard commodities) and coffee, cocoa, sugar, and so on (soft commodities). Futures markets have also been established in gas, oil, and potatoes. In contrast to the United States, few securities dealers are directly involved in the nonfinancial commodities markets. Accordingly, this section restricts itself largely to the ISE and the related financial futures and options market.

The securities industry in the United Kingdom is still in the process of fundamental change. As far as the ISE is concerned, the past 18 months have seen:

- The widening of membership, so that most of the leading firms are now owned by international banks and finance houses
- The abolition of minimum commission rates
- The abandonment of single capacity (that is the rigid separation of the broking and dealing functions)

- The introduction of screen-based dealing systems which has left the ISE trading floor virtually unused
- The development of transaction surveillance by the ISE
- A threefold increase in the number of dealers in the government bond market
- The admission of inter-dealer brokers and clearing firms
- The growing use of book-entry stock transfer systems
- The setting up of transatlantic settlement links

Size

Securities markets in the United Kingdom can be categorized as follows:

- The ISE, on which listed securities (bonds and equities) and options, unlisted securities and Third Market securities are traded
- The Eurobond market
- The over-the-counter (OTC) market (for equity and company loan stocks)
- The London International Financial Futures Exchange (LIFFE)

The market figures for the ISE are illustrated in the following table:

	Domestic Equities	Foreign Equities	Fixed Interest	Government Bonds
Period January to December 1987:				
Turnover (£ billion)	283	103	71	598
Number of trades/bargains				
(thousands)	11,944	1,078	388	761
As of December 31, 1987:				
Market capitalization (£ billion)	378	724	12	246
Number of securities	3,158	753	1,200	1,636

The most readily available index used to indicate the performance of the London stock market is the *Financial Times/Stock Exchange 100 Share Index* ("FTSE") which is based on the prices of the leading 100 shares traded on the ISE and which is calculated on a continuous basis during the day. The FTSE is now more widely reported than the older FT ordinary share index based on only 30 shares. Over recent years the FTSE index has shown the following pattern (next page).

The Unlisted Securities Market (USM) handles companies that wish to raise smaller sums of money, release a smaller percentage of total equities, or those that have too short a trading record for a full listing. The ISE Third Market and the OTC market generally cater to companies that would not meet the requirements of the USM.

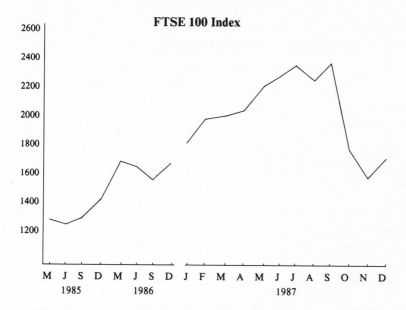

FTSE 100 Index

The Eurobond market is an international market operating principally in London and dominated by the major international banks.

LIFFE commenced operations in 1982. It provides a market in futures and options on interest rate, currency, and stock index contracts.

The International Stock Exchange

Formerly, most of the individual ISE members carried on business in partnerships of varying sizes. As a direct result of "Big Bang" and the fundamental changes occurring in the securities industry in the United Kingdom, many of these firms have incorporated and have become either limited or unlimited companies.

In mid-1987, the ISE firms were classified according to their registered activity as:

	Number of Firms
Broker/dealers	232
Market makers—equities	35
Market makers—gilts	27
Clearing members	3
Money brokers	8
Inter-dealer brokers	8
Option dealers	16
Total	329

209

New Issues

The table below illustrates the 1987 figures for new issues on the ISE.

	Domestic Equities	Foreign Equities	Fixed Interest	Government Bonds
Number of issues	1,032	97	9	62
Proceeds (£ billion)	6.0	1.6	0.3	5.5

Currently, British Funds (gilt-edged securities) are issued by and registered with the Bank of England, which acts as an agent on behalf of the government. The full amount of the stock (wholly or partly paid) may be issued at one time or it may be made available on a "tap" basis, when the Bank disposes of stock gradually in response to demand. Recently, the Bank of England has held experimental gilts auctions; it is unclear whether these will become a permanent feature of the London gilts market.

Gilt-edged securities are normally issued for a term in excess of one year. Shorter term funding requirements are met by the issue of U.K. Government Treasury Bills, traded through the discount houses which are generally not members of the ISE.

Company securities are normally issued through the combined efforts of a merchant bank and a stockbroker who manage the new issue and arrange for the underwriting. The underwriting commission is determined by negotiation and is typically between 1.5% and 2% of the issue price. The issue price is determined by agreement among the merchant bank, the company, the sponsoring broker, and the dealers/brokers who will make a market in the shares. Investors will be offered shares at that price (occasionally they will be invited to tender at a price above a given minimum). Any shares not purchased will be left with the underwriters to hold or to trade out through the normal market mechanisms.

Shares in smaller issues may be "placed" rather than offered for sale. This avoids the need for underwriting, as the shares are purchased directly by investors approached by the sponsoring merchant bank or broker. A designated proportion of shares must be made available to dealers to ensure a liquid market.

Entry requirements for the USM are less stringent than those for a full listing. The USM requires a trading history of three years as compared to five years for a full listing. Only 10% of the shares of USM companies need to be held by outside investors as compared to 25% for a full listing. Entry fees and annual fees also differ for the two markets.

UNITED KINGDOM

Trading Structure

Since 1986, the gilt-edged market has operated in a manner similar to the system operating in the U.S. government bond market. When the market was restructured the Bank of England granted approval to 29 organizations to act as primary dealers and to 6 others who act as interdealer brokers. The primary dealers make markets in government stocks (or a designated range of them) and the inter-dealer brokers trade only between the primary dealers. Trading over the last year is said to have been unprofitable for most of the primary dealers and several have now withdrawn from this market.

The function of money brokers who lend stock to marketmakers and provide secured finance to them has continued under the new system.

The new dealing arrangements for equities allow firms to deal in either an agency or principal capacity, or both, and are based upon the concept of competing marketmakers. Designated marketmakers are required, within defined parameters, to make continuous markets in the stocks in which they deal throughout the mandatory quote period, which is 9:00 to 17:00.

Execution

Execution is effected orally from office to office by telephone, based on prices which are disseminated by SEAQ, an electronic quotation system. Each transaction has to be reported to the central checking system and separately, generally within five minutes, to the ISE for surveillance purposes. Trading takes place in any quantity of shares, not in round lots, and there are no limits on daily permissible price movements.

Settlement and Clearing

There are a number of different settlement systems in operation. Equities and loan stocks are generally dealt "for the Account," which is normally a period of 10 business days, with settlement on the "Account Day," six business days after the end of the Account. Settlement between brokers and marketmakers is primarily through a central clearing service known as Talisman (owned and operated by the ISE and linked to company registrars).

For government securities and corporate new issues, settlement is generally on the next business day after dealing. Delivery of such securities is direct between broker and marketmakers and is of certificate and transfer form against payment. The Bank of England now operates a computerized book-entry transfer system for British government registered stocks.

Clients are due to settle with their brokers on the due dates as described above. The private client is required to settle any outstanding obligations to the broker (whether payment of money or delivery of shares) on the settlement date whether or not the broker completes his obligations to the client on that date. Most institutional clients will, however, only settle against delivery of shares.

A wide range of settlement arrangements apply to foreign securities. This diversity arises not only from differences in Stock Exchange practices worldwide and in the way securities are held and transferred, but also from the different requirements of individual clients. For example, a private client may prefer to pay against a sterling contract note (although his London broker dealt with current settlement in an overseas center), while a U.K. institutional investor may wish to make direct settlement abroad in foreign currency against delivery of stock.

The Eurobonds Market

The market for Eurobonds, whether sterling or other currency-denominated bonds, takes place on an unofficial OTC market operated primarily by banks and some stockbrokers in London. The market is made up principally of institutional investors rather than private individuals. Settlement and custody is handled chiefly by one of two organizations: Euroclear (based in Brussels) and Cedel (based in Luxembourg).

Market Characteristics

Commission Rates. The fixed minimum rates of commission were abolished in October 1986, on de-regulation of the securities markets. Since then, the rates of commission paid by institutional investors have probably halved, to the present level of about 0.2% of the transaction value of equities traded. It is estimated that probably 50% of this business is with marketmakers on a "net price, free of commission" basis. As a direct result of intense competition almost all large government bond transactions are now dealt on a net basis.

Other charges related to dealing are the marketmaker's spread, that is, the difference between the price at which he is willing to buy and sell securities, which can range from 0.75% to 5%, Value Added Tax (VAT) is normally payable at 15% on any commission charged and a transfer stamp levied at a rate of 0.5% on all purchases. There is also a levy of £0.80 per trade of £1000 or more to finance part of the regulatory framework.

Margin Trading. Margin trading as carried out in the United States does not take place on anything like the same scale in the United Kingdom. Instead a minority of business is financed by loans made by stockbrokers to their clients using securities as collateral; this is closely monitored by the Stock Exchange and is subject to detailed regulations. Stock borrowing is permitted for market makers only, and must be conducted through the recognized money-brokers, who in turn borrow the stock from large investors who must be approved by the Inland Revenue. Borrowing and lending both government shares and equities is closely monitored by the Bank of England.

FUTURES AND OPTIONS TRADING

Financial futures and options are both traded in London on LIFFE and options are traded in the ISE. There are two types of options markets on The Stock Exchange: traded options and "traditional" options. "Traditional" or conventional options are traded "over the counter" and positions can only be closed with the original counterparty. They are available in any listed security and are for a period of three months only—they can be exercised at two-weekly intervals within that period.

The traded options market embraces a limited range of securities only (including gilts), but the options are fully transferable. Traded options have lives of three, six and nine months and cover a number of exercise prices which span the current price of the underlying security. There is also trading in index options. Both the ISE and LIFFE trade currency options. Settlement of the option premium for all traded options takes place on the second business day following the day the transaction was entered into, in addition to which the writers of options are required to deposit collateral against the risk of an adverse price movement.

LIFFE is an entirely separate organization from the ISE although many of the large brokers and dealer/brokers are also members of LIFFE. Its membership numbers over 200 firms. This membership includes banks, discount houses, and Stock Exchange firms.

As of January 1988, 20 contracts were traded. These were 13 futures contracts (7 interest rate, 5 currency rate, 1 stock index) and 7 options contracts (4 interest rate, 2 currency rate, 1 stock index).

The clearing house for LIFFE is the International Commodities Clearing House (ICCH) which is owned by a consortium including the four principal U.K. clearing banks. Each properly matched transaction on LIFFE is entered into the clearing system at ICCH and is then subject to a rigidly controlled, centralized confirmation process that includes registration, margining, and eventually settlement and delivery. The standard delivery months are the same for all contracts—March, June, September, and December but in some cases, additional months are available for trading.

Securities Industry Regulation

The new regulatory environment has produced many acronyms. These include:

- FSA—The Financial Services Act 1986 which will regulate all "investment business" in the United Kingdom.
- SIB—The Securities and Investment Board, a special private body set up by the FSA which authorizes SROs and RIEs and whose rule book provides the model on which SROs and RIEs have based their own rules to ensure effective investor protection and acceptable freedom of competition.
- SRO—A self-regulatory organization. There are currently five SROs which regulate members practicing in various segments of the securities market (i.e., stock exchange, futures etc.).
- TSA—The Securities Association. The SRO now responsible for Securities market participants. It has assumed certain regulatory responsibilities of the ISE but in addition covers the Eurobond market and Corporate Finance activities.
- IMRO—The Investment Management Regulatory Organization. The SRO for managers of investment funds of all sizes.
- FIMBRA—The Financial Intermediaries Managers and Brokers Regulations Association. The SRO for investment advisors and intermediaries.
- AFBD—The Association of Future Brokers and Dealers. The SRO for those involved in futures, options, and contracts for differences.
- LAUTRO—The Life Assurance and Unit Trust Regulatory Organizations. The SRO for those involved in the marketing of Life Assurance, authorized unit trust and other collective investment schemes.
- ISE—The International Stock Exchange which is the RIE responsible for dealing with the operation of the securities marketplace and with settlement and transaction reporting. The ISE has part of its regulatory responsibilities to the FSA with the implementation of the FSA on April 29, 1988.
- AIBD—Association of International Bond Dealers. The AIBD is expected to be a DIE.
- RIE—A recognized investment exchange.

214

- DIE—A designated (i.e., overseas) investment exchange.

At the present time (March 1988), the position appears to be:

- The ISE is expected to be the largest of several RIEs and there will be at least one DIE.
- Firms and business houses carrying on securities business have applied to join TSA. Membership is also available to appropriate overseas entities.
- U.K. firms will be members of both ISE and TSA. Overseas firms may join TSA but presumably not ISE. Stock Exchange firms in, say, the Republic of Ireland (i.e., outside the United Kingdom) will probably retain ISE membership but may not need to join TSA.
- Although all SROs have issued rule books these are subject to final amendments and will be kept under review as the new system of regulation settles in.
- Certain transitional arrangements apply to the "client money rules" and to other new and onerous regulations.
- Some of the legal implications of FSA have been the subject of recent discussion. In particular, section 62 of the Act has worried many financial houses. This gives a civil right of action to anyone who suffers loss as a result of any contravention of the rules of an SRO. However, successful lobbying of government has resulted in the operation of the section being postponed until October 1988. Other FSA provisions may prove to be even more important in practice; for example, in order to enforce the rules, SROs have powers, among others, to prohibit an investment business from disposing of its assets and to appoint a trustee to assume control of the business. The full implications of the Act for International Trade will only be established by experience of its operation.

Investor Protection. Until the FSA came into effect, investor protection for ISE transactions was provided by:

- A well-established complaints procedure, which may be backed by disciplinary action against an offending member
- Legal action under common law, which is possible by a client against an investment adviser or broker for breach of agency obligations or for negligence
- A compensation fund in case of failure of a member firm. Payment to each claimant was limited to £250,000 (or £500,000 in certain circumstances)

215

- Transaction surveillance by ISE, including monitoring of price spreads, market aberrations and price jumps
- Insider-dealing laws
- General supervision of the affairs of member firms, including visits to firms' officers, by ISE officials

In 1988, investor protection rules were reinforced by FSA provisions which enable:

- Civil action to be taken under section 61 and 62 of FSA for contravention of regulatory rules
- Criminal proceedings to be taken under section 47 in case of market manipulation (subject to territorial limitation)

Additionally, SRO rules will require:

- Segregation of client money
- Observance of detailed Conduct of Business Rules

and will result in the appointment of a Compliance Officer by each firm.

REGULATIONS AFFECTING NEW ENTRANTS TO THE MARKETS

Membership Requirements

Under the new regulatory structure operational from April 1988, membership of TSA will be granted to any individual, partnership or corporate body who can demonstrate that they are a "fit and proper person." This criterion encompasses such matters as previous history (e.g., convictions for fraud, previous trading experience), capital adequacy, adequate systems for dealing and accounting/settlement, corporate structure and parentage, and so forth. In addition to the corporate membership, each individual responsible for dealing or giving advice must be authorized by passing an exam or by suitable experience and by passing a "fit and proper" test.

All member organizations must comply with TSA financial regulations. Members of TSA are required to prepare monthly capital statements as well as fortnightly calculations of position risk and annual audited accounts within relatively tight reporting deadlines. Each firm is required to maintain a capital base, in approved form, in excess of the sum of

- 3 months' expenses (or a specified minimum sum)

- A position risk requirement, calculated by applying varying percentages to the values of long and short positions in securities, options, futures, and currencies
- A counterparty risk requirement, based on overdue settlements

There is no current requirement to purchase a "seat" on ISE as a condition of membership, although there is an initial fee to TSA and ISE which is dependent on the number of authorized persons employed. There are no restrictions on membership for foreign-owned entities.

Different rules based largely on position risk and administered by the Bank of England apply to Gilt-Edged marketmakers.

OUTLINE OF CORPORATE AND INDIVIDUAL TAX CONSIDERATIONS

Residents

Government Bonds—Current Income. Interest is taxable on a cash-received basis, with adjustments for interest purchased and sold. Most interest is subject to withholding tax at 25%, which is set against any ultimate tax liability with any excess available for repayment. Discount on Treasury bills is taxable on realization by sale or maturity.

Government Bonds—Capital Gains. Capital gains (excluding accrued interest purchased and sold) are exempt from tax provided that the activity does not amount to trading.

Equities—Current Income. *Individuals.* U.K. dividends are taxable for individuals on a cash-received basis. The amount included in total income is 4/3rds of the actual dividend; but a tax credit is given at the rate of 25% on the gross taxable income (1/3rd of the actual dividend), which is set against any ultimate tax liability and any excess is available for repayment.
Corporation. Dividends received from U.K. resident companies are exempt from tax. The tax credit on such dividends may be used to reduce the liability to advance corporation tax on dividends paid by the recipient company. Dividends received from nonresident companies are subject to corporation tax and relief will generally be available both for overseas withholding tax and for overseas underlying tax provided that a specified minimum shareholding (normally 10%) is held.

Equities—Capital Gains. Capital gains and losses are recognized on disposals, subject to relief for inflation as measured by the index of retail prices. Both companies and individuals pay tax on capital gains at the same rate as they would on income.

Traded Options and Financial Futures

Gains on transactions on the ISE, LIFFE, and other Exchanges approved by the tax authorities are taxable as capital gains (unless the activity amounts to trading), but the rules for calculating the chargeable gains and allowable losses are complex. The cost of a traded option writer's closing purchase is disallowed, except for Stock Exchange equity and index options which are cleared through the London Option Clearing House (LOCH). Gains on options and futures on U.K. government bonds are exempt from capital gains tax. Gains from transactions on unapproved exchanges etc. may be taxed as income in some circumstances.

Nonresidents

Government Bonds—Current Income. Interest on certain government bonds is exempt from U.K. tax. Discount on Treasury bills may in practice escape tax by concession. Interest on other government bonds is generally subject to withholding tax at 25%, which is offset against the ultimate tax liability, which is normally calculated at the same rates applicable to residents. Any excess will qualify for repayment and if a double tax treaty is available the U.K. tax rate will usually be limited to a figure less than 25%. There is no adjustment for interest purchased and sold.

Government Bonds—Capital Gains. Capital gains are exempt from tax unless the activity amounts to a trade.

Equities—Current Income. *Individuals.* No withholding tax is levied on individuals, but nonresidents are not entitled to the tax credit referred to above under "Residents" unless a double tax treaty is available. Tax may be chargeable at progressive rates up to 15% of the dividends (unless a double tax treaty is available), but in practice this liability may not be collected.

Corporations. No withholding tax is levied for corporations, but unless a double tax treaty is available, nonresident corporations are not entitled to the tax credit referred to above. No additional tax liability will arise.

Equities—Capital Gains. Nonresident capital gains (as distinct from gains that amount to trading) are exempt from tax unless the gains are attributable to a U.K. branch or agency.

UNITED KINGDOM

Stamp Duty

Purchases of registered shares, convertible bonds etc. are subject to stamp duty at 0.5%. There is no stamp duty on government bonds and certain other bonds denominated in sterling.

PROSPECTIVE DEVELOPMENTS

The full implications of the new regulatory structure, as discussed above, have yet to be seen. Other areas where the ISE is developing a variety of new or improved systems which will include the following:

- TAURUS—A book-entry transfer system for equities which will (over a period of years) eliminate the share certificate
- SAEF—An automated execution service for small transactions (expected to be set at around 1000 shares)

In addition to these, the ISE is developing a broader range of price quotations for overseas securities, together with settlements links with the major overseas markets.

UNITED STATES OF AMERICA

Spicer & Oppenheim
Contact: Joel Press, Tel: (212) 422-1000

Securities and commodities transactions are conducted on a number of Exchanges. The principal Exchanges are:

- American Stock Exchange (AMEX)
- Boston Stock Exchange (BSE)
- Chicago Board of Trade (CBOT)
- Chicago Board Options Exchange (CBOE)
- Chicago Mercantile Exchange (CME)
- Cincinnati Stock Exchange (CSE)
- Coffee, Sugar and Cocoa Exchange (CSC)
- Commodity Exchange (COMEX)
- Kansas City Board of Trade (KCBT)
- Midwest Stock Exchange (MSE)
- New York Cotton Exchange (NYCE)
- New York Futures Exchange (NYFE)
- New York Mercantile Exchange (NYMEX)
- New York Stock Exchange (NYSE)
- Pacific Stock Exchange (PSE)
- Philadelphia Board of Trade (PBOT)
- Philadelphia Stock Exchange (PHLX)

UNITED STATES OF AMERICA

Size

U.S. securities and commodities markets are categorized as follows:

- Stock Exchange—securities such as stocks, stock options, stock indexes, and corporate bonds
- Over-the-counter (OTC) market—securities and options
- Commodity Exchanges—futures, options on futures, and options on indexes
- U.S. government securities market
- Corporate bonds
- Municipal bonds

The 1987 annual market statistics for the New York Stock Exchange (NYSE), American Stock Exchange (AMEX) and the National Association of Securities Dealers Automated Quotation System (NASDAQ) are as follows:

	NYSE	ASE	NASDAQ
Share volume (millions)	47,801	3,505	37,886
Value of shares traded (US$ millions)	2,216,311	53,166	498,301
Average daily volume (millions)	188.9	13.9	149.8
Average price of shares traded (US$)	31	15	13

In 1987, there were 1,647 companies listed on the NYSE, 869 listed companies on the AMEX and 4,706 quoted securities in the NASDAQ system. At December 1987, the NYSE, AMEX and NASD had the following number of member firms: 598, 661 and 6722, respectively.

Eight major U.S. Exchanges—New York, American, Cincinnati, Midwest, Boston, Pacific, Philadelphia, and the NASD—are linked together by the Intermarket Trading System (ITS), an electronic communications network. The system enables brokers, specialists, and market makers to interact with their counterparts on the network whenever the nationwide Composite Quotation System shows a better price. The 1537 issues eligible for trading on ITS at the end of 1987 represented most of the stocks traded on more than one Exchange. Of these stocks, 1335 are listed on the NYSE and 202 on the AMEX. In 1987, ITS share volume climbed to 2.2 billion shares, which represents a 19.2% increase over the previous year's total volume.

At January 1987, the capitalization (defined as ownership equity plus subordinated liabilities) of the 25 largest U.S. broker/dealers ranged from US$186 million to US$3209 million.

Dow Jones 30 Industrial Average (DJIA or the Dow). The Dow is the U.S.'s oldest and most often quoted market indicator. It is a price-weighted average calculated from the prices of 30 blue-chip stocks of primarily major U.S. manufacturing companies and a few service companies. Dow Jones & Company calculates the average by adding the closing prices of the component stocks and using a divisor that is adjusted for splits, dividends, substitutions, and mergers. The DJIA is quoted in points, not dollars.

New York Stock Exchange (NYSE) Composite Index. The NYSE Composite Index is a market-value weighted index composed of four subindexes: the NYSE Industrial, Transportation, Utilities, and Finance indexes, which cover all NYSE listed stocks. The index's base value, set on December 31, 1965, is $50 and point changes are expressed in dollars and cents. The index's value is adjusted to eliminate the effects of capitalization changes, new listings and delistings.

National Association of Securities Dealers Automated Quotations (NASDAQ) Composite Index. Introduced on February 5, 1971, this market-value weighted index is composed of all NASDAQ National Market System (NMS) issues (except warrants) and all other NASDAQ domestic common stocks. The index uses a base value of 100.00.

Standard & Poor's 500 Stock Index (S&P 500). Composed mostly of NYSE-listed companies and some AMEX and OTC stocks, the S&P 500 is a market-value weighted index that measures the change in the aggregate market value of 500 stocks relative to the base period of 1941–1943. It includes the S&P 400 Industrials, the S&P 20 Transportations, the S&P 40 Financials, and the S&P 40 Utilities. The U.S. investment community commonly uses the S&P 500 as a benchmark for comparing the performance of individual stocks, stock groups, portfolios, and investment advisors.

American Stock Exchange (AMEX) Market Value Index (AMVI). The AMVI, along with 16 subindices, was introduced on September 4, 1973, with a base value of 100.00 as of the close on August 31, 1973. Amex adjusted the AMVI to 50.00, half of its original level, on July 5, 1983. It is a market-value weighted index, measuring more than 800 issues including American Depository Receipts (ADRs), warrants as well as common stock, excluding rights, preferred stock on "when issued" stock.

The last 3 years' movements of the Dow are as follows:

UNITED STATES OF AMERICA

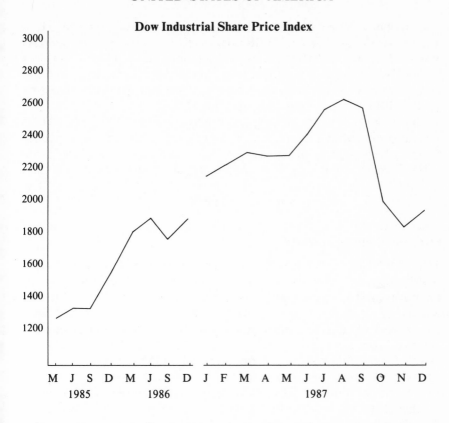

Dow Industrial Share Price Index

OVERVIEW OF THE BOND AND EQUITY MARKETS

The New York Stock Exchange

The NYSE is the U.S.'s largest Stock Exchange, accounting for approximately 80% of all stock exchange volume activity. In 1986 NYSE member firms also generated 77% of all U.S. broker/dealer revenues.

Members of the NYSE are categorized according to the activities they engage in on the trading floor. Those members assigned by the NYSE to deal in particular issues are referred to as specialists, with only one specialist being assigned to each security. The role of the specialist is to help maintain an orderly market, which may require the specialist to buy and/or sell from its own account, as principal.

Broker/dealers who wish to trade securities on the floor of the NYSE become members of the Stock Exchange by buying seats. Memberships

223

organizations. A NYSE seat cost US$625,000 in December 1987. It is also possible under current NYSE rules to lease a seat from a member. As at February 1988, seat lease prices ranged from a high of US$150,000 to a low of US$100,000. In addition, it is possible to communicate directly with members on the floor of the NYSE through an electronic access by paying an annual fee of approximately US$77,000.

Not every public company can be listed on the NYSE. The NYSE evaluates the public's interest in the company's stocks and sets specific financial and other requirements before the company can be listed. One of the primary requirements is that the company may have only one class of common stock outstanding, with equal voting rights. NYSE authorities are currently re-evaluating this requirement.

Over-the-Counter Markets

Trading in OTC markets greatly expanded in 1970 with the introduction of NASDAQ, a computerized quotation system. This network allows potential buyers and sellers of OTC securities to locate the market maker who will buy and sell a particular security in the OTC market. The NASDAQ system provides a continuously updated computer screen that quotes the current bid and offer prices. The NASD charges member firms US$270 per month for the first computer terminal and US$255 per month for each additional terminal that allows access to trade NASDAQ stocks.

In addition to the NASDAQ system, marketmaker identity and quotes in other OTC stocks can be found in a publication popularly known as the Pink Sheets while for bonds they can be found in the Yellow Sheets. Direct telephone contact is necessary to obtain current price information.

Firms are permitted to trade both as agent and as principal. When acting as an agent, the firm reports to its client that it executed the order, acting as a broker between the client and the marketmaker. As a principal, the firm reports to its client that it executed the order as a dealer, acting directly with the client as a trader on the opposite side of the order.

In April 1986, NASDAQ inaugurated its electronic linkage with the London Stock Exchange, the first intercontinental link of major securities markets. NASDAQ plans to provide automated execution capabilities by 1989 in addition to the link's current, actual trade data and international clearance and settlement capabilities. Today, London's TOPIC terminals display the bids and offers of competing U.S. marketmakers for 285 NASDAQ issues. These include the stocks of 200 major U.S. companies and the ADRs of 85 non-U.K. firms. NASDAQ terminals now carry quotations on over 300 stocks from London, including the 100 issues in the Financial Times—Stock Exchange Index.

The key difference between the Stock Exchange markets and the OTC marketplace is that the former are auction marketplaces while the latter is a negotiated marketplace, based on a system of competing marketmakers.

Execution

Most orders to trade listed securities are transmitted to the floor of an Exchange via telephone or teletype and are executed at specific locations known as trading posts. As each trade is executed, it is recorded, immediately processed and announced on an electronic ticker tape. The information on this tape is displayed on other U.S. Exchanges and relayed to investment institutions around the world.

The NYSE also employs SuperDot, an electronic order-routing system, to transmit member firms' market and limit orders in NYSE-listed securities directly to the post where the securities are traded or to the member firm's booth. Once the order has been executed, SuperDot generates an execution report and returns it to the member firm's office over the same electronic circuit that brought the order to the Floor, and the execution is submitted directly to the comparison systems.

As of the end of 1987, 183 member firms were SuperDot subscribers. On an average day, 153,000 orders move through the SuperDot system. On October 20, 1987, the highest SuperDot volume day ever, over 585,000 orders were processed.

The trading unit in stocks is generally set as a "round lot" of 100 shares or an "odd lot" of less than 100 shares. In addition, trades of 10,000 shares or more are called "block" trades.

Settlement and Clearing

Generally, all stock and commodity Exchanges have related accounting, clearance and depository organizations. NYSE transactions are handled by the Securities Industry Automation Corporation (SIAC) and are cleared by the National Securities Clearing Corporation (NSCC). The Depository Trust Company (DTC) acts as a depository for the securities of its members.

The various securities clearing organizations, which generally operate under a Continuous Net Settlement (CNS) process, allow members to clear most transactions directly with the clearing organization instead of with individual broker/dealers. This has greatly reduced the physical receipt and delivery of securities among broker/dealers and has resulted in what has come to be known as a "book-entry" accounting system. Most transactions are completed within five business days after execution, although trading also takes place on a when-issued and de-layed delivery basis.

Initial Public Offering

A privately-held company goes public when it sells securities to the general public for the first time. The Securities and Exchange Commission (SEC) requires most companies to file a registration statement in accordance with the Securities Act of 1933 ('33 Act) before selling securities to the general public. A company may sell securities to the general public by other means, such as private placements, but the term going public usually refers to those instances when a '33 Act filing is required. The process of a company going public for the first time is called the initial public offering, or IPO.

The following overview briefly describes the typical sequence of events that occurs in the course of selling securities to the public.

Writing the registration statement to comply with SEC requirements is usually the most time-consuming (one to four months) step in the process. The month or so between the registration statement's initial filing and the effective date (the SEC's permission date) is referred to as the waiting period. During the waiting period, the SEC will review the registration statement and it will usually respond in four to six weeks with comments and questions through what is known as a deficiency letter. The registration statement will then be modified as necessary, and when the SEC is satisfied, the price will be set and it will be declared effective. In addition to the SEC registration, the company will also have to comply with the securities laws of the states where the stock will be sold. The National Association of Securities Dealers, Inc. (NASD) must also review the offering in accordance with Regulation S-K. Most companies usually file documents to satisfy these requirements soon after they file with the SEC.

The filing of the registration statement with the SEC and the SEC's subsequent permission to proceed with the offering does not in any way imply SEC approval of the issue or its investment merits. The SEC's permission merely indicates that the issue has satisfied legal requirements under the '33 Act.

As soon as the registration statement is filed, the managing underwriter forms a group, or syndicate, of underwriters who will participate in the offering. The syndicate, sometimes comprising as many as 50 to 100 firms, is formed to obtain a broad geographical distribution for the stock and to provide a balance between institutional and individual investors.

A closing is held after the registration statement is effective and the offering has commenced. On the effective date, the stock begins trading either on a Stock Exchange or over-the-counter based on the company's choice and regulatory requirements.

FUTURES AND OPTIONS TRADING

Commodities Markets. A substantial number of registered broker/dealers are also futures commission merchants (FCMs). Trading or investing takes place in futures and forward contracts or in the cash (spot) market on underlying commodities, consisting mainly of grains, livestocks, foods, metals, and financial instruments. The settlement and delivery functions are generally handled by separate clearing organizations. Trading generally takes place on eight Commodity Exchanges (contract markets) around the country.

Financial futures were first introduced on Government National Mortgage Association certificates (Ginnie Mae) in 1975. In addition to the use of financial futures for speculative purposes, these instruments provide an important mechanism to hedge against interest rate fluctuations. Other hedging vehicles include options on financial futures and on stock index futures. Most futures contracts are closed before expiration so that actual delivery of the commodity never takes place. Futures on financial indexes are settled by the payment of cash.

Commodity Exchanges or clearing organizations set initial and maintenance margin requirements. In the light of the markets' volatility since October 1987, these requirements are being reviewed by legislators and regulators with the intention of ensuring an orderly marketplace. All open futures positions are priced daily at current market values with the proceeds (variation margin) settled between the broker/dealer and the clearing organization. There are also price stabilization rules which specify the maximum price changes allowable in any one day. To prevent misuse of client funds or securities, the Commodity Futures Trading Commission (CFTC) requires that FCMs segregate client funds and/or securities into special accounts.

Exchange Traded-Listed Stock Options and Indexes. Options on equity securities and stock indexes are traded on several Exchanges and on a limited basis, in the OTC option market. Listed options are generally traded in 100 share quantities of the underlying security. The expiration dates (generally three-month intervals) and exercise prices are established by the Exchanges. The major difference between stock options and index options is their settlement. The exercise of a stock option results in the

227

delivery of shares of the underlying security. Index option exercises, however, are settled by the payment of cash.

The Bond Markets. In the United States, bonds are generally classified into three broad categories:

U.S. government and agency securities
Corporate bonds
Municipal bonds

U.S. Government and Agency Securities Market. The U.S. government and agency securities market is a very large, liquid market and the government's activities via the Federal Reserve Bank have a major impact on the U.S. economy and capital markets. At the end of 1986, the U.S. government securities market reached US$2.6 trillion in size which corresponds to 45.4% of the entire world's government securities market. The Federal Reserve Bank implements its monetary policy in this market by buying and selling government securities in the open market, dealing solely with 43 primary dealers.

The government securities market is composed of the Federal Reserve Bank and primary and secondary government securities dealers. The market's 43 primary government dealers consist of banks, diversified broker/dealers and bond houses both U.S. and foreign owned that take positions in government securities for trading with primary and secondary dealers and inter-dealer dealers. The primary dealers are required to make markets in these securities, and they must participate, on an auction basis, in the underwriting of new issues made by the government. In addition, primary dealers make daily reports of their inventory positions and market transactions to the Federal Reserve Bank.

U.S. lawmakers enacted the Government Securities Act of 1986 granting the Treasury Department authority over the government securities market. The law authorizes the Treasury Secretary to issue net capital, bookkeeping, financial reporting rules, and to regulate the transfer and control of government securities in repurchase transactions, as well as limiting the use of customers' securities. Approximately 75 previously unregulated dealers were now required to register with the SEC and approximately 300 brokerage firms, banks and savings institutions have filed a special notice with the SEC or one of the banking industry's regulatory agencies.

Corporate and Municipal Bond Markets. For the most part, corporate bonds are traded in the OTC market, although a limited amount of trading in NYSE listed bonds does take place on the NYSE floor.

The trading of corporate bonds generally takes place via telephone and can be settled either physically or through a depository. The substantial volume in the retail municipal bond market is primarily due to the tax-exempt nature of interest on municipal bonds. Taxable municipal securities and put bonds, however, are becoming more prevalent due to recent changes made in the tax laws. Market makers and quotes in the municipal bond market may be found in "The Blue List of Current Municipal Offerings." Some municipal bonds are listed and occasionally traded on various Stock Exchanges, but most transactions are OTC.

Market Characteristics

Commission Rates. To stimulate competition among broker/dealers, the SEC allows them to negotiate commissions between themselves and their clients.

Cash and Margin Trading. Transactions involving the extension of credit between broker/dealers and their clients are governed by Regulation T of the Federal Reserve Board.

For cash transactions with retail clients, regulations require that on settlement date (usually five business days after trade date), clients must pay for all purchases or, if they are selling, must deliver the security sold before funds can be released. Extensions of time are allowed for valid reasons. Most institutional clients, however, trade on a delivery versus payment (DVP) basis. For institutional purchase transactions, the settlement provision is extended under such regulations from five business days to 35 calendar days. Institutional clients are generally required to use the institutional delivery system (IDS), a system created to facilitate the settlement of transactions between such clients and broker/dealers.

Regulation T prevents broker/dealers from extending credit to their clients beyond the "maximum loan value" of the securities purchased, generally 50% of market value. This also applies to listed securities and certain unlisted securities. Clients are also allowed to "sell short", that is, sell a security they do not own. To accomplish this type of transaction, the client must provide 50% in margin.

REGULATIONS AFFECTING NEW ENTRANTS TO THE MARKETS

The structure of the securities industry in the United States today was established in the 1930s by the passage of the Glass-Steagall Act in 1933 and the Securities Exchange Act of 1934 ('34 Act). The Glass-Steagall Act divided the commercial and investment banking industries into two distinct business segments to prevent a recurrence of the excesses that precipitated the Stock Market Crash of 1929.

Broker/dealers in the United States are regulated primarily by the '34 Act. Questionable practices by broker/dealers prompted Congress to pass this Act, subjecting all Stock Exchanges and their members to extensive regulation by the SEC. Any firm wishing to act as a broker/dealer must formally register with the SEC. The CFTC was established to regulate the commodity futures market and FCMs in a manner similar to that of the SEC. Regulatory responsibility over municipal securities belongs to the Municipal Securities Rulemaking Board (MSRB).

Overseas firms and foreign nationals are not legally precluded from registering as broker/dealers or FCMs. They are subject to the same registration requirements as U.S. entities.

While the SEC has ultimate responsibility over securities broker/dealers, it has delegated the daily supervisory and surveillance functions to organizations referred to as Self-Regulatory Organizations (SROs). Every SEC registrant is required to join a SRO. The NYSE, regional exchanges, and the NASD are the primary SROs. Similarly, the CFTC has assigned the self-regulatory responsibility of FCMs to the National Futures Association (NFA).

Broker/dealers are subject to extensive operational and financial reporting requirements designed to protect clients. The most complex and detailed requirements are embodied in the Uniform Net Capital Rule (Rule 15c3-1) and the Client Protection Rule (Rule 15c3-3).

Uniform Net Capital Rule. The net capital rule generally requires broker/dealers to maintain minimum levels of net capital, as defined, ranging from US$2,500 to as high as US$100,000, $6\frac{2}{3}$% of aggregate indebtedness (as defined) or 2% of aggregate debit items computed in accordance with Rule 15c3-3. The amount of net capital required depends on the type of business and the method elected for computing net capital.

Requirements define net capital as net worth (assets minus liabilities) plus qualifying subordinated loans less nonallowable assets (generally illiquid assets) and then less "haircuts," generally equal to a percentage deduction of the market value of proprietary securities, options and commodity positions.

Client Protection Rule. The Client Protection Rule has two basic purposes. First, the rule requires that money owed to the client by the broker/dealer be used only to finance client-related assets. Any excess funds available from the client-related liabilities must be segregated into a special reserve bank account. This rule is designed to prevent the use of clients' funds and securities in financing a broker/dealer's proprietary activities. Second, the rule requires that broker/dealers obtain possession or control, as defined, of all fully-paid-for and excess margin securities of the client.

Financial Reporting Requirements. Financial reporting requirements for broker/dealers are extensive. They are required to file monthly and/or quarterly financial and operational reports (FOCUS Reports) with the regulatory authorities and must also report violations of net capital and client protection rules. In addition, most broker/dealers must file audited annual financial statements, including certain supplementary information with the SEC within 60 days of the broker/dealer's year-end.

Securities Investor Protection Corporation. The Securities Investor Protection Act of 1970 requires registered broker/dealers to become members of the Securities Investor Protection Corporation (SIPC). SIPC membership subjects the broker to an annual assessment fee calculated as 0.25% of securities-related gross revenues with certain allowable deductions.

These fees become part of a pool of funds that ensures the protection of clients' assets in the event a broker/dealer encounters financial difficulties or fails. Because the fund has grown to the SIPC's desired limit, the fee is currently US$100 per year.

OUTLINE OF CORPORATE AND INDIVIDUAL TAX CONSIDERATIONS

Residents

Government Bonds—Current Income. Generally interest income (including original issue discount and market discount) is taxed at ordinary graduated rates (individual, 15–33%, corporate, 15–34%). However, interest income on most bonds issued by state and local governments is tax exempt.

Government Bonds—Capital Gains. After 1987, capital gains arising from the sale of securities held more than six months (one year for property acquired after 1987) are no longer subject to special long-term reduced rates. Long-term capital gains are now taxed at the same rates as ordinary income and short-term capital gains.

Equities—Current Income. Dividends are included in gross income and taxed at ordinary graduated rates. A corporation may receive a 70% deduction for dividend income from domestic corporations. A portion of

UNITED STATES OF AMERICA

the dividend received deductions may not be available to the extent the stock is debt-financed. The effective tax rate will be reduced to 10.2% to the extent the deduction is available. An 80% deduction is available for corporations owning 20% or more of the stock of the issuer.

Equities—Capital Gains. The same rules generally apply for Government Bonds.

Traded Options—Current Income. A distinction must be made between:

- Equity Option—Any option to buy or sell stock, or any option the value of which is determined directly or indirectly by reference to any stock or stock index (other than a broad-based stock index such as the S&P 100)
- Nonequity Option—Any option (other than a right to acquire stock from the issuer) which is traded on a qualified Board or Exchange and which is not an equity option

Nonequity options are taxed annually on a "mark-to-market" basis, for which they are deemed to be sold for fair market value on the last day of the year. Gains and losses are treated as 60% long-term capital gain and 40% short-term capital gain, irrespective of the holding period. After 1987, 60/40 treatment will not result in a lower effective tax rate. In contrast to nonequity options, profit arising from equity options is generally taxed as a capital gain in the year the contract is sold.

Traded Options—Capital Gains. Gain or loss on equity options is taxable as capital gain or loss. The treatment is the same as for Government Bonds.

Financial Futures—Current Income. Profits/gains arising from financial futures are generally treated the same as nonequity traded options.

Nonresidents

Government Bonds—Current Income. Interest income is generally taxed at a flat rate of 30% withholding tax. Reduced rates are available under double taxation treaties. Certain interest income from U.S. sources is not subject to this withholding tax including:

- Interest on most bonds issued by state and local governments and their subdivisions.
- Interest on deposits with persons carrying on a banking business.
- Portfolio interest.

232

In general, portfolio interest is interest on certain bearer obligations and on any registered obligations owned by a foreign taxpayer, issued after July 18, 1984, which are not held by a shareholder with 10% or more voting stock of the debtor.

Government Bonds—Capital Gains. Generally, nonresident aliens in the United States who do not carry on a trade or business in the United States are not liable for U.S. taxes on capital gains. However, the gains (both long-term and short-term) of any nonresident alien who is physically in the United States for 183 days or more in any tax year will be subject to income tax at the rate of 30%. Double taxation treaties may mitigate this provision.

Equities—Current Income. Dividends paid to nonresidents are generally subject to a flat rate of 30% or a lower rate if a double taxation treaty is in force.

Equities—Capital Gains. The 183-day rule applies to capital gains on equities. However, capital gains realized by a nonresident alien are taxable on the disposal of stock of a "U.S. real property holding corporation" as if the taxpayer were a resident. The nonresident may be subject to a 21% minimum tax if that would produce a higher tax than the regular tax. A U.S. real property holding corporation is generally a U.S. corporation with U.S. real property interests whose fair market value is at least 50% of the assets used in its trade or business. An exception applies to a shareholder who does not own more than 5% of the stock of a U.S. real property holding corporation whose stock is publicly traded.

Traded Options and Financial Futures. Profits/gains realized by nonresidents on traded options and financial futures are not subject to any U.S. tax. However, the 183-day rule (as described above under Government Bonds—Capital Gains) also applies to traded options and financial futures.

Stamp Duty

There is no stamp duty. Where applicable, a very immaterial transfer tax may arise.

PROSPECTIVE DEVELOPMENTS

The following are some of the prospective developments that are likely to affect the industry's future environment.

Competition from Banks. U.S. banks are pressing the Congress to eliminate the Glass-Steagall Act so that they may expand into previously prohibited securities activities. Legislators are currently considering a bill that would permit bank holding companies to underwrite all securities except corporate stock. If passed the bill would allow banks to immediately underwrite commercial paper, municipal revenue bonds, mortgage-backed securities and asset-backed securities. Mutual funds and corporate debt could be underwritten after a 180 day waiting period. Additionally, banks could underwrite stock in April 1991 if the Congress approves the bill. As deregulatory and competitive pressures continue, industry observers expect that the distinction between banks and broker/dealers will become increasingly blurred.

New York Stock Exchange Rule Amendments. Prior to October 1987, diversified U.S. broker/dealers had been prohibited from acquiring or affiliating with NYSE specialist businesses. The NYSE modified the rule—in the wake of the October 1987 market break which hurt numerous specialist firms—to allow diversified broker/dealers to enter the specialist business provided certain functional, separation requirements are maintained. Already, several large, diversified securities firms have acquired specialist firms and observers expect this trend to continue.

Amendments to NYSE client margin rules have also recently been approved. These revisions, the first major changes in over 30 years, attempt to simplify and make the rule more efficient.

Post-October 1987: New Regulatory Developments. Virtually every U.S. regulatory group supervising capital markets, from the SEC to the CTFC, has studied the October market break and its effects. The Reagan Administration, despite its deregulatory stance towards financial markets, empowered two groups, the Presidential Task Force on Market Mechanisms (Brady Task Force) and the Working Group on Financial Markets, to analyze and make recommendations on how to prevent a reoccurrence. Among the numerous suggestions made by industry participants and regulators, the following two proposals have created the most controversy:

- The creation of a regulatory "supra-agency," headed by the Federal Reserve Board, with authority over intermarket issues affecting the entire U.S. financial system.
- The use of "circuit breakers," such as price limits and trading halts; in particular, a proposal calling for the NYSE to halt trading for 30 minutes when the Dow Jones Industrial Average (DJIA) declines 250 points and for one hour when the average falls 450 points.

UNITED STATES OF AMERICA

Except for the futures market's installment of limits on price swings for stock-index contracts, regulatory action is still in the proposal stage. Political disputes over regulatory boundaries and measures have erupted both inside and between the SEC and the CTFC. Thus, while new regulations may be forthcoming, it appears that many controversial issues must still be resolved before they are enacted.

FINANCIAL TIMES-ACTUARIES WORLD POUND STERLING INDEX

Pounds Sterling

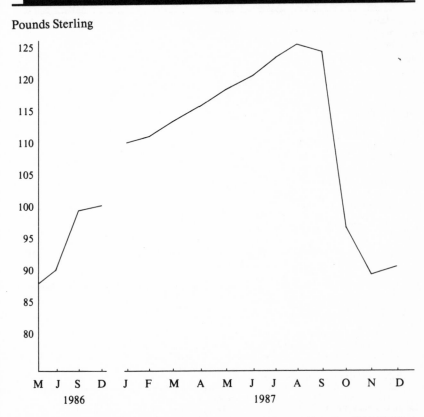

Note: The Pound-Sterling Index is one of the *Financial Times-Actuaries World Indices.*

SPICER & OPPENHEIM'S SECURITIES MARKETS AROUND THE WORLD— A QUICK COMPARISON AS AT MARCH 1988

	Australia	Brazil	Canada	Denmark	France	Germany (West)
Trading in:						
Government bonds	yes	yes	yes	yes	yes	yes
Equities	yes	yes	yes	yes	yes	yes
Traded options	yes	no	yes	yes	yes	yes
Financial futures	yes (6)	yes	yes	yes	yes	no
Minimum commissions?	negotiable	fixed	negotiable	negotiable	fixed (8)	negotiable
Reporting requirements to the Exchange and/or regulatory authority:						
Annual financial statements	yes	yes	yes	yes	yes	no
More frequent financial reports	quarterly	semi-annual	monthly	quarterly	no	monthly/ quarterly
Membership requirements:						
By seat	no	no	yes	no	no	no
Price of seat ($US)	no	no	35,000	no	no	no
Overseas firms admitted	yes	no	yes	no	yes	no
Additional entry requirements for overseas firms	yes	—	no	—	yes	—
Securities dealing by Stock Exchange Members only	yes	yes	yes	yes	yes	yes
Minimum capital requirements:						
Individuals	—	—	—	—	—	—
Firms	A$50,000 –A$250,000	US$486,000 –3,239,000	C$75,000(2)	DKK5m	FFr152,000	DM50,000 –100,000
Investor protection insurance or guarantee fund?	yes	yes	yes	no	yes	no

Notes:
(1) Detailed capital adequacy requirements according to nature and scale of business.
(2) Expressed as a formula related to volume of activity and the firm's business activity.
(3) Minimum capital is R 40,000 for the first two partners or directors and R 10,000 for each subsequent partner or director.
(4) For partnerships and firms requirements are:
  • Not less than $100,000 for each partner of a member firm or director of a member company and $50,000 for each dealer's representative in the member firm or company; or
  • amount equivalent to four times the monthly net brokerage earned, whichever is greater.
(5) For firms applying to manage underwriting syndicates and to undertake public distribution and/or principal dealing or agency business the minimum capital requirement is Y3 billion.
(6) Not generally traded on the main Stock Exchange.
(7) US$2,500 to US$100,000, 6 2/3% of aggregate indebtedness or 2% of aggregate debit items in accordance with SEC Rule 15c3-3.
(8) Fixed up to a certain value of consideration and then negotiable.
(9) Due to commence in 1988.

Hong Kong	India	Indonesia	Ireland	Italy	Japan	Korea (South)
no	yes	yes	yes	yes	yes (6)	yes
yes	yes	yes	yes	yes	yes	yes
no	no	no	yes	yes	no	no
yes	no	no	yes	no	yes	no
negotiable	negotiable	fixed	negotiable	fixed	fixed	fixed
yes	yes	yes	yes	yes	yes	yes
quarterly	no	no	monthly/ quarterly	semi-annual	semi-annual/ monthly	semi-annual
yes	yes	no	no	yes	yes	yes
26,000	60,000	no	no	550,000	16m	no
yes	no	no	yes	no	yes	no
no	—	—	no	—	yes	—
yes	yes	yes	no	yes	no	yes
HK$1m	—	—	—	—	—	—
HK$5m	Adequate	—	(1)	L500m Broker/dealers only	(5)	—
yes	yes	no	yes	no	no	no

(Continued)

Trading in:	Luxembourg	Malaysia	Netherlands	New Zealand	Portugal	Singapor
Government bonds	yes	yes	yes	yes	yes	yes
Equities	yes	yes	yes	yes	yes	yes
Traded options	no	no	yes	yes	no	yes
Financial futures	no	no	yes	yes	no	yes (6)
Minimum commissions?	fixed (8)	fixed	fixed	negotiable	fixed (8)	minimun
Reporting requirements to the Exchange and/or regulatory authority:						
Annual financial statements	yes	yes	yes	yes	yes	yes
More frequent financial reports	no	no	quarterly	monthly	no	no
Membership requirements:						
By seat	no	no	no	no	no	no
Price of seat ($US)	no	no	no	no	no	no
Overseas firms admitted	no	yes	yes	yes	no	no
Additional entry requirements for overseas firms	—	yes	no	yes	—	—
Securities dealing by Stock Exchange Members only	yes	yes	yes	yes	yes	yes
Minimum capital requirements:						
Individuals	—	(4)	—	NZ$59,000	ESC500,000	—
Firms	FLUX5,000,000	M$2m (4)	Banks Dfl 1m Nonbanks Dfl250,000	NZ$500,000	ESC1,000,000	Limited Coy $2m min for others on basis of formula
Investor protection insurance or guarantee fund?	no	yes	yes	yes	no	yes

South Africa	Spain	Sweden	Switzerland	Taiwan	United Kingdom	United States
yes	yes	yes	yes	yes	yes	yes (6)
yes	yes	yes	yes	yes	yes	yes
yes	no	yes	no	no	yes	yes
no	no	yes	no	no	yes	yes
fixed	fixed	negotiable	fixed	fixed	negotiable	negotiable
yes	yes	yes	yes	yes	yes	yes
semi-annual	no	semi-annual	semi-annual	semi-annual	monthly/ quarterly	monthly/ quarterly
no	yes	no	no	yes	no	yes
no	no	no	no	2,800,000	no	625,000 (NYSE)
no	no	no	no	no	yes	yes
—	—	—	—	—	no	no
yes	yes	no	no	yes	no	yes
—	—	—	—	—	—	—
(3)	—	SEK500,000	SFr500,000	NT$30 Million	(1)	(7)
yes	no	no	yes	no	yes	yes

INTERNATIONAL SECURITIES INDUSTRY CONTACT PARTNERS

Warwick Higgs
52 Phillip Street
Sydney 2000
AUSTRALIA
Telephone No: (02) 250 9555
Telex No: AA 26051
Fax No: (02) 251 3663

Americo Campiglia
Avenida Paulista 1439 - 40 andar
C/43 e 44
Caixa Postal (PO Box) No 6.172
01311 Sao Paulo SP
BRAZIL
Telephone No: (011) 288 0822, 289 3280,
289 3570
Telex No: 1134523 CAMG BR
Fax No: -

Robert Landori-Hoffman
1445 Don Mills Road
Don Mills
Toronto
Ontario - M3B 3N6
CANADA
Telephone No: (416) 391 2900
Telex No: -
Fax No: (416) 391 2748

Søren Jensen
Vimmelskaftet 42A
Postboks 2247
1019 Copenhagen K
DENMARK
Telephone No: (01) 14 35 80
Telex No: 16156 ESANO DK
Fax No: (01) 14 04 55

Patrice de Maistre
68 Boulevard de Courcelles
75017 Paris
FRANCE
Telephone No: (1) 47 66 28 05
Telex No: FAESANO 641537F
Fax No: (1) 42 27 14 65

Jurgen Ott
Plaza Hamburger Allee 2-10
6000 Frankfurt am Main 90
Frankfurt
GERMANY
Telephone No: (069) 77 20 06
Telex No: 416703 OTWP D
Fax No: (069) 7071804

Nicholas Heywood-Waddington
Spicer & Oppenheim
20/F Hong Kong Club Building
3A Chater Road
Central
HONG KONG
Telephone No: 5-2110421
Telex No: 89630 ESANO HX
Fax No: 5-292734

Homi Bilpodiwala
Bank of Baroda Building
Bombay Samachar Marg
Bombay 400 023
INDIA
Telephone No: (22) 204   77 22/23,
204 29 61, 204 48 18, 204 59 63,
204 66 47
Telex No: 0116150 STCA IN
Fax No: -

INTERNATIONAL SECURITIES CONTACT PARTNERS

William Macdonald
Jl K H Wahid Hasyim No 2
PO Box 92/Jkt
Jakarta
INDONESIA
Telephone No: (21) 327860, 333554
Telex No: 61460
Fax No: -

Noel Fox
43/45 Northumberland Road
Ballsbridge
Dublin 4
REPUBLIC OF IRELAND
Telephone No: (01) 688644
Telex No: 30593 OFCO EI
Fax No: (01) 689755

Attilio Arietti
Via Paolo da Cannobio 11
20122 Milan
ITALY
Telephone No: (02) 870141, 870975
Telex No: 220159 CONSUL I
Fax No: (02) 870141

Gareth Jones/Tohru Takihi
Shin Aoyama Bldg
Twin West 20th Floor
1-1 Minami Aoyama 1-Chome
Minato-Ku
Tokyo 107
JAPAN
Telephone No: (03) 475 1711
Telex No: 242 3206 OVICON J
Fax No: (03)475 1769

Byong Nam Kim
12th Floor
Seohung Building
68 Keonji-Dong
Jongro-Ku
Seoul
KOREA
Telephone No: 735-0241
Telex No: ESPILEE K23647
Fax No: -

Claude Faber
15 Boulevard Roosevelt
2450 Luxembourg
LUXEMBOURG
Telephone No: 2 56 26
Telex No: 2834 FIDUFA LU
Fax No: 46 20 19

Michael Goh
5th Floor
Loke Yew Building
Jalan Mahkamah Persekutuan
50050 Kuala Lumpur
MALAYSIA
Telephone No: (3) 2922937, 2912824
Telex No: MA 40362 EPCO
Fax No: -

Eppo Horlings
Koningslaan 30
1075 AD
Amsterdam
NETHERLANDS
Telephone No: (020) 769955
Telex No: 14613 HOBOL
Fax No: (020) 764478

Owen Pierce
7th Floor
Westpac Securities Tower
120 Albert Street
PO Box 2219
Auckland 1
NEW ZEALAND
Telephone No: (09) 792 950
Telex No: MGNZS 63034
Fax No: (09) 32830

Jose Paiva Novo
Rua Tomas Ribeiro 50-1
1000 Lisbon
PORTUGAL
Telephone No: (1) 543 770
Telex No: 63146 CTEAM P
Fax No: -

Eric Tan
47 Hill Street, 05-01
Chinese Chamber of Commerce
and Industry Building
SINGAPORE 0617
Telephone No: 336 3355
Telex No: FKTAN RS 26005
Fax No: 3372 197

Geoff West
FHS House
15 Girton Road
Parktown
Johannesburg
SOUTH AFRICA
Telephone No: (011) 643 7361, 643 7301
Telex No: 4-30086 SA
Fax No: (011) 643 2229

Jorge Escudero
Antonio Maura 10, 3
28014 Madrid
SPAIN

Telephone No: (1) 521 91 10
Telex No: -
Fax No: (1) 522 48 99

Pierre Rossier
Am Schanzengraben 23
8002 Zurich
SWITZERLAND

Telephone No: (1) 201 71 71
Telex No: 816 036 EXPE CH
Fax No: (1) 201 14 71

Van-Fred Long
7th Floor, No 41, Section 1
Chung Hsiao W Road
Taipei
Taiwan R O C
TAIWAN

Telephone No: (2) 3114040
Telex No: 21593 TPSANYEI
Fax No: (2) 3718767

Peter Oliver
Friary Court
65 Crutched Friars
LONDON
EC3N 2NP

Telephone No: (01) 480 7766
Telex No: 884257 ESANO G
Fax No: (01) 480 6958

Joel Press
7 World Trade Center
New York
New York 10048
U S A

Telephone No: (212) 422 1000
Telex No: 66249
Fax No: (212) 669 6997

WORLDWIDE OFFICES OF SPICER & OPPENHEIM

Argentina	Estudio Perel
	Buenos Aires, Cordoba, Mendoza
Australia	Duesburys
	Adelaide, Brisbane, Burnie, Canberra,
	Darwin, Hobart, Hurstville, Mareeba,
	Melbourne, Mooroka, Newcastle, Perth,
	Sale, Scone, Surfers Paradise, Sydney,
	Wagga, Wollongong
Austria	Allgemeine Kontroll und Treuhand Gesellschaft
	m.b.H. Nfg. KG
	Vienna
Bahrain	Jawad Habib & Co.
	Manama
Belgium	Bertels, Van Meerbeeck & Co.
	Antwerp, Brussels
Bermuda	Spicer & Oppenheim
	Hamilton
Brazil	Campiglia & Cia. S/C Auditores Independentes
	Brasilia, São Paulo
Canada	Friedman & Friedman, Montreal
	Mintz & Partners, Toronto
	Campbell, Saunders, Vancouver
Cayman Islands	Spicer & Oppenheim
	George Town
Channel Islands:	
Guernsey	Spicer & Oppenheim
	St. Peter Port
Jersey	Spicer & Oppenheim
	St. Helier

245

WORLDWIDE OFFICES OF SPICER & OPPENHEIM

Cyprus	Pavlou, Poyiadjis & Co.
	Nicosia
Denmark	Scan-Revision I/S
	Aalborg, Arhus, Brønderslev, Copenhagen,
	Frederikshavn, Fredensborg, Haderslev,
	Hirtshals, Hjørring, Hobro, Randers,
	Saeby, Skagen
France	Société Française d'Audit et d'Expertise
	Avignon, Bordeaux, Draguignan, Lyon, Marseille,
	Nantes, Paris, Pau, Pointe-à-Pitre,
	Toulon, Tours, Strasbourg
Germany	BTR Beratung und Treuhand Ring G.m.b.H.
	Wirtschaftsprüfungsgesellschaft,
	Augsburg, Bremen, Düsseldorf, Essen,
	Frankfurt, Freiburg, Gummersbach, Hamburg,
	Hannover, Köln (Cologne),
	München (Munich), Stuttgart
Gibraltar	Spicer & Oppenheim
	Gibraltar
Greece	Kolokotronis-Papakyriacou & Co.
	Piraeus
Hong Kong	Spicer & Oppenheim
	Hong Kong
India	Sharp & Tannan
	Bangalore, Bombay, Madras,
	New Delhi, Secunderabad
Indonesia	Drs. S. Reksoatmodjo & Co.
	Jakarta, Surabaya
Ireland	
(Republic of)	Oliver Freaney & Company
	Dublin
Italy	Consulaudit S.a.s.-Arietti & Co.
	Genoa, Milan, Rome, Turin, Verona
Japan	Spicer & Oppenheim
	Kyushu, Nagoya, Osaka, Tokyo, Yokohama
Korea	Samduk Accounting Corporation
	Seoul
Kuwait	Bader, Al-Wazzan & Co.
	Safat-Kuwait
Lebanon	Usamah Tabbarah and Co.
	Beirut

246

Luxembourg	Fiduciaire d'Organisation et de Revision Fernand Faber Luxembourg
Malaysia	Ahmad Abdullah & Goh Kuala Lumpur, Penang
Malta	Mizzi, Scerri, Said & Co. Sliema
Mexico	Gossler S.C. Aguascalientes, Chihuahua, Delicias, Guadalajara, Hermosillo, Juarez, La Paz, Matamoros, Mexicali, Mexico City, Monterrey, Navojoa, Obregon, Tijuana, Torreon
Netherlands	Horlings Brouwer & Horlings Amstelhoek, Amsterdam, Voorthuizen
New Zealand	Kirk Barclay Alexandra, Auckland, Blenheim, Christchurch, Hamilton, Invercargill, Kawakawa, Kerikeri, Matamata, Queenstown, Rotorua, Wellington, Whangarei,
Nigeria	Sulaimon & Co. Jos, Kaduna, Kano, Lagos, Sokoto
Oman	George Mathew & Co. Muttrah
Pakistan	S. M. Masood & Co. Islamabad, Lahore
Peru	Rodolfo Retamozo y Asociados Lima
Portugal	Consulteam Consultores de Gestão, S.A. Faro, Lisbon
Saudi Arabia	Usamah Ali Tabbarah Dammam, Jeddah, Riyadh
Singapore	Spicer and Pegler (locally Foo, Kon, & Tan) Singapore
South Africa	Fisher Hoffman Stride Bisho, Cape Town, Durban, Grahamstown, Johannesburg, Port Elizabeth, Pretoria
Spain	Audihispana, S.A. Barcelona, Bilbao, Madrid, Marbella, Málaga, San Pedro de Alcántara
Swaziland	Fisher Hoffman Stride Mbabane

247

Switzerland	Experta Treuhand AG Basel, Bern, Geneva, Lausanne, Lugano, Zug, Zürich
Taiwan	Van Fred & Co. Taipei
Thailand	Y-Na Thalang & Co. Bangkok
United Arab *Emirates*	Spicer and Pegler Dubai
United Kingdom	Spicer & Oppenheim Aberdeen, Belfast, Birmingham, Bolton, Bournemouth, Bristol, Cambridge, Cardiff, Chester, Croydon, Dudley, Edinburgh, Glasgow, Hull, Leeds, London, Manchester, Newark, Newcastle upon Tyne, Nottingham, Peterborough, Southampton, St. Albans, Uxbridge
United States *of America*	Spicer & Oppenheim Chicago, Dallas, Denver, Fort Lauderdale, Houston, Los Angeles, Miami, New York, San Francisco
Venezuela	Guillen, Poleo y Asociados Caracas